HISTORIC
CAPITAL

HISTORIC CAPITAL

Preservation, Race, and
Real Estate in Washington, D.C.

CAMERON LOGAN

UNIVERSITY OF MINNESOTA PRESS

MINNEAPOLIS · LONDON

Every effort was made to obtain permission to reproduce material in this book. If any proper acknowledgment has not been included here, we encourage copyright holders to notify the publisher.

Illustrations in this book were funded in part or in whole by a grant from the SAH/ Mellon Author Awards of the Society of Architectural Historians.

Portions of chapters 2 and 4 were published as "Mrs. McCain's Parlor: House and Garden Tours and the Inner-City Restoration Trend in Washington, D.C.," *Journal of Urban History* 39, no. 5 (2013): 956–74. Portions of chapters 4 and 5 were published as "Beyond a Boundary: Washington's Historic Districts and Their Racial Contents," *Urban History Review* 41, no. 1 (2012): 57–68.

Published by the University of Minnesota Press
111 Third Avenue South, Suite 290
Minneapolis, MN 55401-2520
http://www.upress.umn.edu

The University of Minnesota is an equal-opportunity educator and employer.

Library of Congress Cataloging-in-Publication Data
Names: Logan, Cameron
Title: Historic capital : preservation, race, and real estate in Washington, D.C. / Cameron Logan.
Description: Minneapolis : University of Minnesota Press, 2017. |
Includes bibliographical references.
Identifiers: LCCN 2017042178| ISBN 978-0-8166-9234-7 (pb) | ISBN 978-0-8166-9232-3 (hc)
Subjects: LCSH: City planning–Social aspects–Washington (D.C.) | Historic preservation–Social aspects–Washington (D.C.) |
    Federal-city relations–Washington (D.C.) | Land use–Social aspects–Washington (D.C.) | BISAC: ARCHITECTURE / History /
    Contemporary (1945-). | SOCIAL SCIENCE / Sociology / Urban. | ARCHITECTURE / Urban & Land Use Planning.
Classification: LCC NA9127.W2 L64 2017 | DDC 720.9753–dc23
LC record available at https://lccn.loc.gov/2017042178

Contents

Abbreviations

ADSW	Art Deco Society of Washington
AIA	American Institute of Architects
CECO	Capitol East Community Organization
CFA	Commission of Fine Arts
CHRS	Capitol Hill Restoration Society
DCCA	Dupont Circle Citizens' Association
DCPL	District of Columbia Preservation League
DCRA	Department of Consumer and Regulatory Affairs
DTID	Don't Tear It Down!
ECR	Emergency Committee on Recreation
FHA	Federal Housing Administration
GSA	General Services Administration
HPO	Historic Preservation Office
HPRB	Historic Preservation Review Board
HSW	Historical Society of Washington, D.C.
JCL	Joint Committee on Landmarks
MICCO	Model Inner City Community Organization
NCPC	National Capital Planning Commission
PPS	Providence Preservation Society
RLA	Redevelopment Land Agency
SWNA	Southwest Neighborhood Association
ULI	Urban Land Institute

From "Life Inside a Monument" to Living in Historic Neighborhoods

In 1974 local activist and neighborhood newspaper editor Sam Smith published *Captive Capital: Colonial Life in Modern Washington*, a wide-ranging and racially salient critique of municipal government and daily life in Washington, D.C. In the first chapter, "Life Inside a Monument," Smith suggested that Washington's ever-expanding federal core was an empty theatrical set, a mere backdrop for national politics and pageant that was largely irrelevant to inhabitants and antithetical to the development of a satisfying and humane urban environment.[1] Charles Dickens inaugurated Smith's theme of a bloated and enveloping monumentality in the 1840s with his famous dismissal of Washington as a "city of magnificent intentions."[2] But in the second half of the twentieth century the idea of Washington as an unnaturally puffed-up evocation of the classical past became a touchstone for architectural and urban critics of the capital city. Reviewing the new Senate office building for the *Architectural Forum* in 1959 under the heading "Saying Nothing, Going Nowhere," Douglas Haskell cited Washington's predilection for a watered down and meager version of the classical language of architecture as evidence of "a state of architectural illness" and "extreme mental confusion."[3] In the same publication a few years later prominent late modern architect and educator Paul Rudolph described the means of achieving monumental effects in Washington as "banal and meaningless."[4] In 1968 critic and prominent historic preservation advocate Ada Louise Huxtable memorably complained that Washington is an "endless series of mock palaces built for clerks, not for kings."[5] Huxtable, Rudolph, and Haskell led a band of critics who viewed much of Washington's historically inflected, twentieth-century monumental architecture as dishonest and incompetent—empty signs. Even before the architecture critics rounded on the national capital Alistair Cooke, the low-key, urbane BBC correspondent who would become something of a monument himself, got in on the act. In a 1949 broadcast Cooke suggested that in the late nineteenth century Washington had developed a taste for grandiose plaster-of-Paris facades and ever since it "has lusted after these Roman monsters like a girl guide after Mark Antony."[6]

Sam Smith acknowledged in the 1970s that for the many tourists who visit the city this was all very well. "To visit the other side of the television screen," he wrote, "and see the stage sets of the evening news is enthralling."[7] Visiting Washington has long been a kind of civic pilgrimage for Americans, a right of citizenship, and the desire of visitors to experience what M. Christine Boyer has called "synthetic city tableaux," carefully imposed scenes of historical and visual order, is more than satisfied by Washington's federal core.[8] Smith noted that for the "temporary residents who float in and out of Washington with the tide of national administrations the arrangement of the city . . . is at least adequate and sometimes exhilarating."[9]

For Washington's permanent inhabitants, however, Smith argued that the seemingly unstoppable expansion and replication of this monumental image throughout the twentieth century was decidedly unhealthy. The growth of great congressional office complexes, for example, was not only a sign of the moribund nature of the traditional language of architecture, as architectural critics had insisted, it was a kind of creeping urban blight (Figures 1 and 2). The removal of houses and local businesses to accommodate these great palaces of administration, especially the "grotesque and gargantuan" Rayburn House Office Building, between the 1940s and the early 1970s, diminished the urban scene and paid no regard to the interests of the city's inhabitants.[10] Smith argued that such demolitions contributed to the sense that Washingtonians were mere house servants of the federal government, most appreciated when they could not be seen. So while the stage set of the federal area might prove satisfying for tourists and amenable to the functioning of the federal government, it obscured the interests and ideals of the city's inhabitants, consigning them to a menial, if not invisible, position.

Figure 1. The U.S. Capitol, Washington, D.C., with surrounding office accommodation, including the Rayburn House Office Building in the foreground on the left. Architect: Harbeson, Hough, Livingstone and Larson. Source: HABS/HAER Collection, Prints and Photographs, Library of Congress.

Sam Smith was neither the first nor alone in complaining of the invisibility of Washington's inhabitants. A number of observers suggested that African Americans, who became a majority in the city in the postwar period, inhabited what was in effect a secret city, in the midst of the televised version, but invisible and subordinate to it. Historian of Washington Constance McLaughlin Green made the point explicitly with the title of her 1967 book, *The Secret City*, in which she documented the history of slavery, segregation, and race relations in the capital.[11]

For Sam Smith and Green as well as an emerging group of black leaders that included Walter Fauntroy, who acted as the city's nonvoting delegate to Congress in the 1960s, and Marion Barry, who would later become the city's so-called mayor for life, the fundamental problem with D.C. was the lack of a local political franchise. The city could only address racial injustice and the problems associated with urban planning by congressional fiat if local political authority could be established on a much more democratic basis. Section 8 of the U.S. Constitution mandated that a federal district be created for the seat of the national government and that it should be subject to the authority of Congress. Consequently, for most of its history, the District of Columbia was governed in spirit and in effect by the U.S. Congress. But the proper scope of congressional control was the subject of ongoing controversy. For a steadily growing group of Washingtonians in the 1950s, 1960s, and 1970s, the establishment of municipal "home rule" and statehood for the District of Columbia were the keys to a more just and enriching city.

Historians of Washington such as Howard Gillette Jr. have placed this battle to establish meaningful, local, political representation at the center of the D.C. story in the postwar decades.[12] But this book argues that the problem of political representation, or the absence of local control, was intrinsically linked to a much wider realm of cultural representation and environmental perception. Critics of the city sometimes described Washington as a company town.[13] But across the century neighborhood organizations fought to dispel the idea that inhabitants were simply a garrisoned clerical army or, worse, house servants of the government. The home-rule campaign was the most politically explicit rejection of that status. But it was only one part of a decades-long effort to make the city home. Across the twentieth century inhabitants of the national capital persistently asserted their entitlements as citizens who formed communities and articulated their aspiration to become Washingtonians in a fuller sense. Such place-based citizenship required, Sam Smith observed, "a local memory."[14] This was something that federal officials, who were

Figure 2. Life Inside a Monument. Drawing by John Wiebenson. Courtesy Abigail Wiebenson and Ronit Eisenbach.

responsible for running the city, conspicuously lacked. But it was also something about which inhabitants felt uncertain, and it thus required careful cultivation. Neighborhood groups, civic organizations, and a new breed of local political actor all took great care to foster local memory.

This book examines the ways in which inhabitants of Washington's intown neighborhoods used historic preservation to cultivate stronger affinities with their city. Washington is both exceptional and typical in this respect. The capital's inhabitants were like those of other large and small American cities in this period in wanting to do more to protect valued buildings and historic neighborhoods and play a bigger part in decisions about the future of their city. But the specific conditions in Washington—the lack of democratic municipal government, the strongly symbolic and national character of its urban core, and the apparent transience of a large part of its population—made the task of identifying with the city and caring for its neighborhoods even more urgent. The history of historic preservation in Washington is thus intensely local, unusually connected to the national level in policy terms, as well as powerfully representative of national trends. This book, therefore, is both a history of Washington through the lens of its historic preservation movement and a history of historic preservation in the United States that takes D.C. as its case study. It is different from most books about historic preservation as it is not an attempt to explain preservation or advocate for it. Instead it puts preservation at the center of the history of a major city. *Historic Capital* focuses on the maturation of historic preservation in the United States in the second half of the twentieth century when the movement came of age as local environmental politics and urban policy.[15]

In Washington local advocates and neighborhood-based organizations, encouraged and assisted by sympathetic planners and architects, insisted that the city's neighborhoods, not just its monumental core, should be protected and preserved. Those neighborhoods, they argued, were also a powerful source of memory, cultural meaning, and economic value. Insisting that neighborhoods and the houses, schools, and shops of which they were composed should be protected, that they had cultural value not just for the current inhabitants but to a wider public and to those not yet born, was a powerful assertion of a public interest in and right to the city. Historic area zoning, later known as historic districting, proved to be the most powerful planning tool for achieving this goal. Between 1964

and 1985 advocates and experts defined a wide arc of central-area neighborhoods as historic places. The rate and nature of environmental change
in much of the city, an area stretching from tony Georgetown in the west
to the struggling Anacostia neighborhood in the city's Southeast quadrant, was carefully controlled as a consequence of this historic districting
process (Map 1). The strong legal and regulatory system that underpinned
those protections reflected wider trends in American cities in the period.
But Washington was also agenda-setting. Preservation politics and process

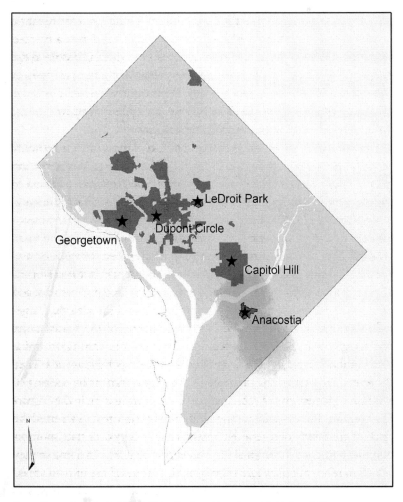

Map 1. Historic districts in the District of Columbia. Created by and copyright Matthew B. Gilmore.

in Washington were, like other exemplary reforming public projects in the national capital, an "example for all the land."[16]

PRESERVATION

In the period from 1960 onward Washington's restoration and preservation advocates were notable for their capacity to create a positive vision for the older sections of the city's residential landscape. The English architectural historians Elaine Harwood and Alan Powers have described the years between 1965 and 1985 as "the heroic period of conservation."[17] This redeployment of the architect Alison Smithson's influential formulation of the 1920s as "the heroic age of modern architecture" was a pointed way of highlighting that far from being merely reactive and hostile to the new, the global historic preservation (heritage conservation) movement was a form of historical agency. In its own way, it possessed a positive vision for making cities and the environment underpinned by a social movement and a sense of moral and ethical mission.

Harwood and Powers's depiction of the global movement is certainly accurate for Washington in the decades from 1965 to 1985. Preservation in D.C. became much more than a hobby pursued by a narrow band of building fanciers and antiquarians. The movement and its policy apparatus were central to the process of redefining the cultural value and meaning of the city. Preservationists not only rejected the idea of the intown area's obsolescence and inevitable failure, they identified the value of residential neighborhoods and the ordinary environment in historical terms. They rejected automatic priority being given to the projects, interests, and image of the federal government, and they rejected the idea that large-scale state intervention and expansive reformation of the spatial order of the city was necessary. This set of refusals was the basis upon which preservation-focused groups also helped to propel a positive agenda. They became a key part of the campaign for self-government by seeking to establish a greater level of local control of the environment in the District of Columbia. Preservation and neighborhood-action groups asserted the value of continuity over redevelopment, civic activity over state sponsorship, and resident decision-making over expert planning. In doing so they helped to reorient policy and reimagine the future of the intown areas.

But the process of asserting greater control over physical change was far from harmonious. Competing interests and priorities, not to mention full-scale rioting, threatened to derail the project of restoring houses and neighborhoods. While housing restoration and neighborhood preservation were community-building efforts to some, especially newly arriving, mostly white, urban pioneers, they were a species of what we now call gentrification to others, especially incumbent African Americans of modest means.

In Washington, D.C., inhabitants and political decision-makers viewed questions of social change, real estate, and cultural value through the lens of race. Indeed they viewed almost everything through the lens of race, and the historic preservation movement was no exception. When the preservation movement really began to grow in strength in the 1960s Washington possessed a great range of historical and patriotic societies as well neighborhood organizations and block groups. These were all repositories of local memory in one way or another. But such groups were organized, either explicitly or tacitly, along racial lines. The most numerous of the local groups were the neighborhood-based citizens' and civic associations. The citizens' associations were white, and the civic associations were black. While local government passed pioneering antidiscrimination measures in the 1870s, Jim Crow became a central feature of neighborhood and civic life in Washington in subsequent decades. Some new neighborhood groups formed in the 1960s, 1970s, and 1980s attempted to work around this division or across it, but they emerged from this racialized structure. As such Jim Crow left a powerful imprint on all kinds of community activism and citizen participation in local affairs.

PRIVACY

The racial bifurcation and tensions that characterized the process of urban restructuring in the 1960s, 1970s, and 1980s, which form a key part of this history, did not entirely prevent the formation of shared projects and aspirations that transcended the city's racial fault lines. The ambition to take greater control of city government was the most politically potent of these. But underlying that political project, this book argues, was a cultural conviction that inhabitants of the city ought to feel at home in Washington. Living in the city should not be a question of lodging, but of making a home and, through that process, exercising one's entitlements as a citizen. Consequently the house and the neighborhood both became prominent sites for articulating the politics of home rule. The term itself, borrowed though it was from decolonization struggles and the Irish troubles, suggests that home was a keyword for people in D.C. in the period. The insistence on the values of homeliness and familiarity in remaking the city were not merely expressions of ascendant, middle-class social values, they were also a direct counter to the unhomeliness of the federal realm and the assumption that Washington was a place you went when you left home.

The extensive effort to identify and promote Washington as a city of inhabitants and of homes was driven, in part, by an objection to the negative effects of the city's insistent and too-new monumentality. In the 1940s the influential British town planner and critic William Holford remarked of Rome's triumphal commemoration of Victor Emmanuel that "its monumentality, like that of a colossal cheese, is not yet ripe."[18] Critics of Washington's government buildings, including the city's growing band of neighborhood activists and preservationists, likewise viewed the U.S. capital's newer classical monuments, as well as its redeveloped residential quarter in Southwest, as unripe. In contrast, they found a maturity in the city's older houses and neighborhoods that could be savored. Here, they believed, were the city's authentic monuments.

The shift in consciousness, or monumental awareness, occasioned by an intense period of neighborhood-based historic preservation activism is an index of wider changes in historical awareness itself. The landscape historian J. B. Jackson noted this shift in his 1980 essay "The Necessity for Ruins." "With us," he wrote, "the association seems not to be with our politically historical past, but with a kind of private vernacular past—what we cherish are mementos of a bygone daily existence."[19] Even if those associations were not always with their own family histories, neighborhood restorationists in the District of Columbia saw the value of what John Ruskin once described as a "warm monument in the hearth and house" as a more lively connection to the past than the cold, marble monuments of the National Mall.[20]

The strong focus among preservationists in Washington in the 1960s, 1970s, and 1980s on the low-key historic environment, the homely red bricks of row house and neighborhood, is attributable to the very particular circumstances of living in the national capital. Because the city's civic realm was shared with the nation at large it was characterized by a sense of distance or unhomeliness for Washingtonians. This was in part because inhabitants had a double relationship with the city. Introducing readers to a special issue of *Architectural Forum* in 1963, critic Peter Blake noted that "it has often been said that every American has two home towns—his own, and Washington, D.C."[21] Such a formulation presumed, of course, that nobody was actually from Washington or considered it to be their true hometown. But inhabitants had to make a home and form their local connections amid the markers of national meaning. The theorist of American citizenship Lauren Berlant has rhetorically asked, "Can national identification survive the practical habitation of everyday life in the national locale?"[22] But for the city's inhabitants, especially those in the intown residential areas, the inverse was just as pressing. How could local identification emerge from the practical habitation of everyday life in the national locale?

The inhabitants of the District of Columbia thus confronted the question of how they could make the city their own in historical and cultural terms. The visitor, newcomer, and inhabitant alike might recognize, as Ada Louise Huxtable did in 1967, that "Washington has a solemn, full-blown beauty."[23] But for inhabitants that solemn beauty, for all its familiarity, remained distant. For most, as Peter Blake noted in 1963, Washington was "a pretty strange home town."[24]

Washington's strangeness, and the difficulty it presents in relation to managing one's identification with the nation, has inspired a very particular response among some of its best-known inhabitants. The literary historian Sarah Luria has argued that prominent public figures in Washington in the late nineteenth century carefully orchestrated and publicized their particular vision of homeliness. Frederick Douglass used his homes, first a large house on A Street, Capitol Hill in Northeast, and then Cedar Hill, in the Anacostia neighborhood, and the private domestic world he cultivated in those houses as a public commentary on the racialized social conventions of the city (Figure 3). Henry and Marian Adams used their Henry Hobson Richardson–designed house, the Hay-Adams House (1884–87) on Lafayette Square, and their own conspicuous privacy in that house as a reproach to the social habits of Washington's political elite. In different ways the owners of these properties made a public point of their own right to privacy and private property. Both Cedar Hill and the Hay-Adams House were far from conventional or typical places in Washington. But the owners in both cases made explicit

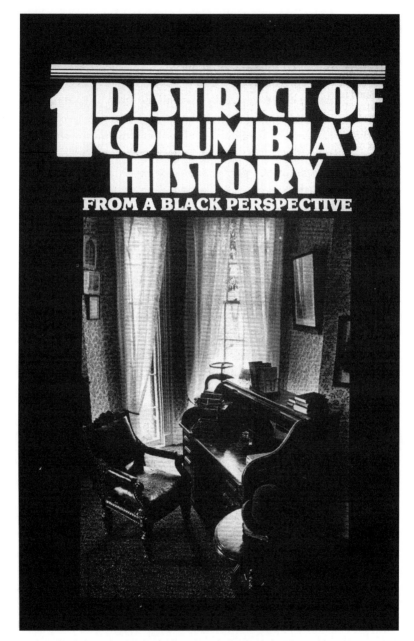

1 DISTRICT OF COLUMBIA'S HISTORY
FROM A BLACK PERSPECTIVE

Figure 3. Interior of Cedar Hill, the home of Frederick Douglass, Anacostia, Southeast Washington, D.C., as it was presented to visitors by the National Park Service in the 1970s. Photograph by Hoke Kempley. Source: Ron Powell and William D. Cunningham, *Black Guide to Washington* (1975).

the wider cultural significance of the private realm. They publicized their private, domestic arrangements.[25]

The historic preservation movement in the twentieth century was likewise explicit in proclaiming the public cultural importance of private dwellings. The preservationist opposition to the reforming project of urban renewal—represented in Washington, D.C., by the reconstructed Southwest—appears from today's perspective as an almost reflexive architectural conservatism.[26] But such a characterization does not capture the real interests and anxieties of preservationists in the period. Preservationists worried about what a redeveloped intown environment would do to the subtle relationship between private dwellings and the public conviviality of the street and, therefore, to the relationship between neighborhood and city. The series of thresholds that framed and mediated the relationship between home and city, private and public were entirely reformulated in the Southwest urban renewal area. The spatial order of the new Southwest, the relationships it established between individual dwelling units and the public domain, made it more difficult to dramatize one's private dwelling. As such, it deprived its inhabitants, or so neighborhood preservationists believed, of the capacity to enact one's citizenship by caring for house and neighborhood.

PROPERTY

Exemplary citizenship, therefore, required publicity, but exemplary citizens insisted on the value of private property as well as privacy itself. For most participants in Washington's preservation and restoration movement private property was the medium in which they exercised their right to the city. This apparent paradox between advocating for shared cultural resources on the one hand and insisting on acquiring a private interest in property on the other is in fact perfectly consistent with wider American traditions, especially republican traditions, that placed private property at the center of the political and conceptions of the public good. Indeed, the success of Washington's housing restoration movement, the thing that underpinned neighborhood preservation activity, was basically coextensive with its success in promoting the value of individual property ownership. But it also depended on a certain kind of speculation in real estate. The professed preservationist bias in favor of urban and architectural forms inherited from the past was also a speculation on the economic value of old houses and neighborhoods in the future. Preservationists in Washington invested financial capital, mostly in small sums, in older dwellings and neighborhoods in the hope and expectation that their value would grow over time. This was how history, at least that part of it represented by property, became a kind of capital, and how the historic preservation movement helped to reshape the social landscape of Washington's intown areas.

The reliance on property—the close connection between property ownership and good citizenship and the dynamics of rising real estate value—was a source of great strength for preservationists in Washington across much of the twentieth century. Restoration created what looked like a virtuous circle. Social investment in neighborhood organizations and financial investment in old houses helped create demand for property in formerly moribund areas. This in turn induced further demand, and real estate values in many cases stabilized and began to grow.

But over the longer term the encircling role of private property also destabilized the preservation movement, undermining some of its core claims. In the 1960s, 1970s, and 1980s, preservation's heroic period, advocates insistently argued that the restoration culture and historic preservation controls underpinned social diversity and were a vital grassroots mechanism for achieving environmental justice and democratic control of the urban process. But these core claims became increasingly difficult to reconcile with the economic incentives and logic of the preservation movement. The success of preservation in valorizing capital in the form of real estate, even at a relatively modest scale, unquestionably magnified the disadvantage of those who did not own real estate in the restoration areas. It is now quite clear that in the largest, most expensive U.S. cities, of which Washington is one, property-centered preservation did not address the very obvious inequalities in housing or those of wealth based on housing.

As historians of American cities and its real estate from Miami to Oakland to Chicago have overwhelmingly demonstrated, the property game has been one loaded in favor of middle-class whites in the United States. It is not that blacks have been unaware of or uninterested in the benefits to be obtained from owning real estate. In the last two decades of his life Frederick Douglass argued consistently that African Americans in Washington should acquire property to take their proper place in American life. The private domain was more important, he suggested, even than public accommodations in the battle to establish racial equality. And property along with savings would mold ex-slaves, he argued, into middle-class citizens. To assert equality, Douglass believed, blacks had to possess what whites wanted. But Jim Crow policies and culture thwarted African American aspirations to property. Financial institutions, local politics, federal policy, and, most of all, entrenched beliefs about race and real estate almost ensured a situation in which ethnic minorities, especially African Americans, were property poor by comparison with whites.[27]

This is not to say that preservation and restoration advocates in Washington were to blame for this disadvantage. Discussion of housing affordability in central cities was much less prominent in earlier decades than it is today, and "gentrification" was a term unknown to most of the protagonists in this history. But the housing restoration and preservation movement is implicated within this wider story of property privilege and disadvantage. Conflict about the role of preservation in initiating social change in Washington, especially the whitening and *embourgeoisement* of intown areas, was already a notable source of neighborhood tension by the late 1960s. In the 1970s the idea that the restoration culture was hurting the interests of existing inhabitants, especially poorer blacks, was at odds with the movement's self-conception as a force for social diversity and neighborhood empowerment. But the criticism had some resonance. Ultimately the runaway success of the restoration and preservation movement in market terms robbed it of its animating moral mission. The strength of the movement in protecting and creating areas of choice in big cities, real estate success stories, was also a story of growing pressure on the poor. In Washington, in the 1960s, 1970s, and 1980s, that meant pressure on blacks.

Despite the tensions that arose around gentrification and its racial implications in Georgetown, Capitol Hill, and Dupont Circle in the 1960s and 1970s, and the growing social scientific literature that addressed the problem in the 1980s, policy makers and public debate remained focused on how to improve safety, avoid property devaluation, and guard against signs of decay in intown areas. That is, most who actively engaged in the process of shaping the city believed their task was to make it more amenable to middle-class and well-to-do audiences, not guard against gentrification. In such a context the vision pioneered by citizen activists that focused on piecemeal upgrading of housing and preservation of historic districts proved very durable. And that vision was not just popular with citizen groups composed of white-collar workers and cultural intellectuals. Government agencies adopted strategies that drew extensively from the preservationist vision.[28]

Yet as housing has become less and less affordable in many of Washington's intown areas—and beyond—in the twenty-first century, the ideal elaborated by neighborhood restoration groups and preservation societies has begun to seem more and more problematic. If the current period is to be defined as "a time of gentrification" in Washington, as one recent review of historical literature on the city asserts, then it is almost certainly the case that the vision of urban vitality and citizen-led decision making that emerged from the heroic period of preservation is no longer operative. In Washington the ideal of the row-house neighborhood, revived by sweat equity and community spirit, has now withered.[29]

So when did the vision of Washington's row-house neighborhoods as the defining identity of the local city—of the terrain of D.C., as opposed to official Washington—finally expire? While such questions are rarely clear-cut, there is a compelling case to say that in Washington it was sometime toward the end of 2002. It was at that time that the inhabitants of the Potomac Place complex, formerly known as Capitol Park Apartments, one of the earliest completed projects in the Southwest urban renewal area, successfully delayed an infill development project by arguing that it was a historically significant place. They thus asserted, successfully as it turned out, that postwar urban redevelopment was itself now a historically significant cultural legacy that ought to be protected. Many of those who could remember the original impact of the Southwest redevelopment project and abhorred its alien presence in the city were surprised and perturbed by this development. But others saw a natural evolution, and the city's leading architects of the period—Chloethiel Woodard Smith, Charles Goodman, and Francis Lethbridge—were reappraised and newly appreciated.

Of course Washington cannot be seen in isolation. The period immediately before and after the 2006 death of the great urban and architectural critic Jane Jacobs marked a turning point in thinking about the American city and its twentieth-century legacy. The Jacobs polemic against postwar project planning and design had held sway among activists, academics, and city planners for perhaps a quarter of a century. But as individual preservation groups reassessed the historical significance of the formerly despised "tower in the park" developments and architectural historians wrote appreciatively of the legacy of the welfare state and its architecture, the Jacobs moment also came to an end.[30]

This shifting sense of what is valuable about the past and what is desirable in our cities brings the period covered by this book into relief as a distinct historical period. In its long development that period spans the entire century, covering the development of preservation sentiment in Georgetown in the 1920s and 1930s right through to the concerns about protecting the redeveloped Southwest in the 2000s. But most of what follows is focused on the period 1960 to 1990, when citizen engagement with the historic resources in their environment underwent a period of intensification. That intensification of activity was partly a rescue mission for decaying neighborhoods, partly a rejection of government-directed transformation, and partly a financial and cultural speculation on a preserved urban environment.

SOURCES

In the course of the research for this book I spoke to a number of participants and informed observers about preservation in Washington during the 1970s and 1980s in particular. But this book is not based on oral accounts or the memories of protagonists. The evidence that I rely on is drawn from archival sources, most of them held in public collections in Washington, D.C. Wherever possible my intention was to capture the views and actions of Washingtonians as articulated in the period. During the period in which I researched the book the proliferating discussion of gentrification transformed the discourse on preservation. That shifting frame for understanding the legacy of preservation is an important reason to write this book now. But I did not want the evidence that underpins it to be colored by the prominence of those current concerns.

STRUCTURE

The book is organized according to a thematic-chronological framework. The historical development of the city and its preservation movement is built up through these thematic layers. Chapters 1 and 2 focus on the two great drivers of the preservation enterprise, value and taste, the economic and the cultural. The success of the preservation movement is impossible to understand if one does not understand the dynamics and interaction of these forces. The core economic argument of neighborhood preservation—that restoring old properties and creating meaningful land-use controls creates high-quality environments that protect and enhance the value of urban land—was articulated quite clearly in the 1920s and 1930s. But the range of places that attracted restoration activity and preservation sentiment before World War II was very limited. In Washington it was really only Georgetown. But as the destructive specter of urban renewal loomed in the late 1950s and early 1960s, the taste for the past began to change, and with it the scope and possibilities of the restoration culture expanded. In the 1960s and early 1970s architects, planners, real estate agents, and a wider public all reevaluated the formerly reviled legacy of the Victorian era. That reevaluation transformed the prospects of the existing fabric of much of the intown environment—the old City of Washington—much of which was developed or redeveloped between the end of the Civil War and the 1910s.

In Washington the federal government was, in many ways, the economy and the culture. Its policies and its projects had a major impact on both the value and character of the urban environment. Chapter 3 argues that federal activity inspired and strengthened the arm of the local preservation movement in Washington in the 1960s by both its positive and negative example. The Kennedys were at the heart of this, and what happened in the environs of the White House, first at Lafayette Square and then along Pennsylvania Avenue, galvanized the preservation movement. Lafayette Square revealed the possibilities of area preservation plans, while the Pennsylvania Avenue redevelopment project, with its planned demolition of cherished landmarks such as the Old Post Office building, inspired a citywide voice for local preservationists in the form of the not-for-profit advocacy group Don't Tear It Down!

Growing community support and political legitimacy, however, did not make preservation immune from criticism. Beginning in the late 1960s, community groups in several neighborhoods, usually representing or speaking for low-income African Americans, launched strong attacks on the restoration societies and other organized preservation groups. The core of the critique was that restoration was a deliberate process of upscaling that had adverse consequences for incumbent residents of limited means. Chapter 4 examines the sources and substance of this criticism, the reaction from preservationists to it, and the emerging scholarly research that took up the link between preservation and gentrification. The criticism of the movement was the first hint that preservationist claims about the social and community efficacy of their movement might not be reconcilable with its economic justification in the longer term.

But in the 1970s, the decade of the neighborhood as one urban historian has described it, Washington's neighborhood groups were undeterred and pursued preservation goals and promoted the restoration culture with greater vigor than before or since. They defined new historic districts and expanded existing ones, they advocated for stronger legal protections, and they worked to strengthen local control of municipal affairs. Chapter 5 argues that the expansion of the monumental footprint of Congress on Capitol Hill and the rapid growth of the westward extension of the downtown office district near Dupont Circle produced this heightened energy and activity. These two separate building campaigns were in fact closely tied together. The expansion of the federal government produced and was influenced by a growing government-influencing sector in Washington across the decades 1965–85. The two neighborhoods most affected by these building campaigns possessed some of the most well-organized and effective neighborhood action and preservation groups. Their confrontations with establishment monumentality on the one hand and commercial banality on the other both promoted and sharpened neighborhood preservation politics.

The energy and moral purpose of Washington's preservation movement in the 1970s was a source of great strength. Even when its leadership erred politically as it did around Dupont Circle during the successive historic district expansion efforts, the overall mission of promoting and expanding historic districting was still maintained. African American neighborhood groups in U Street and Shaw ultimately aligned themselves with the preservation process after initially rejecting the right of Dupont Circle preservationists to define the historical significance of their area. This difficult episode of conflict and reform was also a moment of regeneration and expansion. But the growing powers and especially the professionalization of the preservation field in the 1980s proved trickier still. During a seven-year-long battle over the fate of the Rhodes Tavern, the subject of chapter 6, it became clear that participants in the preservation movement disagreed quite fundamentally about the aims of preservation and the proper role of preservation advocacy. The book argues that the cogency and energy of the movement never fully recovered from this episode. Preservation's procedures were regularized, and in the late 1980s and 1990s the system put in place in the 1960s and 1970s operated with considerable success, but its political dynamism and its creativity as urban policy were no longer evident.

In the first years of the new century the story of preservation and of Washington's intown environment came full circle. The transformative and destructive urban renewal project in Southwest was now the subject of its own redevelopment pressures. Chapter 7 explores the series of ironies and misunderstandings around the attempt by residents and preservation activists to preserve Capitol Park (1959). The Chloethiel Smith–designed project was one of the urban renewal area's most architecturally distinguished and interesting developments. But the proposal to preserve it was still quite shocking to veterans of neighborhood preservation battles in the 1960s and 1970s. Was bulldozer-driven urban renewal with its hygienic modernism and expansive open spaces now a culturally significant legacy in its own right? It was a proposition that many design professionals and scholars regarded as quite obvious but that many citizen activists from other sections of the city simply could not see or accept.

But as this book reveals again and again, the possibility of such reevaluations is in fact at the heart of the preservation enterprise. The historical volition of any building or fragment of the urban landscape is unstable and can become significant to us unexpectedly. Preservationists and citizens generally should welcome this. After all, such shifts in what we value about the past become the basis upon which we reimagine the possibilities for our cities in the present and the future. Retrospective city making, if we can call it that, is not merely academic, a game for antiquarians and architectural connoisseurs. It is a powerful form of urbanism in its own right. Twentieth-century Washington, D.C., is testament to that.

CHAPTER I

Value

Property, History, and
Homeliness in Georgetown

Histories of U.S. architecture and the built environment most often depict Washington, D.C., as an exemplar of planning, visual order, and legal control. Height limited, overtly monumental, generously endowed with public space, and possessing a number of prominent experiments in coordinated community planning, it appears as though Washington is the great exception to the commercial rule of American urban life.[1] Historic preservation, the other principal subject of this book, likewise seems, at first glance, to be based on noncommercial foundations. The judgments of cultural and historical value upon which preservation depends take, in theory, a disinterested view of economic value in the built environment. But closer inspection reveals that commercial interest and the value of property are at the center of both Washington's history and the history of historic preservation. This chapter explores how propositions about the economic worth of the city's real estate were intertwined with the forms of cultural and historical evaluation that underpinned preservation politics in the city. The preservation movement did not—as though in a moment of madness or revelation—leap into the arms of the market and mainstream urban development in the 1980s, as accounts such as Mike Wallace's history of the preservation field suggest. The longer history of preservation activity in Washington, D.C., reveals that the preservation agenda was always tied to concerns about real estate, just as much as it was to certain characteristic images and ideas about civic identity, architectural character, and urban form. The preservation movement, therefore, did not abandon its grassroots

for big business in the 1980s. But some of the contradictions within preservation practice did emerge more powerfully as cultural and economic
values became more difficult to resolve.[2]

In 1967 the great urban historian John Reps demonstrated that the physical forms and social structure of Washington, D.C., are in fact steeped
in the culture of property, much as in other American cities. This was
true from the very beginning. In the 1790s George Washington promoted
speculative investment in the new federal territory, believing that such
investment might provide much of the needed capital to fund accommodation for the incipient federal government.[3] Later historians of the
city have documented the ways in which Washington's most important
municipal leader and most notorious local politician of the nineteenth
century, Alexander "Boss" Shepherd, head of the D.C. Board of Public
Works (1871–73) and briefly the District's territorial governor (1873–74),
enriched himself and his circle via a "comprehensive improvement plan"
that provided infrastructure—new water and sewage systems, tens of
thousands of shade trees, and an extensive system of street illumination.
That program of works dramatically improved amenity in large areas of
the city and in turn underpinned rapid rises in the value of much of the
city's prime, residential real estate.[4] Most recently, scholarly attention has
turned to the history of postwar urban renewal and the ways in which
civic leaders in Washington successfully pushed to implement an ambitious program of urban redevelopment intended to address declining
central city real estate values.[5] In each case, it was not merely a visionary
goal for imposing physical order on the city that motivated advocates
of remaking the urban environment, but also a strong sense of how the
city's property value might underpin such visions.

Urban historians typically look to the physical landscape of U.S. cities
for evidence of cultural and technical change that manifests via planning
innovation and shifts in architectural expression. However, urban landscapes are also records of the regimes of investment and belief in real
property that shaped decision making and flows of capital. The uptown
residential landscape of Manhattan, the skyscrapers of the Chicago Loop,
the "foothills ecology" of Los Angeles, the midcentury industrial suburbs
of Oakland, and the ghostly hulks of industry in North Philadelphia and
East Baltimore, each speak of waxing and waning forces of investment,

of uneven urban development, of locational advantage and sudden shifts in real estate belief and practice.[6]

Howard Gillette Jr. has argued that Washington's history can be a read as an ongoing battle between justice and beauty, social welfare and national pageant. But Washington's urban landscape must also be read as a history of land values. The highly rationalized office landscape of K Street, the carefully restored colonial and early republican image of Georgetown, the enormous, classically inflected congressional office complexes, and the carefully preserved rows of nineteenth-century middle-class housing that lie beyond them each contain lessons about real estate value. Each of those lessons in turn teaches us something about social change in the city, about race, neighborhood, work, and home. While the cultural symbols and architectural sources that underline the exercise of power in Washington are decipherable to any visitor carrying a *Frommer's* guidebook, or indeed a smartphone, a properly historical view of Washington, D.C., must encompass the wider landscape within which those symbols sit. One of the keys to understanding that wider landscape, though frequently overlooked in historical accounts, is the shifting terrain of real estate value. What did people believe about real estate value and why? These questions have the potential to explain a great deal about the shape of the city and the social patterns that that shape supports.[7]

Washington, D.C., presents some particular problems owing to its intentional monumentality and the intensity with which its inhabitants sought to protect much of its nineteenth-century residential fabric. This latter characteristic in particular—a pattern of unintentional monuments or historic environments that are the focus of this study—has played an unusually prominent role in the city's history since the end of World War II, determining the value, character, and shape of its built environment.

After a generation or more of scholarship focused on twentieth-century residential real estate practices such as redlining, blockbusting, and racially restrictive covenants, urban, architectural, and planning historians are familiar with the impact of these practices on American cities, especially the way they affected patterns of slum formation, racial segregation, and campaigns for redevelopment and renewal. The impact of historic preservation protections on land value in the twentieth century, however, has not been discussed in U.S. urban historiography. Yet there is no question that throughout the century, experts and advocates in Washington formed strong views and shaped policies and practices around precisely this question. Planners, economists, downtown business groups, citizen activists, and legislators were all concerned with the ways in which old buildings and historic protections affected urban neighborhoods. They were interested—both curious and in some cases also financially invested—in how the construction of apartment buildings affected house prices, whether the metropolitan real estate market could be managed via demolition and staged redevelopment, and most importantly for this history, the ways historic preservation protections affected residential real estate values and related social phenomena such as gentrification and the displacement of incumbent residents.

In 1972, an audience of preservationists in Washington listened while planning and policy expert Barclay G. Jones explained that preservation must be considered as a collective good for its economic benefits to make sense. He concluded that "preservation activities have positive economic value" but also warned that "for the individual, the economics of preservation will too often be negative." As such, he argued, "ways must be found to see that the burden of preservation's cost is widely distributed."[8] Insights such as this spurred preservation activists and policy makers to find new ways of providing private incentives to achieve the public goods that they were so keen to define and protect in this period. But this happened not only during the heyday of policy innovation in historic preservation law and economics between the early 1960s and 1980s. Across the twentieth century, restoration advocates, preservationists, and city planners articulated their belief that the correct deployment of historic protections, zoning rules, and tax incentives would have a salutary impact on property use and value.[9]

The pragmatic concern with this question of value as it played out in Washington, D.C., opens onto a larger theoretical and historical question: Under what conditions has cultural and historic value been translated into economic value? One of the central premises of preservation protections is that there are forms of value—cultural and historical—that should be irreducible to monetary value. At its heart—and this is one of the reasons that such protections were seriously challenged in the United States—legal preservation protections constrain the entitlements of the property owner by asserting that a place possesses community or national significance and embodies a collective good. When a place is protected by effective preservation laws the property right can only be exercised in such a way that does not diminish the cultural significance of that place.[10] Historian Graeme Davison has noted that the wave of new statutory protections for historic places around the world in the 1960s and 1970s reflected a growing conviction in many developed nations that there is a public or national interest in such places. He also noted, however, that many, if not most, of those places had "traditionally been regarded as private in nature."[11] Public or collective interest in those private places thus assigned a new form of value to them. This in turn has affected their economic value. Understandably, therefore, questions of real estate value have encircled the historic preservation enterprise throughout the twentieth century.

Cultural theorist Patrick Wright has argued that in the United Kingdom historic preservation activism and legislation profoundly challenged established patterns of capitalist accumulation in the built environment:

> Capitalist property relations can only be preserved if they are reproduced through new accumulative cycles, and preservation of these relations seems in this sense to necessitate the constant transformation of life in both town and country. The preservation of capital is therefore predicated on widespread social change and, indeed, actual demolition. . . . This is the dereliction which brings capital into conflict with the (historic) preservation lobby.[12]

This is a significant point and one that helps explain the social conflict occasioned by historic preservation movements around the world, including in Washington's central area neighborhoods in the 1960s, 1970s, and 1980s. Preservationists insisted on collective goods, either explicitly or implicitly, and therefore inspired a strong counterreaction from those whom the historian Mike Wallace has called the "Propertied."[13] Such propertied people have rejected the legitimacy of such cultural entitlements. Nevertheless, the history of historic preservation efforts in Washington over the course of the twentieth century confirms other recent research on the development of historic preservation in the United States, which has found that historic district protections, in particular, are a form of social politics based in the progressive reform traditions of the early twentieth century and the community politics of the 1960s and 1970s.[14] Max Page and Randall Mason begin their introduction to an edited collection of essays on the history of preservation in the United States by asserting that preservation is "one of the broadest and longest-lasting land use reforms in this country."[15] In other words, its most far-reaching implications have been in its capacity to shape land use and value. This is a very different emphasis from that of the preservation movement's most influential early chronicler, Charles Hosmer, for whom it was primarily a mode of establishing cultural continuity and identity in the face of the rapid transformations wrought by modernity.[16]

It would be wrong to assert that preservation politics in the United States has been anticapitalist either in intent or in effect, even though preservation campaigns have incited powerful opposition from property-owning interests. It is probably fairer to say that preservation has been ameliorative in intent, an attempt to shape and control real estate markets rather than reject the logic of capitalist accumulation in the built environment. In Washington, D.C., exercising such control in residential districts has been part of a wider tradition that is focused on the conspicuous protection and promotion of the realm of domestic, private life. The earliest and by far the most influential example of such activism was in Georgetown, where these two key aspects of preservation— conservative valorization of domestic private life, and collective action on behalf of shared amenity and real estate value—came together in a long effort to restore and preserve the area's residential landscape. To understand the wider arc of how preservation activism addressed questions of residential real estate value across the twentieth century, it is useful to go back to that prototypical effort in Georgetown.

PRESERVING THE VALUE OF HOMES: JOHN IHLDER'S "GEORGETOWN HOMEOWNERS"

Georgetown is older than Washington, D.C. It was founded in 1751 as a tobacco and wheat trading port on the Maryland side of the Potomac River at the furthest navigable point upriver from the Chesapeake Bay (Figure 4). The town maintained a separate political identity from Washington until 1871, despite being enclosed within the boundaries of the District of Columbia by Andrew Ellicot and Benjamin Banneker's 1791 survey. During more than a century of steady growth from the mid-eighteenth century until the late nineteenth, Georgetown became a commercial town of some substance. It fostered the growth of the "federal seat" on the other side of Rock Creek and was home to many of those who made the City of Washington, both physically and politically. However, during the half century that separated the Civil War and World War I, Georgetown gradually lost its prominence in the life of the capital as Washington grew rapidly and a series of high-status neighborhoods, including Logan Circle and Dupont Circle, developed in the city's Northwest quadrant. By the early twentieth century Georgetown was a very different place, one much reduced in its political and social influence. One chronicler of the section has described it in this period as "dowdy and unfashionable, a backwater."[17]

But the period of economic stagnation that affected Georgetown from the 1880s onward acted as something of a preservative and provided the conditions that would underpin its emergence as a historic place from the

Figure 4. Topography of the Federal City, 1791, by Don Hawkins. The grid of Georgetown streets is visible at upper left. Source: Library of Congress.

1920s onward. Over the decades between the mid-1920s and the mid-1960s the area acquired a new form of value, one based in its distinctive legacy of colonial- and federal-era houses and the atmosphere of history associated with them (Figure 5). The transformation in perceptions of the area saw it go from "dowdy" to become Washington's most fashionable address. Moreover, its rise to prominence as a neighborhood of choice became the single most important precedent for the citywide housing restoration and neighborhood preservation movement in the 1960s, 1970s, and 1980s, the heyday of restoration and preservation activity in D.C.

The steady transformation of Georgetown indicated that choosing to purchase and repair an old house rather than buy or build a new one might not just be wise from a financial perspective, but also confer cultural distinction and social prestige on those who made the choice. Such cultural capital could not be claimed by city dwellers—including many Georgetowners—who lived in central Washington because of economic or racial constraints that effectively prevented them from moving elsewhere. But the cultural prestige accumulated by those who could afford that choice was intimately bound up with efforts to protect the historic character of the place. That historic character was in turn tied to the traditional domestic associations of the area's houses and its townscape. By this process, Georgetown became a symbolic place in Washington during the twentieth century, an influential model for a number of neighborhoods that saw in its example a path to physical revitalization and social distinction. Underpinning Georgetown's leadership in this was a steady increase in the value of property in the area.[18]

Georgetown's name was regularly intoned as the ideal toward which inner-city areas should strive as restoration activity spread in Washington in the 1950s, 1960s, and 1970s. Residents and restorationists in Capitol Hill enthusiastically compared themselves to Georgetown. In the early 1950s Elizabeth Kohl Draper, who was active in the incipient restoration of the residential neighborhoods close to the Capitol, gave a "Progress Report" to the Columbia Historical Society in which she suggested that "the architecture need not be eighteenth century, but the [Capitol Hill Southeast] section should be just as attractive as is the western approach to Georgetown."[19] In 1963 Donald Canty noted in *Architectural Forum* that as a result of restoration activity "Capitol Hill is fast becoming another Georgetown."[20] In 1970 a feature writer for the *Washington Daily News*

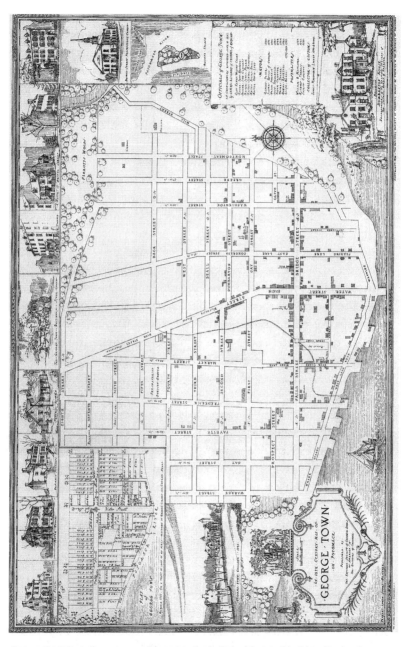

Figure 5. An eighteenth-century map of Georgetown by the National Society of the Colonial Dames of America, District of Columbia, 1934. Source: Colonial Dames of America in the District of Columbia.

called Capitol Hill the "neo-Georgetown" of contemporary Washington.[21] People in other areas of the city soon adopted a similar habit. In 1973 a *Washington Post* writer posed the unlikely question of the rundown Logan Circle neighborhood: "The Next Georgetown?"[22] A few years later a restorationist living several blocks to the east of Mount Vernon Square, in a neighborhood much less affected by restoration and gentrification than even Logan Circle, breathlessly asked a newspaper reporter, "it looks like Georgetown doesn't it?"[23] New infill development in some older sections of the city was also advertised during the 1970s in ways that invoked Georgetown and its "Federal architecture." More than a socially and aesthetically distinctive place, by the 1970s Georgetown stood for restoration itself in the minds of Washington's real estate boosters, journalists, and preservation advocates. Georgetown was the realized example of the hoped-for revival of the intown areas. It embodied the economic potential conferred by the atmosphere of history and the cultural distinction derived from that atmosphere.

Socially, there were three separate but overlapping sets of interests that instigated the protection of Georgetown's residential fabric in the early twentieth century. In the 1910s incumbent residents exhibited a burgeoning interest in the history of some the area's earliest and most substantial houses and the great figures that had inhabited them. Places such as Tudor Place, Dumbarton, and Montrose were especially prominent in such descriptions. A second group that contributed to Georgetown's renewal in the early twentieth century came from outside the District and was much less interested in questions of social pedigree. Members of this group instead focused their energies on improving living conditions by upgrading old houses in the area. Composed mostly of government workers and junior military officers and their wives, they arrived in Washington during World War I, having been brought to the capital to work for the federal government because of the war emergency.[24]

But the most important catalyst for organized protection and improvement of the area's built environment was provided by a group of influential newcomers who arrived in Georgetown in the 1920s and 1930s. This group laid the organizational and social foundations for the framework of protections that underpinned Georgetown's reputation in subsequent decades. Most had no previous associations with Georgetown, but they quickly formed a nucleus of citizens' groups and saw themselves as defending the good of the community. Dean Acheson, who would become Harry Truman's secretary of state, was ultimately the best known of those newcomers. But it was the housing reformer John Ihlder (1876–1968), later the head of Washington's slum reclamation agency the Alley Dwelling Authority and then the National Capital Housing Authority, who was the driving force in the group and the one who possessed expertise in matters of urban real estate and the technical issues related to urban planning, especially zoning.[25]

Ihlder, who moved to Washington in 1920 to organize a "Civic Development Department" at the U.S. Chamber of Commerce, was already in possession of a wealth of experience in the fields of housing and urban reform when he arrived in the capital. Working on New York's *Evening Sun* as a cub reporter he had met journalist and reform advocate Jacob Riis in 1900, a meeting he later cited as a decisive inspiration for his career. After moving to Grand Rapids, Michigan, Ihlder became involved in municipal affairs and worked with business and civic groups campaigning for "a city plan, a new water system, a playground within half a mile of every home, and the city manager form of government."[26] Municipal reform, housing activism, and city planning formed a constellation of interests that he developed during his time working as a journalist. In 1910 he returned to New York to work for the National Housing Association and in that capacity traveled to the United Kingdom and Europe to study housing conditions—experience he then utilized as an advisor to civic associations across the United States. In 1917 he became the director of the Philadelphia Housing Association, where he was also a member of the zoning commission from 1917 to 1920. This eclectic experience in the incipient housing and city-planning field provided Ihlder not only with his powerful convictions about housing justice and urban reform, but also a great purview on American real estate more broadly and especially its dynamics in aging urban environments.[27]

On his arrival in Washington Ihlder purchased Nordern at 2811 P Street in Georgetown and quickly involved himself in the civic affairs of his new neighborhood. In 1924, as chairman of the newly formed Georgetown Homeowners' Committee (a committee of the existing Georgetown Citizens' Association), he wrote a widely publicized pamphlet on the organization's behalf under the title *The Future of Georgetown* (Figure 6).[28] The pamphlet argued strongly for amending Washington's 1920 zoning

GEORGETOWN
PEABODY ROOM

The Future
of Georgetown

ALVIN M. WEST
26 JACKSON PLACE
WASHINGTON, D. C.

Figure 6. Cover of a pamphlet, *The Future of Georgetown*, produced by the Georgetown Homeowners' Committee, 1924. Source: Kiplinger Research Library, Historical Society of Washington, D.C.

act to lower heights in residential sections of Georgetown and prohibit any building erected for use as an apartment house, flat, or hotel. In the pamphlet Ihlder contrasted the existing value of Georgetown with the immanent threats to that value. He unfavorably compared the recent "intrusion of apartment houses" with what he called the "private homes" that composed the basic residential pattern in Georgetown. "If George-town is to remain a *home* community," he warned, "the time to act is now." It was an attempt to mobilize the public-spirited, private property owner against the commercial interests of the apartment house devel-oper. He equated the homeowner with a strong investment in commu-nity while the apartment house, he suggested, encouraged transience. Where private homes and their owners encouraged the protection of "natural beauty" and "individuality," apartment houses, he argued, "bor-row light and air from open spaces and invade the privacy of homeown-ers."[29] Ihlder thus evoked a familiar Washington theme: that a settled domestic life and the feeling of continuity that it encouraged were con-stantly threatened by the sense of transience that prevailed in the city. But what made Ihlder's viewpoint different from that articulated, for example, by Henry and Marian Adams a few decades earlier, who relied upon their own exemplary domestic arrangements, was his evocation of the themes and emerging tools of urban planning. That is, regula-tion and collective action could be mobilized, Ihlder argued, on behalf of stability and continuity.

While couched in the language of moral order and environmental amenity, Ihlder's argument for a zoning amendment for the residential area was, like zoning more generally and Clarence Perry's neighborhood unit idea that appeared just a few years later, fundamentally concerned with the proper shaping of real estate value. Indeed issues of environmen-tal order and property value, he believed, should be considered together.[30] Ihlder argued that apartment development held out the possibility of great increases in land value, but only for selected parcels of property. The overall effect would be a loss of amenity and an accompanying decrease in value for the remaining houses. He warned that

if the people of Georgetown do not protect themselves, the town in the next twenty years will become, not a solid mass of apartment houses, but a nondescript area with one or two or three in each block. And under their shadows will be the remaining private dwellings, for sale at a fraction of their present potential value; because home seekers will no longer be looking toward Georgetown, and many present owners will have sold out and moved to other districts which are protected against invasion.[31]

Ihlder urged Georgetowners to recognize the changes that had occurred in their district during the past five years—especially the restoration and preservation of existing houses and the enhancement of the area's character that came with it. "Note the increase in property value *because of these changes*," he implored his reader. "Would it not be folly to stop this improvement by spoiling the character of the community?"[32] In this way, he introduced the idea that preserving elements of the past and the existing character of the place could count as improvement of the district, not just individual properties (Figure 7).

Ihlder's pamphlet and the subsequent strategies pursued by the Georgetown Citizens' Association and the Progressive Citizens Association of Georgetown (PCAG) brought together some of the basic ideas that would be touchstones for neighborhood preservation and historic districting in Washington in later decades: a promotion of the idea of home as the single-family house, an invocation of the progressive planning idea of the neighborhood as a collective household, a sense that this neighborhood and community ideal was threatened by urban growth and rapid change, and a belief that such growth and change was a form of uneven development that provided great financial benefits to a few real estate developers and a loss of value and amenity to the community at large. In contrast to the urban intensification pursued by property developers, Ihlder promoted a model of realizing value in residential property that assumed that enlightened self-interest, the defense of environmental amenity, and community development were complementary. He also argued for citizen vigilance against commercial exploitation and environmental degradation, and for social and political investment in the district in addition to financial investment. Such views were shared and promoted by most preservation advocates in Washington in subsequent decades.

Ihlder's main arguments were clearly manifestations of his experience as a progressive reformer as well as his contact with urban-planning discourse and its evolving legal tools. But histories of planning have tended to ignore neighborhood preservation and its emergence alongside zoning

Have you noticed what is taking place in Georgetown today? On street after street old dwellings are being renovated in accordance with the traditions of the community; vacant spaces are being occupied by attractive little dwellings; in one instance already an old stable has been converted into a dwelling that is an ornament to the town and so desirable that the owner sold it before it was finished. Look back five years and note the number of changes of this kind, due to the present charm of Georgetown and to its promise of becoming more and more attractive to the home buyer. Note the increase in property values because of these changes. Would it not be folly to stop this improvement by spoiling the character of the community?

A recent hearing before the Zoning Commission was enlightening. The owner of a dwelling in what a few years ago was considered one of the best residence districts of Washington proposed to

Five

Figure 7. Page 5 of *The Future of Georgetown*, illustrating the qualities in the environment that the Georgetown Homeowners' Committee wanted to protect and describing the positive impact of restoration activity on real estate prices. Source: Kiplinger Research Library, Historical Society of Washington, D.C.

and other urban reform tools. Understandably, influential models of development such as those pioneered by Clarence Stein and Henry Wright at Radburn, New Jersey, and powerful environmental controls such as the New York Zoning Resolution of 1916 are the most commonly cited textbook case studies. Yet the very same rationales that drove such innovations in land-use control were also standard features of neighborhood-driven restoration and historic preservation efforts from the 1920s onward. As advocate and historian Vince Michael has argued by reference to the well-known early historic districts in Charleston, South Carolina, and New Orleans, "historic district preservation was not an evolution in zoning but present at its inception."[33]

The Georgetown example also reveals that so-called promarket preservation has a longer history than has generally been recognized. Preservation efforts prior to World War II were not simply elite measures to create aesthetically privileged enclaves to protect amenity against market forces, as Mike Wallace has argued. In at least some cases, they were genuine attempts to shape and control real estate markets and to enhance property value by restoring houses and preserving the scale and character of neighborhoods. While Ihlder's efforts were partial by comparison, they certainly predate and almost certainly influenced the better-known work of Antoinette Downing in Providence, Rhode Island, in the 1950s and 1960s.[34]

Preservation-oriented local organizations in Washington such as the Georgetown Citizens' Association, the Capitol Hill Restoration Society, and the Dupont Circle Citizens' Association recognized the efficacy of zoning for promoting orderly development and environmental control throughout the twentieth century. Such values were arguably as significant for preservation in the latter decades of the twentieth century, if not more so, than the ideas of Jane Jacobs, with her celebration of mixed uses in the urban environment and of social diversity. That is, it was not simply the romance of the aging cityscape, but also its environmental control and economic prospects that motivated the great wave of restoration and preservation. To miss this is to misunderstand the true character as well as the surprising success of historic districting.[35]

John Ihlder's ideas about the link between neighborhood preservation and homeowner citizenship, therefore, were prototypical. But he was also successful in the short term in his own domain, achieving the program he laid out on behalf of the Georgetown homeowners. With the help of friend and Chamber of Commerce colleague Bernard Wycoff and the twenty-six other households that composed the membership of the Georgetown Homeowners' Committee, Ihlder succeeded in persuading the U.S. Congress to pass an amendment to Washington's zoning ordinance limiting new construction to a height of forty feet in the residential sections of Georgetown. The amendment had the desired effect of making new apartment construction economically unappealing to developers and thereby slowing the pace of redevelopment. By so doing the amendment helped to preserve older buildings on larger lots, which in turn encouraged people to purchase and restore existing houses in the vicinity.[36]

Ihlder's knowledge of early zoning efforts in the United States meant that he was aware of the possible benefits to be obtained from both functional and density zoning. Washington's 1920 zoning law dealt with the former but ignored the latter. Or, in Ihlder's view at least, the ordinance had not been strict enough on maintaining lower densities in what he described as established "home communities." Just as significantly, Ihlder understood the power of a well-organized group of local citizens. With firsthand experience of the growing cultural sentiment in support of land-use controls, and what would later be called historic preservation, as well as the organizational structures that publicized their value, the newcomers to Georgetown in Ihlder's orbit took a leading role in promoting the idea that Georgetown, the District of Columbia's oldest section, might also become its most attractive and fashionable residential neighborhood.[37]

The impulse to protect the qualities of Georgetown was clearly inspired on the one hand by a growing recognition of the cultural value of the houses in the district and on the other by a belief that an increased scale of development was about to transform the area. Newcomers noted with alarm the dilapidated condition of many of the great houses that dated back to the late eighteenth and early nineteenth centuries. Meanwhile Ihlder saw the potential for rapid change that might come with increased apartment construction and traffic enabled by the new bridge across Rock Creek Park at Q Street. The cohort that valued the old houses quickly grasped the threat posed by Georgetown's changing identity, a change they themselves had helped to promote. So even as they promoted the cultural value of the area's architectural legacy, investing as much money in renovating houses as they might have in building new ones, they moved to defend the area against rapid development and the destruction that seemed certain to follow its increased desirability. This difficult balance between promoting physical and economic revitalization while defending against an increased scale of development was in many ways a defining challenge for all of the groups who would subsequently promote housing restoration in Washington and in central-city neighborhoods around the United States.[38]

The vigilance Ihlder counseled for Georgetowners was ultimately justified by reference to property value. The 1924 Georgetown zoning amendment was designed to protect residential uses and minimize what the Georgetown Homeowners' Committee viewed as the negative impact of apartment construction. Ihlder and his like-minded neighbors were convinced that property value should not be subject to major fluctuations caused by speculative development and rapid social change. Instead, they believed property value should grow steadily and evenly, ensuring social and physical continuity as well as encouraging investment in existing dwellings and property maintenance. Neighboring areas such as Dupont Circle and Cleveland Park did not possess the legacy of houses with recognized historic interest that Georgetown had. But residents in Dupont Circle also successfully utilized density zoning to reduce the incentives for redevelopment in the 1920s and 1930s. Cleveland Park citizens followed suit and successfully lobbied to have their neighborhood "downzoned" in 1940.[39]

This view of how residents could control development and simultaneously enhance property value held sway in Georgetown in the ensuing decades and underpinned the effort to have much of the area designated as a historic district. After more than a decade of lobbying by the PCAG, Congress eventually passed the Old Georgetown Act in 1950, creating the Old Georgetown Historic District (Map 2). This supported the intent of the 1924 zoning amendment in working to maintain the existing scale of development, but it also protected against incremental and thoughtless diminution of the aesthetic qualities of the district.[40]

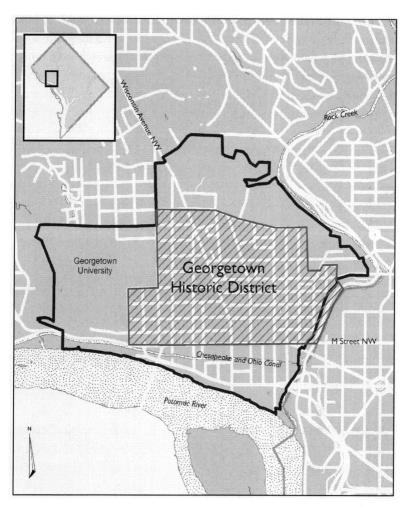

Map 2. The current Georgetown Historic District is enclosed in thick black outline. The hatched area indicates the original 1950 Old Georgetown Historic District. Created by and copyright Matthew B. Gilmore.

EXCEPTIONAL HISTORY:
LOUIS JUSTEMENT'S PLAN FOR TOTAL REDEVELOPMENT

Even as the Georgetown citizens' campaign to preserve existing buildings and the environmental setting for their district reached maturity with the successful designation of a historic district in 1950, such efforts seemed destined to be regarded as exceptional in Washington. The period saw the emergence of an invigorated housing and redevelopment agenda allied to a compelling new architectural and urbanistic image furnished by the modern movement. The success of planners and architects in persuading policy makers and city leaders of the urgent need to act on a large scale was based on a powerful conviction about the negative trajectory of land values in aging urban districts. Historic district protection and downzoning of historic areas was, in the opinion of most leading postwar experts, not sufficient to address the problems of devaluation that bedeviled most aging U.S. cities. It is a well-recognized irony, however, that the destructive means employed to redevelop urban areas at a project scale in the postwar decades became perhaps the greatest driver of sentiment to protect old buildings in areas designated as obsolete. As such it is vital to understand the postwar redevelopment agenda, its core motivations, and its evolution in Washington.

Among the most influential figures in the redevelopment field in Washington at the time was architect-planner Louis Justement (1891–1968). The title of his far-reaching 1946 study *New Cities for Old* signaled quite clearly his approach to the problem and helped set the direction of urban redevelopment when it got underway in the 1950s. The book proposed an expanded field of cooperation through which architects, planners, and municipal governments together might transform the prevailing conditions in American cities and stabilize the financial value of their land. He stated his underlying approach to the problem of devaluation quite plainly. "It is really not so difficult," he wrote; "all we have to do with our cities over a long period of time is to tear down all the buildings."[41] It is a statement that would have alarmed preservationists of subsequent decades and sounds extreme in light of the expansive development of historic preservation activity in the last third of the twentieth century. But it was a viewpoint that enjoyed wide support in the immediate postwar years. Like many of his architectural colleagues in the United States, Justement was broadly modernist in his architectural orientation by the end of World War II. As such, he believed that living conditions could and should be substantially improved for the great mass of people in cities by rehousing them in better-designed dwellings. These would be functionally oriented, rationally constructed, and more salubrious than those they replaced. The organization of the city itself should also make a substantial contribution to that improvement. Urbanistically Justement's proposals exhibited a cautious acceptance of the urban program advocated by the Congrès internationaux d'architecture moderne (CIAM) since the early 1930s. He believed that cities should be redeveloped according to a pattern of superblocks and high-speed roads provided to connect the different districts within the city (Figure 8). He also saw the advantages of separating the so-called four functions—dwelling, work, recreation, and transportation.[42]

Justement saw the problem of devaluation and the related issue of slum or substandard housing conditions as connected to badly managed urban land, based on improper economic incentives and impediments to

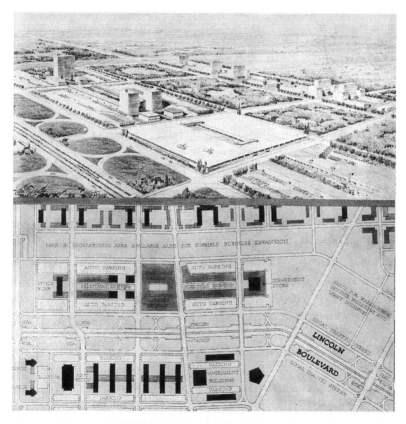

Figure 8.   Plan and perspective of a proposed redeveloped inner ring of Washington, D.C., by Louis Justement. The drawing highlights the separated functional zoning preferred by Justement. Source: Louis Justement, *New Cities for Old* (1946).

large-scale action. Characteristically for the immediate postwar period, he viewed the possibilities that lay ahead in distinct contrast to the first half century of professional planning. "Real city planning," he suggested, "will involve the complete reconstruction of the city; as we must devise financial mechanisms that will permit the ultimate destruction of all existing buildings."[43] The centerpiece of his program for the reform of the city—for which he used Washington as the case study—was a system of planned obsolescence in the field of housing. This could be achieved most effectively by extending the pattern of municipal control over urban infrastructure—what historian Daniel Rodgers has described as "the self owned city"—into the realm of residential landownership.[44] This would occur by a process of gradual condemnation, as Justement believed that almost every neighborhood would become blighted in the course of time, "for blight is, generally speaking, a function of the age of the neighborhood."[45] By this process the city, via a municipal realty corporation, would eventually come to control almost all of the available residential land within its boundaries. This would enable the city, he believed, to undertake large-scale redevelopment work without being constrained by the possible adverse effects on the value of particular parcels of property. With effective control over land, the municipality could set about improving the quality of the housing and the urban system more widely. Justement was certainly aware that in Stockholm, for example, where the architect Sven Markelius was the city planner, municipal landownership was a decisive factor in planning and tended to produce what like-minded experts of the period believed to be a high-quality urban environment. As G. E. Kidder Smith noted in his postwar study of Swedish architecture, "Municipal land ownership is the key to much of the attractiveness of Sweden's cities."[46]

While Justement saw an expanded role for government in respect to municipal land, with the municipal authority controlling the economic conditions under which land could be developed and exchanged, he was adamant that responsibility for providing housing should be left in the hands of private enterprise, which would compete to provide a valuable commodity to the city's inhabitants. Indeed this was his idea of how to avoid the need for public housing. His model was a bit like that which had evolved to accommodate motor vehicle transportation. The responsibility for the underlying infrastructure and the regulation of the conditions of its use were to be furnished and controlled by government, with private enterprise manufacturing the vehicles; in the case of housing, the dwelling units.[47] The key driver within the plan was that "at the end of the fiftieth year, the building is demolished, thus automatically making way for its successor."[48] Under such a plan the economic incentive in housing would be shifted from controlling space to producing housing of a continuously improving quality. The model was intended not just to do away with slums, but to improve the housing situation overall by providing more efficient and rational incentives for the production of dwellings.

So what did Justement's system of planned obsolescence imply for an area such as Georgetown? The district contained a large number of houses not just older than fifty years, but many that were 100, 150, and even 200 years old. Justement acknowledged that some neighborhoods may be so carefully maintained as to avoid the need for acquisition by the municipal authority. In fact, he specifically cited Georgetown as an example of the kind of exception he had in mind:

> Old Houses in Georgetown defy the general rule that the value of a building is in inverse relation to its age. If the building lasts long enough the rule sometimes operates in reverse. Two principal factors are involved: It has become fashionable among certain people to live in the old original houses because they have the value of scarcity, like precious stones; furthermore, these houses have an aesthetic appeal because they are the culminating product of the handcraft era. Georgetown, far from becoming a blighted area, has shown a remarkable renaissance in the past two decades. This same rejuvenation cannot be applied generally to other portions of the city. Only a few blocks in Georgetown and Alexandria have this historic, sentimental and aesthetic interest.[49]

He believed, therefore, that some historically significant buildings and residential districts might be retained. But they would be quite small and exceptional within the overall urban pattern, owing to the fact that their value was based on rarity and preindustrial craft qualities in their construction. What was worthy of protection in Georgetown, he argued, was certainly not substantial enough to undermine the general impetus toward condemnation and redevelopment. For the time being at least, revitalizing historic neighborhoods along the lines suggested by John Ihlder for Georgetown would remain a very limited activity confined to a handful of districts with widely acknowledged historical significance. On the other hand, condemnation, clearance, and redevelopment should take place on a large scale to ensure, as far as possible, the efficacy of the financial investment.

SOUTHWEST

In the postwar decades the federal government assumed responsibility for reinvigorating the value of central-city real estate via its expansive urban redevelopment program. The provisions included in Title I of the Housing Act of 1949 encouraged cities to access federal money for redevelopment, enabling them to attack urban blight. Vague in its definition but seemingly pervasive in reach, blight was viewed analogously to sickness in a living organism. It could spread from part to whole and undermine the entire organism. Devaluation and physical blight in central area residential neighborhoods was considered especially troubling as it threatened desirability and viability of neighboring downtown office and retail districts and the fixed capital investments on which they relied.[50] The thrust, therefore, of much of the urban renewal program was to create housing and neighborhoods in central areas that appealed to middle- and upper-income segments of a city's workforce. Planners and political leaders believed that the presence of these middle-class inhabitants would push up rents and reinvigorate land value more widely.

The presence of physically deteriorating areas in Washington, D.C., was also troubling for city leaders and federal officials because they perceived such areas as a threat to the dignity of the federal area. Visitors to the city enacted the rights of citizenship in the area in and around the National Mall. As such, decay in its immediate environs represented a symbolic threat to the national project. Places such as Southwest, a substantial but somewhat isolated section of the city between the National Mall and the Potomac River; the slum districts of Capitol Hill, immediately adjacent to the U.S. Capitol Building; and the area historically known as Swampoodle, an impoverished and shrinking residential district north and west of Union Station, each threatened to infect the historical tableaux of the National Mall. The urban renewal plans developed by the National Capital Planning Commission (NCPC) and published as the "Urban Renewal Workable Program" in 1957 reflected a strong concern with these deteriorated residential sections (Map 3).[51]

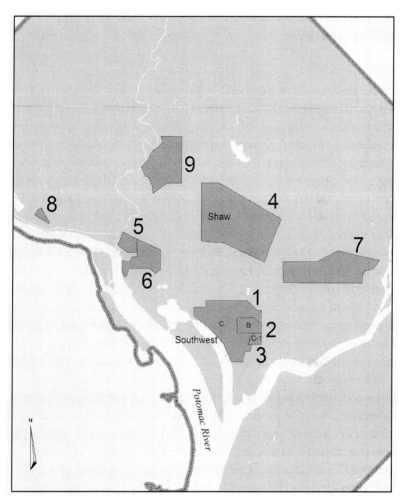

Map 3. Urban renewal areas based on the 1957 Urban Renewal Workable Program Map created by the District of Columbia Redevelopment Land Agency (RLA). When created, the RLA map identified the wide scope of bulldozer-driven urban renewal proposed for Washington's intown areas. Areas 1, 2, and 3 were part of the Southwest project; 4 was Shaw/Swampoodle; 5 and 6 were Foggy Bottom/West End; 7 was Capitol Hill, Northeast; 8 was Georgetown Waterfront; and 9 was Adams Morgan. Map redrawn by and copyright Matthew B. Gilmore.

The District of Columbia Redevelopment Land Agency (RLA) was established prior to the influential 1949 Housing Act and was thus well placed to take advantage of the federal legislation. In 1952 the RLA asked Louis Justement and the Washington architect Chloethiel Woodard Smith to produce a plan for the Southwest quadrant of Washington, one of the city's oldest quarters and an area that was an established source of concern for mortgage lenders and insurers. In the 1930s the U.S. Federal Housing Administration (FHA) mapped a series of negative statistics about the area's physical conditions and economic value onto what FHA officers clearly believed to be a related set of social conditions. The maps documented the median age of properties (comparatively old), average rental prices (low), and percentage of structures needing repairs (high). The social features of the neighborhood considered relevant to its value were "percentage of dwellings occupied by people other than white," "spread of colored population," and "residences of juvenile delinquents."[52] Government agencies and mortgage lenders assumed that the link between social features and physical decline was self-evident. But Justement had argued in *New Cites for Old* that the age of the area's housing alone was justification for demolition and redevelopment. The houses were almost all between 50 and 150 years old, and in Southwest there was little or no restoration of the type that was taking place in Georgetown. In Justement's view the area was an obvious candidate for urban renewal.

In many respects the 1952 Justement-Smith plan for Southwest was an elaboration of the redevelopment proposal Justement had included in *New Cities for Old*, though some of the book's more radical reform ideas, notably the idea of full municipal ownership of urban land, were politically untenable by 1952 and did not form part of the proposal. The plan envisaged the construction of tall residential buildings, the provision of high-speed automobile access and ample parking, and the provision of large areas of open space for communal recreation. The key, as Justement had argued in his book, was to act on a large scale. But instead of the city taking control of large parcels of land with the aim of establishing effective control over its value, this project had the more limited, and more politically conservative, aim of raising the value of the redevelopment area by attracting a sizable group of middle and upper-middle income earners.[53]

The Justement-Smith proposal never became a master plan for Southwest, and the designated renewal area was divided into three sections and eventually involved a host of different designers and developers, most famously I. M. Pei with the powerful New York developer William Zeckendorf. But, like the Senate Park Commission Plan (known as the McMillan Plan) half a century earlier, which provided a new physical framework and architectural image for the National Mall, the Justement-Smith plan was a publicity coup.[54] It won the admiration of Washington's newspapers and influential supporters in the building industry and in key civic organizations such as the Federal City Council. During the latter part of 1952 boldness became the keyword in the public debate about how to proceed in Southwest. Justement had consistently warned against timidity and piecemeal action, arguing that to plan effectively and rebuild cities would "require a bold program of action."[55] The Justement-Smith plan was contrasted with the earlier Albert Peets plan on behalf of the NCPC, which the Washington Building Congress described as "too timid."[56] The Peets plan had called for incremental redevelopment and physical forms more in keeping with Washington's intown residential environment.[57]

The Justement-Smith proposal, apart from providing impetus for a more far-reaching redevelopment agenda, set down general planning and design principles that exerted a strong influence over the Southwest project as a whole. The plan, and the debate that it invited, were about establishing a trajectory for the redevelopment of the city, and in that moment, the Justement-Smith plan appeared to many observers as a blueprint for success in stabilizing and improving the value of urban land. Historic preservation and the renewal of existing communities and physical forms was given little more than token consideration as the project unfolded. In the end a new city, or at least a new district, replaced the old.[58]

For all its promise and all its power to mobilize support on paper, the reality of the large-scale redevelopment project in Southwest Washington ultimately had an even greater power to inspire opposition. The negative reaction to the project that emerged in the late 1950s and early 1960s did not prevent its success as an individual project. Measured against its own aims Southwest was extremely successful. The 560-acre site was cleared of old buildings, and a modern, well-equipped group of neighborhoods built in their place. The project revived the value of a large area of residential land and promoted the formation of a community with a long-term tenure in the area and a high level of engagement in neighborhood affairs. But in the short-to-medium term the project also became a byword for undesirable urban renewal in Washington's central area neighborhoods. Its efficacy as a model of redevelopment and renewal was undercut as the legitimacy of urban renewal aims themselves faltered.[59]

By the 1960s, large-scale redevelopment was constrained by a political reaction to its destructive premises. Stabilizing and increasing central-city land values and establishing the conditions for successful community building along middle-class lines generally depended on the disruption of incumbent, usually poor, black neighborhoods. In the context of a growing civil rights movement, such schemes were viewed as unjust, even cruel. In the sixties a steadily growing group of observers regarded "negro removal," as James Baldwin famously described the consequences of the urban renewal program, as an unjustifiable cost for renewing the value of inner-city real estate.[60]

In a 1966 study Harvard University urbanologist James Q. Wilson noted the depth and breadth of the reaction to urban renewal nationally. Strongly negative in its overall character, this reaction was articulated both within policy debates and by popular movements, and it helped define new objects of political activity focused on urban form and the social life it sustained.[61] In Washington religious leaders, politicians, planners, and citizen activists all rounded on the Southwest project. Walter Fauntroy, at that time an outspoken young minister from the New Bethel Baptist Church in the Shaw neighborhood, and later a major figure in D.C.'s home-rule movement, told a newspaper reporter in 1960 that the Southwest urban renewal program "has dispossessed the very families and income groups who need help most and whose housing needs Congress intended the urban renewal program should meet."[62]

While the forced displacement of incumbent residents was the principal concern of critics and policy makers, other observers were also appalled at the scope of the physical destruction in the built environment and the paucity of meaningful preservation of buildings. In later years some chroniclers of the period argued that the purported decay and hopelessness of old Southwest as portrayed by reformers and modernizers was simply a misnomer. How such neighborhoods were perceived depended entirely on one's viewpoint. For example, photographs by Joseph Owen Curtis of neighborhood life in Southwest Washington from the 1930s and 1940s exhibit a deep affection for the patterns of everyday life and the neighborhood environment in which it was conducted. Rich in its depiction of human activity, Curtis's work has been cited by one chronicler of the period as evidence of the "ordered community of intricate social relationships that urban planners had missed" when they earmarked that area for demolition.[63]

PRESERVATION AS RENEWAL

When those observations about the destruction of community in Southwest were published in the 1980s they were mainstream, common sense. But two decades earlier the situation was very different. Wilson's 1966 book about the reaction to urban renewal documents the swift-moving tide of opinion. Commonsense redevelopment of the early 1960s was widely attacked by the middle of the decade and a byword for Jim Crow urban policy by the end of the decade. As the civil rights movement grew in strength urbanists, housing advocates, and preservationists began exploring alternatives to bulldozer-driven renewal.

One of those experts was the influential Washington-based planning consultant, architectural critic, and historian Frederick Gutheim (see Figure 14, chap. 3). Gutheim established the Washington Center for Metropolitan Studies in 1960, the Preservation Roundtable in 1969—an informal gathering of key preservation policy-makers and advocates in Washington—and later initiated a graduate program in historic preservation at George Washington University (1976). Gutheim regarded himself as a mainstream urbanist, and he supported coordinated redevelopment and renewal efforts in the 1950s and 1960s. But by 1960 he also clearly believed that historic preservation should be a central plank in that effort. He argued that the protection and revitalization of historic areas and historic towns would be a vital task of planning in the 1960s. In a keynote address to the "Annapolis Roundtable on the Growth of Historic Towns," held in May 1962, Gutheim observed that

> in the entire Urban Renewal handbook, without which no local public agency makes a move, there is no mention of the preservation of historic buildings or historic areas. . . . Directions and specifications are offered on

almost every conceivable subject to be encountered in the redevelopment process, but not on the preservation of buildings or areas.[64]

The nationally significant objective of the conference, he went on to proclaim, should be to change that, to provide guidance and explicit support for preservation-based renewal efforts. Gutheim, therefore, expressed his regret at the absence of one of the scheduled speakers at the Annapolis gathering, the commissioner of the federal government's Urban Renewal Administration, William L. Slayton. But he welcomed Slayton's representative, Margaret Carroll.

In the following year, 1963, Gutheim realized his objective. The Urban Renewal Administration jointly sponsored a conference and subsequent publication with the Housing and Home Finance Agency with the title *Historic Preservation through Urban Renewal*. Its author was Margaret Carroll. The publication highlighted Philadelphia's Society Hill project. This was an innovative renewal plan, led by the prominent planner and urban thinker Edmund Bacon, that became very well known in subsequent years for its sensitivity to existing physical patterns and its willingness to preserve a large number of buildings. But the Renewal Administration's publication also cited lesser-known initiatives underway in Portsmouth, New Hampshire; Mobile, Alabama; and Monterey and San Francisco, California, among others. Based on these examples, they concluded that urban renewal could play a vital and useful role in the nationally significant effort to "preserve, restore and rehabilitate historic structures and sites."[65] That year they also joined the National Trust for Historic Preservation's annual conference to host a day-long session on the topic of salvaging historic areas.[66]

The change of policy direction from the Urban Renewal Administration was an important acknowledgement that federal money was reshaping cities in ways that were often socially disruptive and physically destructive. However, the Carroll-authored publication highlighted the central importance of local initiative and responsibility for ensuring that redevelopment and renewal align with the interests of the community. She asserted that "if a community is willing to work at it, plan for it and provide strong leadership, there are not many preservation problems which occur in connection with urban renewal that cannot be solved."[67]

Frederick Gutheim, William Slayton, and Margaret Carroll were all aware of the energy that was going into housing and neighborhood restoration efforts in some of Washington's intown areas by this time. Gutheim cited activity in Georgetown and Alexandria, Virginia. He would also have been aware of the efforts in the Capitol Hill residential area and Foggy Bottom, a small neighborhood just to the west of the White House that was still predominantly residential in the 1960s.

By 1960 locally driven efforts that focused on regenerating the value of urban land and providing a range of housing options by rehabilitating existing buildings were underway in a number of urban areas around the country. These included Hyde Park and Kenwood in Chicago, Powelton in Philadelphia, and several working-class neighborhoods in Pittsburgh. But perhaps the best-known example and certainly the most explicitly preservationist in intent began in Providence, Rhode Island, in 1956, with the founding of the Providence Preservation Society (PPS).

Led by resident Antoinette Downing and John Nicholas Brown (scion of the famous Brown family of Rhode Island), this promarket preservation project for the inner-city College Hill district was the most influential of the postwar decades. While Downing and her colleagues drew on their knowledge of preservation efforts elsewhere, including in Georgetown, they were the first to access Urban Renewal Administration funds for the purposes of rehabilitation and historic preservation. In other words they did not mobilize preservation sentiment against urban renewal or against conventional private property relations, but harnessed the urban renewal process to historic preservation aims and vice versa. The centerpiece of the PPS plan to renew the North Benefit Street section of Providence was a carefully researched historic resources study that included ordinary dwellings alongside architecturally notable buildings. The project involved collaboration between the PPS and the Providence City Plan Commission, but its intellectual driving force was unquestionably Downing.[68]

The College Hill Historic District was designated in 1960 following the completion of a comprehensive survey of the affected area and included 500 buildings, 348 identified as "contributing structures." In 1967 a revised version of the historic resources study revealed that seventy-five houses in the district had been restored since the program got underway in 1960.[69]

The Providence program was underpinned by the same rationale John Ihlder had applied in Georgetown three decades earlier. Restoration and preservation, it was argued, if tackled from a comprehensive perspective, lifted the value of property and could thus revive the fortunes of an inner-city residential district, while preserving and promoting particular qualities in the built environment that could never be re-created. But the Providence project promised a much wider field of action than had been imagined in Georgetown. The Providence demonstration project was designed not only to promote restoration activity in an area with obvious appeal for the middle class and urban elite, but also to address the problems of devaluation and decay in neighborhoods that otherwise had no obvious prospects for revival. North Benefit Street, where the project was focused, was more like Southwest Washington, D.C., than it was like Georgetown. It was an area of concentrated social disadvantage subject to so-called blight conditions. To persuade inhabitants and the city government of the prospects of successfully renewing the area by restoring houses rather than clearing blocks, Downing and her collaborators saw that the urban landscape must be viewed in realistic terms. That is, rather than seeing the state of disrepair in the College Hill area as a sign of total failure, one that demanded an entirely new environment, the Providence study argued that such conditions could be reversed and remediated and that the buildings in the area would not need to be erased. The Providence program asserted that such areas must not be viewed in the narrowly analytical terms deployed by redevelopment agencies and other midcentury experts. On the contrary, Downing insisted that Providence was a total environment and a human environment.[70]

In subsequent years the reputation of the Providence program grew and with it Downing's own reputation as preservation champion and innovator. In Washington Downing's influence filtered in via published reports and articles as well as via sympathetic planning experts such as Gutheim, who had a national purview. Downing also appeared in person, most notably at an influential conference held in Washington in 1972 that was attended by many members of the burgeoning neighborhood preservation and restoration societies in D.C. The significance of the PPS's approach was that it encapsulated a noticeable shift in preservation thinking, one that moved the field away from its earlier focus on isolated monuments and shrines to historical heroes, toward what one historian has described as "the utilization of a neighborhood's historic fabric as an instrument of revitalization."[71] This shift in mission was promoted not just in Providence but also in different ways by prominent planners and preservationists around the country such as Edmund Bacon in Philadelphia, Arthur Ziegler in Pittsburgh, and Leopold Adler in Savannah, as well as by a host of neighborhood preservation groups in Washington, D.C.

Between the mid-1960s and mid-1970s profitable preservation, prodevelopment preservation, and preservation as renewal were all central topics in the flourishing preservation discourse. Such strategies gained traction in debates about the urban crisis, which was engulfing central cities by the late 1960s and influencing perceptions about the trajectory of urban life. Crucial to this discussion was the ordinary and everyday built environment, the so-called background buildings that constitute the majority of structures in any city, neighborhood, or town. By this time preservationists generally shared a belief that the real economic value of preservation strategies would be derived from protecting such background buildings, which were not in themselves culturally or historically significant. The contribution that such anonymous buildings made to what Frederick Gutheim had described in the early 1960s as the "total fabric" made those buildings significant from the point of view of the real estate value of a historic area. Likewise, what architect Seymour Auerbach variously described as the "character" and "atmosphere" of an urban area were intangibles that could nevertheless play a vital role in maintaining and reviving the value of property in a district.[72]

By the end of the 1960s preservation advocates and specialists writing in preservation-oriented publications were sanguine about the possibility of using historic preservation to foster property value and were mostly in agreement that it was necessary to consider "the total environment" not just outstanding individual works and places of special historical significance. In a speech delivered to the National Trust for Historic Preservation's 1969 conference D. K. Patton, commissioner of the Department of Commerce and Industry in New York City and member of that city's Brownstone Revival Committee, asserted that "judicious preservation is not antithetical to economic vitality and growth. Properly applied principles of historic preservation complement and support the whole process of urban economic growth."[73] Likewise, Leopold Adler stressed the importance of educating local communities, noting that the Historic

Savannah Foundation concentrated on "making Savannahians aware that historic preservation goes hand in hand with economic progress."[74]

So the 1960s, the decade that saw the most significant legislative milestones for historic preservation in the twentieth century, also saw the consolidation of a fundamentally different approach to the urban environment and its economic value. That approach had been around for some decades but had been overwhelmed by the energy and optimism of the postwar redevelopment agenda. From about 1960 preservationists, both in Washington and all across the country, claimed that this new approach balanced environmental awareness, humanistic cultural values, and an embrace of economic growth. In other words, the rise of preservation in the period was not simply a story of Jane Jacobs–inspired insurgent activists versus planning czars with their hubristic schemes to rebuild the cities. It was also a story of resources redirected and new models of rehabilitation crafted. This redirection of energy occurred within the planning profession and government as well as being shaped by pressure from without.

CONCLUSION

Max Page and Randall Mason have argued that national stories about historic preservation, such as Mike Wallace's, which focus on key legislative and regulatory changes made at the federal level, while interesting and worthy of discussion, are not the most important stories about the movement. The local level is where the real action is, where the economic conditions are felt and disputes about land use and redevelopment are acted out. In a sense, Page and Mason suggest, all preservation is local. Certainly what happened in Georgetown from the 1920s onward, and what happened in connection with the redevelopment of Southwest in the 1950s and 1960s, tells us a great deal about specifically Washington conditions. But it is equally clear that those local stories were bound up with national trends. John Ihlder, Louis Justement, and Frederick Gutheim all left a powerful imprint on the city via their activities. But each of them developed their thinking in the context of national and international policy discussions and design trends. Local actors in other places, people such as Antoinette Downing, influenced thinking in Washington as much as the particular social dynamics within the city. Moreover, urban development trends in Washington, D.C., across the middle decades of the twentieth century were a lodestar for the nation as they had been at the turn of the twentieth century and earlier. The success of Georgetown in one period and the ambition of Southwest in the next were noted beyond Washington and shaped the local debates elsewhere, not least because they were also the examples that national policy-makers and administrators such as William Slayton witnessed firsthand.

It is hard to overestimate the significance of real estate value as a driver for the preservation movement. Yet value is not formed in a vacuum or according to some abstract calculus. It is formed in relation to cultural perceptions and forms of representation. Thus far we have only just touched upon those issues. To really comprehend why Georgetown emerged in the way that it did, to figure out how Washington's Victorian cityscape recovered from the brink of oblivion to become a beloved landscape worthy of recognition and preservation alongside Georgetown, and to understand why the modernist urban redevelopment agenda faltered and now seems like an exception requires that we understand the perception of the physical qualities of the urban environment as a historical process. That is, to understand the shifting terrain of value and how historic preservation influenced that terrain demands a history of taste.

CHAPTER 2

Taste

Architectural Complexity and Social Diversity in the 1960s

In 1960 Roberta McCain, the wife of Admiral John S. McCain Jr. and mother of the future senator and presidential aspirant John McCain, opened the family's row house for the annual house and garden tour of the Capitol Hill Restoration Society (CHRS). Mrs. McCain told a neighborhood newspaper reporter on the day of the event that she had fled her house for the duration of the tour, but had "instructed her maid, stationed strategically at home, to report any comments she happened to hear."[1] Unfortunately there is no record of what the maid heard that day and consequently no way of knowing exactly how visitors to the family's home reacted to Mrs. McCain's row house, her choice of furnishings, or her standards of housekeeping. Nevertheless, Mrs. McCain's concerns provide a clue to the cultural assumptions and social character of the restoration movement in Washington in 1960. With bulldozers still busy in Southwest Washington and highway builders contemplating which streets and houses to excise from D.C.'s intown landscape, Mrs. McCain and others in her orbit opened their houses to exhibit their own preference for the city's existing historic fabric. This well-publicized preference was a quiet but clear reproach to the prominent urban redevelopment agenda of the day. This group of mostly elite tastemakers utilized the house and garden tours as an invitation to others to come and look at their restored houses and follow their lead.[2]

While the Capitol Hill area was far behind Georgetown in terms of its prestige as a restoration area and in the value of its residential real estate, as many as seven hundred people came to look at the McCain House and

twelve others in the surrounding neighborhood that day. The great interest generated by this display of restored houses presaged a significant
expansion of the restoration trend underway at the time in Washington.
That expansion was twofold. It involved a new level of interest from a
broader middle class, those not part of Washington's political or military
elite. The audience for housing restoration expanded as tastes broadened.
In particular, affection for Victorian architecture and urbanism grew rapidly. Consequently, whole swathes of the intown residential landscape
that were not recognized as part of the accepted terrain of historically
significant, pre-Victorian, or "handcraft era," neighborhoods in earlier
decades were gradually deemed worthy of restoration and preservation
interest. This greatly assisted efforts in the Capitol Hill area as well as in
the intown areas of Northwest.[3]

The McCains and others like them who participated in the early house
and garden tours in the Capitol Hill area were part of the same social
class that drove the restoration of Georgetown. But their participation also signaled a growing acceptability, even prestige, for areas other
than Georgetown, areas that, broadly speaking, were middle class and
Victorian. Mrs. McCain and the others who participated in the CHRS
tours in the late 1950s and early 1960s were a sort of bridge for the restoration movement, one that carried the movement out of Georgetown
and beyond its almost exclusive concern with the colonial and federal
periods.

The active promotion of restoration via the house and garden tours
was the most important means of expanding interest in neighborhood
restoration. But the focus on exhibiting the fruits of the restoration
effort, of asking others to look at restored houses, reflected a growing
concern with the wider environment. As the restoration trend evolved
into a movement, there was a shift in focus. The restoration movement
was not only concerned with display. Participants also looked outward
and encouraged their neighbors to do the same and observe what was
going on around them just as John Ihlder did in Georgetown in earlier
decades. There was a growing focus, in other words, on tending the restoration effort and protecting the value of what restorationists had already
achieved. In 1963 the CHRS published a pamphlet entitled *Capitol Hill
Vigilantes*. The front-page sketch depicted a group of "vigilant" residents
in caricatured fashion peering out in different directions from a typical

Washington row house (Figure 9). One mustachioed "gentleman" wields his binoculars, presumably on the lookout for tasteless additions and inappropriate development of all kinds. Another, in suit and tie, sports a raccoon-tail hat, Davy Crockett style, and raises a hand as though he is swearing allegiance to something. A young woman waters her garden but remains watchful, ostentatiously observing the surrounding neighborhood. An elderly woman carefully peruses a petition. Even a small child and his pets can be seen keeping watch on their community. The image is gently self-deprecating, but the pamphlet was a seriously intentioned call to arms for property owners (presumptively white in this image) in the Capitol Hill area.[4]

As the image on their pamphlet makes clear, the CHRS invoked the myth of the frontier, just like the "brownstone revival" movement in New York and "urban pioneers" in Baltimore, Wilmington, Philadelphia, and elsewhere in the United States.[5] For the CHRS and the other neighborhood and civic groups that pursued similar aims in the 1960s and 1970s, the restoration of housing and neighborhood heralded the restoration of ideals of citizenship in the intown areas and was thus cast as a revival of values drawn from the past. In fact it was a specifically Jeffersonian call for "eternal vigilance." This invocation of vigilance was tied to private property as something that required physical care and also social watchfulness, a kind of stewardship that sought to reshape the neighborhood environment in all its dimensions. On the inside of the *Capitol Hill Vigilantes* pamphlet was the text of a speech delivered to the CHRS by the National Trust for Historic Preservation's Tony P. Wrenn, in which he argued that such active, vigilant citizenship was the necessary cornerstone of any attempt to renew the resources and social life of the city. Such an attempt, Wrenn believed, should be based on the careful preservation of valued places.[6]

The conscious exercise of good taste and, indeed, an expansion of what was considered good taste were both necessary to build Washington's restoration movement from its historical base in Georgetown. But assertions of taste—formal or aesthetic appreciation of the city's aging building stock—were not, in and of themselves, sufficient to protect existing buildings and urban patterns. Throughout the twentieth century, restoration and preservation groups recognized that effective neighborhood preservation depended upon vigilant citizenship at the local level.

Capitol Hill
Vigilantes

If the "Hill" is to be stablized and preserved, that
is just what we must become, and what we must remain.

Produced as a
Community Service
by
THE CAPITOL HILL
RESTORATION SOCIETY

Figure 9.   Cover of Capitol Hill Restoration Society pamphlet, *Capitol Hill Vigilantes*, 1961. Source: Kiplinger Research Library, Historical Society of Washington, D.C.

Across the whole period from the late 1950s through until the end of the century a growing group of property owners in the Capitol Hill area and elsewhere in Washington drew on the example established in Georgetown and participated in the rites of display encouraged by the house and garden tours while heeding Wrenn's call for vigilant property ownership. Being fully part of the restoration culture implied an expansive set of concerns. In many places the issues of rat abatement, trash collection, and crime reduction remained the bread and butter of neighborhood vigilance. But in a steadily expanding group of intown neighborhoods, this concern with the savory qualities of public areas and street activity was augmented by attentiveness to the historical qualities of the built environment. In the Capitol Hill neighborhoods, Dupont Circle, Kalorama Triangle, and sections of Foggy Bottom, Cleveland Park, Burleith, and Mount Pleasant, physical threats to that historical ambience catalyzed resident group concerns and swelled the ranks of historic preservationists. Proposed innovations and realignments of the city's transportation and circulation system (which threatened the underlying spatial order of the L'Enfant Plan), incompatible new architectural forms and building details (which threatened the apparent coherency and "human scale" of the built environment), and a growing number of buildings and sites being utilized for nonresidential purposes, such as headquarters for industry bodies, were all galvanizing forces in the period. Preservation-oriented groups such as the CHRS, the Foggy Bottom Restoration Association, the Dupont Circle Citizens' Association (DCCA), and later the Dupont Circle Conservancy promoted the idea that the visual and architectural qualities of their neighborhoods and the social activities they sustained were subtly linked. These links, they asserted, made the historical and aesthetic qualities of the built environment a legitimate point of activist concern.[7]

Capitol Hill residents, for example, insistently argued against slum clearance and the expansion of the U.S. Capitol's auxiliary buildings, while restoring Victorian-era fireplaces and mantels and cultivating ornamental gardens. Over in the city's Northwest quadrant, during the 1960s and 1970s Dupont Circle residents rallied against the encroachment of Washington's new office building district in the K Street area, while also arguing against new curb cuts and satellite dishes, and strongly recommending that residents not replace timber window frames with aluminum varieties.[8]

The story of how this advocacy for historic fabric grew and spread around the intown areas, and the aesthetic convictions on which such advocacy was based, intersects closely with the story of real estate value across the century. Structural, economic factors played an important part in the process. A rent gap between Washington's central areas and its suburbs opened up in the 1960s as the costs associated with developing new suburbs grew and demand for suburban housing remained strong. As that gap grew, the financial incentive to choose central-city areas and rehabilitate properties there became greater. Yet the restoration trend in Washington did not emerge as an automatic response to structural conditions. Nor was such demand created by the spontaneous awakening of a new sensibility, which saw value and meaning in the central city in contrast to the suburbs. As geographer Neil Smith has noted, the "demand for gentrified housing can be and is created, most obviously through advertising."[9] Attitudes to the aging cityscape shifted during the 1960s and 1970s, but did so with the help of a concerted publicity campaign that advertised the value of the intown neighborhoods as a living environment and the architectural merits of its housing.

The publicity that promoted the merits of aging neighborhoods relied on particular norms of taste and structures of feeling. Questions of architectural style were of course bound up with those structures. This chapter examines how changing patterns of architectural taste and the changing social composition of the restoration movement underpinned the growing influence of historic preservation in the 1960s, 1970s, and 1980s. The almost universal revulsion for the architecture of the Victorian period that underpinned the architectural taste culture of the early twentieth century persisted well into the postwar decades. But by 1960 a new air of tolerance was evident. This shift in sentiment was vital to the expansion of the culture of restoration that gathered momentum in the 1960s and the preservationist politics that accompanied it.

COLONIAL ARCHITECTURE AND NATIONAL FEELING, 1900–1960

From the early years of the twentieth century through until perhaps 1960, ideas about what was true and good in the domestic architecture of the past were remarkably stable in the United States. High-style traditionalists, mainstream modernists, and middle-class suburbanites all converged around the idea that colonial- and federal-era architecture was authentically American and embodied the virtues of honesty, good taste, and restraint. In 1904, writing of the Georgian-influenced houses that were so pervasive in the eastern United States, architect Joy Wheeler Dow remarked that "they are intensely American in every line."[10] As the enormous popularity of Colonial Williamsburg attested, a broad pattern of eighteenth-century and early nineteenth-century buildings, not just its most famous historical shrines—Mount Vernon, Independence Hall, the John Hancock House—constituted a national heritage. Architectural commentators in the early twentieth century drew a stark contrast between what they viewed as the authentically American colonial styles and the "foreign importations" of the later decades of the nineteenth century, which they associated with an apparent collapse of taste.[11]

This cultural preference for colonial- and federal-era architecture was one that proved to be remarkably persistent in the United States. In 1960, Robert J. Lewis, the *Washington Star*'s home and real estate editor, explained to his readers why he thought colonial- and federal-era domestic architecture was so universally admired. Under the title "The Neat and Orderly Colonial Facade" Lewis catalogued the qualities of the style, asserting that its appeal lay in its "pleasantness," "its ease," and "its homeliness." He went on to enumerate what he saw as the most pleasing details—small paned windows, shutters, wrought iron railings, entrance lanterns—and to highlight its orderly system of proportion. While he acknowledged that there was great regional variety in the domestic architecture of the eastern United States from the period 1680 to 1830, he asserted that "good taste is the common denominator." In other words, the appeal of this period of domestic design—revived and reproduced insistently in the twentieth century—was its capacity, in Lewis's view, to transcend passing fashions. Here was an architecture, he concluded, that encapsulated good taste and domestic comfort in any era. "For centuries they have been tried, and for centuries they have been found true."[12]

During the half century from 1910 to 1960 the taste for federal-era domestic architecture, in particular, was a driving force of the restoration movement in Georgetown. For John Ihlder and his Georgetown Homeowners' Committee in the 1920s the area's "mellow old dwellings, its gardens, and its long history" were essential to its charm and, therefore, its ongoing value. The historical pedigree of the houses was far from incidental, and the houses that were illustrated in Ihlder's pamphlet

The Future of Georgetown were colonial- and federal-era houses. In 1944, with the restoration trend in Georgetown well established but formal preservation protections still some years away, the American Institute of Decorators sponsored the publication of *Georgetown Houses of the Federal Period* (Figure 10). It was perhaps the most explicit articulation of the taste culture that underpinned the restoration trend in Georgetown across this whole period. While the authors acknowledged the presence of houses

GEORGETOWN
HOUSES

OF THE FEDERAL PERIOD
1780 ~ 1830   WASHINGTON·D·C

DEERING·DAVIS
A·I·D
STEPHEN·P·DORSEY
and
RALPH·COLE·HALL

Foreword by
Nancy McClelland A·J·D

Figure 10.   Cover of *Georgetown Houses of the Federal Period, 1780–1830*, originally published in 1944.

from all periods of Georgetown's history, they asserted the superiority of the federal period: "Federal, Classic Revival, Victorian and Modern homes—all are here, but the architectural significance and the greatest charm of the town is in those structures built during the first fifty years of the nation's existence."[13] The authors connected the salient architectural qualities of Georgetown's federal-era houses to what they viewed as the moral attributes of the period itself. "A consistency of restraint and simplicity prevail in these structures which remind one of the general 'quality' evident in the life and effort of the new Republic."[14] The acknowledgment that many of the great patriots and political figures of the period—Thomas Jefferson, George Washington, John Adams, and Francis Scott Key—lived in or frequented Georgetown enhanced this supposed reciprocity between the moral and aesthetic qualities of the district. One's capacity to identify with both the local environment and the national story at once was also enabled by this connection to the morally exemplary figures of the early republic and the quality of their cultural world.

But the moral and aesthetic pedigree affirmed in *Georgetown Houses of the Federal Period* also included a wider social group that were a vital part of the mythology of the area during the twentieth-century restoration effort. In the 1910s William A. Gordon, a member of one of Georgetown's longest-standing families and an inhabitant of the Colonel John Cox House (later published in *Georgetown Houses*), delivered two papers to the Columbia Historical Society discussing the physical and social history of Georgetown. In addition to highlighting the architectural and landscape qualities of the area, Gordon defined Georgetown's social character in terms that would have strong appeal for neighborhood restorationists and historic preservationists in Washington for much of the twentieth century. Gordon described Georgetowners of the first half of the nineteenth century as "industrious, intelligent and enterprising; good citizens, self-reliant and proud of their town."[15] Moreover, he suggested, "the owners of the places mentioned were not men of wealth in the present acceptation of the word; but they were men of birth, education, high character and influence for good in the community."[16] It was the ideal of strong citizenship, the investment in the civic life of the town, not just its association with wealth and national power that Gordon identified as the enduring quality of the place. Three decades later the authors of *Georgetown*

Houses reiterated this focus on solid citizens by dedicating the greatest number of illustrations and descriptions to what they described as "typical, small houses." Taken together these typical houses, constructed in the half century from 1775 to 1825, constituted, they argued, an "urban type of dwelling with a distinct local idiom adapted to the lives of its builders and to local climate and materials."[17] The book implied, therefore, that there was an authentic connection between the stylistic characteristics of Georgetown's federal-era houses and the good character of their owners. The place was proportionate, and this quality was what gave the town as a whole its strong environmental character.

The architectural preferences articulated by Gordon and other Washingtonians in the first half of the twentieth century were characteristic of wider sentiment in the United States in the period. In 1912, for example, author and tastemaker Mary Northend opined that "Colonial is synonymous of the best and objects created during its influence are always of a higher degree of perfection than the best of other periods."[18] Nationalist endorsement of the colonial and federal architectural image and nationalism was a standard feature of design discourse in the first half of the twentieth century. Design historian Bridget May, for example, has documented the prevalence of such views in the shelter magazines such as *House Beautiful* in the early twentieth century. May argues that positive evocations of the colonial house "gained power from their association with the founding of the country, ancestral homes and a strong family life—what many middle-class members regarded as the foundations of American life, values and institutions."[19] This middle-class preference was a patriotic affirmation of the architectural habits and everyday environment of the revolutionary period. At the same time it was an ethnocentric affirmation of the superiority of the traditions of Anglo-European settlers who came to the United States in the seventeenth, eighteenth, and early nineteenth centuries. Support for this constellation of architectural images from the eighteenth and early nineteenth centuries became noticeably stronger in a period when many saw a threat to the cultural norms and political hegemony of native-born, white Protestants.[20]

The convictions of John Ihlder and his colleagues in the planning profession about real estate value and neighborhood amenity were thus joined to a set of genteel assumptions that dominated architectural taste and preservationist opinion. The embrace of the colonial and federal image in domestic architecture was almost universal among both progressive and conservative elites in the period. While there was great variety under the rubric "colonial architecture" what was most important about its use was the implied rejection of the recent past: Victorian architecture broadly conceived. As the museums scholar and critic Barbara Kirshenblatt-Gimblett has remarked, "Bad taste is one of the ways in which good taste announces itself—the finger that points to the breach points to the rule."[21] The presence of Victorian stylistic tendencies and habits of design were an unambiguous marker of poor taste and thus a way of constituting the boundaries around good taste.

Probably the greatest testament to this hegemony of the colonial and federal image was the fact that through several decades during the first half of the twentieth century Georgetown houses designed and built in the post–Civil War period were remodeled into what one amateur enthusiast in the early 1960s described as "bastard colonial."[22] That is, the external markers of Victorian architectural taste (bad passing fashion) were excised and replaced with ornamental details that evoked the architecture of the colonial and federal eras (durable good taste). Colonialized Victorian-era houses were, paradoxically, understood as updated and modernized, even as they sought a more respectable historical pedigree.

The belief of real estate columnist Robert J. Lewis, therefore, in the universal appeal of the neat and orderly colonial facade was based on a long-standing tradition of commentary that linked the colonial and federal periods of design to strong sentiment for family and nation and a rejection of Victorian bad taste. By 1960, however, when Lewis affirmed its immunity to fashion, that colonial revival consensus was clearly fraying. The certainty that pervaded the 1920s and 1930s, with its celebrated Williamsburg restoration and reconstruction, gave way to a very different set of cultural and architectural images. The rule of taste established in the early decades of the twentieth century was about to be overthrown, and Lewis's praise for the shared ideals of American domestic architecture was, in fact, something of a eulogy. If Americans of widely varying means and outlook had broadly agreed on what constituted tasteful and morally sound domestic architecture—which in many ways they did between 1900 and 1960—in the 1960s that consensus unraveled.

During the 1960s and the 1970s Washingtonians' interested in restoring old houses showed a remarkable elasticity and inclusiveness in the buildings they considered worthy of preservation and restoration. Taste was no longer to be governed by simple, commonsense values. The quiet repose, "the sobriety," "restraint," and orderliness of colonial-era domestic architecture was no longer the only appealing image of the past. New recruits to the restoration and preservation cause discovered the pleasures of Victorian domestic architecture, embracing its restless energy and formal complexity. This embrace of Victorian inclusiveness and eclecticism signaled both a move away from the genteel consensus in the restoration movement and a growing unease about the trajectory of modern architecture.

THE TASTE FOR GINGERBREAD

In 1957 John Maass made one of the first published contributions to the effort to revive the reputation of Victorian-era architecture and design in the United States with a richly illustrated book, provocatively titled *The Gingerbread Age*. Maass argued that the aesthetically conformist 1950s could learn something from Victorian architects and builders. In his view, rather than being gloomy, superficial, and shallowly eclectic as many accused, Victorian residential architecture was vigorous, innovative, and playful. Maass saw nothing wrong with the applied ornament that was such a conspicuous aspect of Victorian architecture. Instead he saw an analogy with clothing of the period. With the mass manufacture of architectural details—not just brackets and moldings but almost every imaginable detail, including masonry gargoyles—a medium of cultural communication became available to a much wider group in society than ever before, just as cheaper textiles encouraged both a diffusion and new sense of inventiveness in clothing fashions during the same period. Moreover, Maass argued that the bold definition of form that emerged in Victorian clothing fashions was an apt parallel to the domestic architecture of the period, when the complex program of the house became a point of departure for design rather than a problem to be overcome.[23]

The Gingerbread Age was at odds with mainstream taste as well as high-style criticism and scholarly opinion. Almost all of the major figures who wrote about American architecture in the first half of the twentieth century took a predominantly negative view of the late Victorian era, or what was also often called the Gilded Age. While Lewis Mumford acknowledged that there were great exceptions, most notably the work of Henry Hobson Richardson, he wrote that the architecture of the Gilded Age was marked by "the dispersion of taste and the collapse of judgment."[24] Louis Sullivan's biographer Hugh Morrison thought it was "all completely and irremediably bad."[25] As late as 1948 the man who would subsequently become the dean of historic preservation education in the United States, James Marston Fitch, described the architecture of the high Victorian age as a "turgid flood."[26]

As it turned out Maass was not an eccentric contrarian. Within just a few years of the publication of *The Gingerbread Age* specialists in the field were openly expressing a new level of appreciation for, and understanding of, Victorian architecture. In 1964 Alan Gowans argued that American architecture of the 1870s and 1880s was not "some inexplicable, collective aberration," but the "product of deep forces making for inexorable social and cultural change."[27] Whatever your personal view of it and in spite of its relentless individualism, Gowans argued, the architecture of the high Victorian period was just as much a historical style as those that came before it. In 1966 the Victorian Society of America was founded as a sister organization to the English Victorian Society (1958), and by the mid-1970s the effort to protect the architectural and urbanistic legacy of the Victorian period, viewed as an eccentricity just fifteen years earlier, was accepted as perfectly normal. While Gowans's evenhanded historical assessment had precedents in the work of Henry-Russell Hitchcock and Wayne Andrews, such appreciation for the historical specificity of Victorian architecture had been uncommon in the highly polemical context of architectural discourse in the postwar decades.[28]

In Washington it was amateur enthusiasts more than the scholarly critics and historians who had the greatest impact on changing perceptions. John Maass's *The Gingerbread Age* resonated with a lawyer by the name of Henry Glassie, father of the well-known folklorist and historian of vernacular architecture of the same name. Glassie senior occupied an office in a distinctively Victorian row house near Dupont Circle and became curious about the building and others like it. In *The Gingerbread Age* Glassie found the appreciative language that gave voice to the pleasure he took in the building that housed his office, and he subsequently transposed its arguments to the national capital in an article titled "Victorian Homes in Washington." Glassie shifted Maass's time frame, and in so doing focused on some different tendencies in design, but he adopted the

same rhetorical posture as Maass, disavowing scholarly specialization and
foregrounding his affection for the period. Glassie's article, like Maass's
book, acknowledged the pleasures derived from the highly expressive
ways in which Victorian builders and architects modeled form, and at the
same time reveled in eclectic associations with other places and times.[29]
Glassie also perceptively outlined how the system of urban development in Washington in the late nineteenth century created environmental characteristics overlooked by design professionals and critics of earlier
decades because of the widespread antipathy toward Victorian architecture. Architect-planner Louis Justement was typical in this respect. In
the 1940s he was so focused, as he wrote, on "getting rid of the buildings
erected during the architectural nightmare in which we have been living
for the past hundred years"[30] that he completely failed to recognize the
great environmental qualities bequeathed to Washington by that period
of development. In contrast, Glassie highlighted such qualities noting,
for example, the great trees that lined many of the residential streets that
were developed and planted in the 1870s and 1880s.

Glassie's appreciation for this legacy also led him to an appreciation
of the part played by the District's controversial territorial governor
Alexander "Boss" Shepherd. From the Progressive Era onward Shepherd
was seen as the emblematic figure of Washington's version of the local
political machine, a man dedicated to his own power rather than public
service. Glassie was one of the first in a growing group of historians and
journalists that began to rehabilitate Shepherd's reputation. For Glassie,
Shepherd was himself a picturesque dimension of Washington's Victorian past.[31]

This more positive attitude to Shepherd spread, and in 1972 the *Washington Post*'s architecture critic Wolf von Eckardt put Shepherd's influence
at the center of his appreciative account of the architecture and urban
qualities of Logan Circle, a traffic circle and intown neighborhood in
Washington's Northwest quadrant.[32] Borrowing from Maass, von Eckardt
described Logan Circle, developed in the 1870s and 1880s, as a "wonder-
ful, uninhibited concoction of gingerbread and *joie de vivre.*" This section
of the city was characterized, von Eckardt said, by its "never ending towers and turrets, gables and bays, French windows and portholes, arches
and columns, balconies and loggias, stairs and stoops, mansards and double mansards, which, stunned out of any more accurate description, we

Figure 11. Composite drawing of houses on Logan Circle by Historic American Buildings Survey, circa 1992. Courtesy of Library of Congress.

call High Victorian" (Figure 11).[33] "Boss" Shepherd's reputation, therefore, was consonant with that of the domestic architecture that thrived around the time of his political influence. For decades a source of embarrassment if not disgust, from about 1960 onward both the man and the architecture were newly appreciated as big, bold, and rarely boring.

HOUSE AND GARDEN TOURS

This reevaluation of what constituted an acceptable architectural image of the past among experts and amateur commentators exercised some influence on the growing restoration organizations. Notably the house and gardens tours, which were central to the restoration movement's promotional apparatus in its period of great growth between 1960 and the mid-1970s, reflected this change in taste. In Washington, D.C., between the 1920s and 1940s Georgetown was typically the focus of discussions about neighborhood restoration and preservation. In 1952, however, Elizabeth Kohl Draper reported on the progress of Capitol Hill, Southeast as a restoration area, and by 1960 restoration activity was well advanced in several central-city neighborhoods, including Foggy Bottom and Kalorama. The main reason for this was the rapid growth in the organizational apparatus dedicated to restoring buildings and neighborhoods in the late 1950s and early 1960s. Organized groups established and promoted the reputations of several central-city neighborhoods as restoration areas.

New neighborhood-based preservation and restoration groups such as the CHRS and the Foggy Bottom Restoration Association (both founded in 1955) emerged in the period, and their activities quickly became locally prominent. House and garden tours became a central feature of their activities, catalyzing interest in their neighborhoods. The display of family homes by the McCain family and others like them reveals cultural assumptions and patterns of taste that reshaped expectations and ideals related to domesticity, neighborhood, and the city. The headlines of the early 1960s focused on the potential and the problems of large-scale urban renewal efforts. But the pages of the weekend lift-out sections from this period evidence a fine-grained pattern of urban change. This arguably had as great an impact on the perceptions and trajectory of Washington's central area neighborhoods in the last third of the twentieth century as the story of urban renewal and outward conflict playing out on the front pages.[34]

But this neighborhood restoration movement in Washington and elsewhere—Boston, New York, Savannah—in the latter decades of the twentieth century did not spring from nothing. That is, it was not the spontaneous awakening of a fundamentally new consciousness and moral vision as "back to the city" proponents in the 1970s suggested. Rather the movement required careful tending and promotion and a dedicated organizational infrastructure. In Washington, D.C., between the 1950s and the 1970s house and garden tours became the most publicly visible aspect of organized restoration activity. Aside from showcasing individual houses, the tours raised money for local preservation and citizens' groups and created awareness of the activities of such groups throughout the metropolitan area.[35]

As with other markers of what the urban geographer Dennis E. Gale has called "the culture of restoration" in Washington, Georgetown was the model. The first Georgetown house and garden tour was conducted in 1927, and the event has been held almost every year since. But in the 1950s and 1960s the house and garden tour idea began to spread to other sections of the city where restoration activity was just getting underway.[36]

The regular house and garden tours held in the suburban and rural counties surrounding the District of Columbia in the 1950s and early

1960s undoubtedly also influenced the intown groups that rose to prominence at that time. The *Evening Star* and *Sunday Star* "Society-Home" section frequently publicized such events, illustrating the "gracious houses"
and manicured gardens that were their highlights. The Maryland House
and Garden Pilgrimage, the Potomac Country House Tour (first held in
1956), the House and Garden Tour of McLean, Virginia, the house tour
of the Alexandria Association, and the Northern Virginia Garden Tour
all focused on grand houses and the historical worthies who had built
or inhabited them. Newspaper and magazine articles that publicized the
events implied that the tours would provide a glimpse of the gentry in
Washington's nearby hinterland. For example, the owners of Habre de
Venture in Charles County, Maryland, the house built by Thomas Stone,
a signer of the Declaration of Independence, opened the property for a
1961 tour. In the same year Robert and Ethel Kennedy showed Hickory
Hill, their house in McLean, Virginia, dating from the early nineteenth
century.[37]

Owners who opened their houses for these events tended to view
their property in patrimonial terms. This patrimony was composed not
just of the architecturally distinguished houses but also their landscape
settings and their contents—books, antique collectibles, and furnishings.
The individual objects and the properties as a whole linked the property
owners to the federal era and early republic and the mythologized figures associated with the period. In this way the rural properties opened
for these tours complemented the growing reputation of Georgetown.
Exhibiting such connections through house tours was intended as exemplary, a way of demonstrating to a middle-class audience how places and
objects could make tangible links to a valorized past.

The patrimonial idea of history that was enacted, with its authoritative
cultural tradition and focus on a moment of intense patriotic interest—
the federal period—was different from the restoration culture that developed in the late 1960s and 1970s. As Richard Ernie Reed's book, *Return to
the City* (1979) attests, self-discovery and community formation become
central themes of the restoration culture in that later period. Yet a wider
view of the continuities of the restoration movement also reveals that
these patterns of display, with their patrimonial ideological underpin-
nings, mixed quite easily with the growing focus on self-discovery and
self-expression that became more important to the restoration movement

in later years. The negative ideal against which urban pioneers and the restoration movement of the late 1960s and 1970s contrasted itself was not the propertied elite, but the suburban middle-class. Elite urbanites in Washington and in its rural hinterland actually formed part of the picturesque diversity of the city as it was increasingly construed by restoration and preservation advocates in the late 1960s and 1970s.[38]

CAPITOL HILL RESTORATION SOCIETY
HOUSE AND GARDEN TOURS

The CHRS initiated its annual house and garden tour in 1958, and by 1960 the organizers sold over seven hundred tickets to the event. This level of interest is clear evidence of a burgeoning restoration constituency and highlights the fact that urban residential neighborhoods, not just the hamlets of the rural hinterland, enjoyed growing historical interest and cultural prestige. The effort to foster interest in the neighborhoods immediately to the east of the U.S. Capitol and assist, as the CHRS brochure stated, the "preservation and restoration of historic buildings on Capitol Hill" involved a deliberate and sophisticated publicity campaign. Aside from distributing artfully produced flyers and posters around the metropolitan area, promoters persuaded the editors of the city's major newspapers, several weekly magazines, and neighborhood newspapers to publicize the event with short pieces and/or pictorial spreads. Material produced for the CHRS tours inverted the earlier visual trope that showed slums in intown neighborhoods with the Capitol dome looming up behind. Now, instead a stylish, historic house or tidy streetscape appeared in the foreground with the dome looming up behind (Figures 12 and 13).[39]

Typically held during spring, when gardens were at their best and the residential real estate market picked up, the house and garden tours were a showcase for individual renovations and for private market-led neighborhood revitalization. For organizations such as the CHRS and later for the DCCA the tours were the equivalent of the commercial builder's display homes. They created increased interest in restoration neighborhoods, which in turn helped to sell houses to potential restorers and remodelers. An article published in the neighborhood newspaper *The Intowner* in the early 1970s, promoting a Dupont Circle house tour, was typical of the way the tours were publicized. It noted that the tour "is

CAPITOL HILL

RESTORATION SOCIETY

Annual Tour Of
HOMES and GARDENS
On
CAPITOL HILL
2 P.M. - 6 P.M.
Sunday, May 15, 1960

Figure 12. Ticket for the 1960 Capitol Hill House and Garden Tour. Source: Jessie Stearns Buscher Collection. Courtesy of Nancy and Norman Metzger.

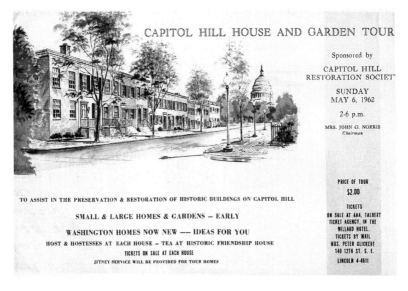

Figure 13. Advertising flyer for the 1962 Capitol Hill House and Garden Tour. Source: Jessie Stearns Buscher Collection. Courtesy of Nancy and Norman Metzger.

especially recommended for those of our readers looking for ideas in remodeling their homes or apartments."[40] The active participation of local real estate agents was also a prominent aspect of the events. But rather than enumerating the standard features of houses in the manner of a typical real estate advertisement, the tour brochures focused on the distinctive ways in which the inhabitants had furnished and decorated the houses and cultivated their gardens.[41]

In the promotional and interpretive material that accompanied the tours some effort was made to identify the period in which houses were built, but during the 1950s and 1960s there was little evidence of systematic research into the history of the individual buildings. C. Dudley Brown, who had a long involvement with restoration projects on Capitol Hill and in other parts of Washington, has recalled that at that time there were a lot of efforts to "early them up"—meaning that Victorian-era houses were frequently given new shutters, doors, and other details in historical styles that had little or no basis in the history of the building.[42] The studied historicism that became associated with historic preservation in the 1980s in particular was not yet a pronounced value. Instead old houses were generally treated as an opportunity and site of inspiration for the expression of taste in the decorative arts.

Descriptions published in tour brochures focused on interior details such as fireplaces and mantels as well as furnishings and collectibles and the ways in which inhabitants restored and incorporated these elements into functionally modernized interiors. A marked feature of the Capitol Hill house and garden tours in the 1960s was the value placed on eclecticism and exoticism. The 1964 tour brochure vividly illustrates the point. The huge living room in the Claiborne house, we learn, was "a blending of Victorian and modern styles, complemented by Chinese sculptures, lithographs and Oriental rugs." Mrs. Hendricks's house was "filled with magnificent pieces from many countries and periods. An urn more than a thousand years old is displayed in an early American cabinet on top of a 17th century Italian buffet."[43] Attendees at the 1964 tour also saw the interior of the Hogan house with its "collection of old family watches from Ireland . . . a crystal chandelier from Czechoslovakia in the dining room and a 1780 Sheffield Coffee Urn."[44]

It is unlikely that these descriptions reflect a conscious revival of Victorian habits of collecting and decorating. The design of *Breakfast at Tiffany's* (1961) probably exercised greater influence. But the annual Capitol Hill tour, like the new appreciation for Victorian architecture in the 1960s, was an index of the shift away from an idea of good taste as restraint. Like British Victorians, Washington's 1960s remodelers nurtured a somewhat romantic idea of remote places that equated those places with the past. Likewise, regional and historical styles were not an authoritative guide to restoration and decoration. Rather the past and foreign places were more like a treasure trove that provided the raw materials for personal expression, for the creation of a kind of interiorized universe. As Walter Benjamin noted of the nineteenth-century middle-class parlor, "for the private individual the private environment represents the universe. In it he gathers remote places and the past. His drawing room is a box in the world theatre."[45] This ideal of private life and the private environment was manifestly part of the self-identity of Washingtonians who opened their properties, and thereby their "universe," for public display as part of house and garden tours in the 1960s.

Restoration efforts, especially those in Georgetown, had long been associated with prominent figures in the State Department, many of

whom had spent a great deal of time outside the United States, and some
of whom became standard bearers of worldliness and cultural sophistication in Washington. The same group, as historian David Johnson has
pointed out, were also stereotyped and disparaged in some quarters in
the 1950s as "rich, red and queer" and liable to be found, according to
tabloid journalists Lait and Mortimer, "prancing behind the walls of
their restored townhouses."[46] Publicity also highlighted the taste of those
who had spent time outside the United States. For example, the local
newspaper *Capitol Hill Spectator* highlighted the purchase of a row house
by "Mr. and Mrs. Richard Conroy of the State Department, who have
just returned from a tour in Vienna."[47] Indeed, such reports included a
wide range of prominent people, from congressmen and their families
to artists and intellectuals. Later stereotypes of urban, liberal elites were
not yet stamped, but the elements were all there.[48]

In the early CHRS house tour materials, however, retired military
leaders—paragons of conventional masculinity—and their families were
most prominently represented. The prominence of military families reflected the ongoing links between the residential community in Capitol
Hill, Southeast, and the Washington Navy Yard in this period. The 1960
tour included the McCain house as well as the residences of another
admiral and a retired colonel, and in the following few years there was
always at least one tour house on display that was occupied by a high-
ranking, retired military person. An inventory compiled by the CHRS
indicates that fourteen military officers opened their houses for such
tours in the decade between 1958 and 1968 (Map 4). One might assume
that the decorative tastes of these tour participants would be more conservative than others. But tour information from these years highlighted
the provenance of the very eclectic range of objects that the military men
and their wives had collected while overseas, much as for other participants. The 1961 Capitol Hill tour information described Brig. Gen. and
Mrs. Thomas J. Betts's house and its "many curios, including two beautiful jade ducks from Shanghai . . . a Japanese wall screen describing an
amusing story . . . a Coromandel screen from the Indian Ocean area . . .
a Polish candelabra," and numerous other collectibles from Europe and
Asia.[49] A pictorial spread in the *Sunday Star* in 1960 showed the interior of
Colonel Robert Burns's house, which apparently included a "400 year old

Spanish castle warmer table . . . bull fight plaques he picked up in Spain," and his antique brass Punch and Judy set that he used as bookends.[50]

Not everyone who was active in housing restoration in the early 1960s was socially or professionally prominent in Washington. It is obvious, however, that those who organized the tours and otherwise promoted housing restoration felt it was useful to highlight the presence of notable people in the intown areas. Jacqueline Kennedy, who lived in restored houses in

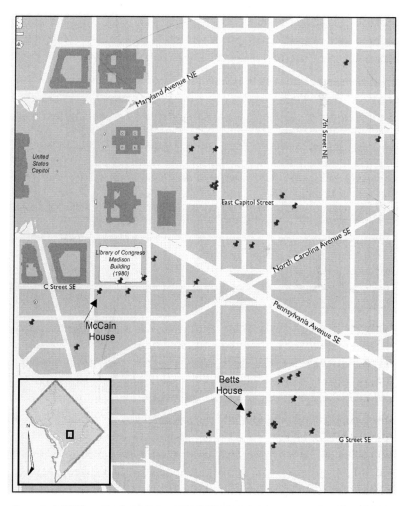

Map 4. Capitol Hill Restoration Society House and Garden Tour house locations, 1959–61. Created by and copyright Matthew B. Gilmore.

Alexandria, Virginia, and Georgetown before and after her period in the White House, was undoubtedly the best-known preservation advocate in the Washington area in the 1960s. But many other politically and socially prominent people also lived in remodeled houses in the early 1960s. As early as 1949 it was reported that Supreme Court Justice William O. Douglas had purchased a "historic house" in the southeast section of Capitol Hill. The *Washington Post* generously publicized the restoration effort of former attorney general Francis Biddle and his wife, the poet Katherine Garrison Chapin, in 1960. And in 1961 the *Star* reported that economist and diplomat Eleanor Lansig Dulles, member of the Dulles diplomatic dynasty that included Secretary of State John Foster Dulles, was a major catalyst for restoration activity in the Foggy Bottom neighborhood, where she had purchased and remodeled five houses. Groups such as CHRS viewed the confidence of such prominent figures in the economic health, social life, and cultural patterns of intown areas as a valuable means of promoting the safety and desirability of those neighborhoods.[51]

There were potential pitfalls, however, in emphasizing elite leadership in restoration publicity. By the late 1960s focusing on the cosmopolitanism and the air of international sophistication of prominent restorationists was potentially inconsistent with the focus on community building and participation. The restoration movement dramatically broadened its reach during the 1960s by emphasizing the importance of investing financial, cultural, and personal resources in the city's intown neighborhoods and pointed to the qualities of vigilant homeownership and community participation as desirable objectives. In his 1963 speech to the CHRS Tony Wrenn of the National Trust highlighted these themes, warning his audience that they must "be alert" and "willing to work" if they are to protect the qualities of the residential environment on Capitol Hill.[52] On the one hand there was the charisma of the natural aristocracy, those for whom good taste apparently came effortlessly. On the other hand there was the increasing focus on the need to work hard and be vigilant so as to maintain the beauty and increase the value of urban neighborhoods by preserving their architectural and environmental qualities.

While restoration advocates did not explicitly address such social distinctions at the time, efforts were made to manage the possible contradictions in the quickly evolving restoration movement. In the context of the Capitol Hill neighborhoods there was at least one attempt to describe the harmony of interests between incumbent residents of "good taste" and enthusiastic pioneers. A 1960 booklet about the Capitol Hill area included a section on restoration, which described the CHRS in the following terms:

> After getting off to slow start a few years ago it began to attract a much larger membership, and now for the last three years has been conducting spring house tours which arouse a good deal of interest and enthusiasm and draw many new residents to the Hill.[53]

The author went on to note, however, that new residents drawn into the restoration trend "have sometimes been unaware that this eastern arrondissement had never been entirely abandoned by its old families." These families who, the reader is told, have "good taste and the money to gratify it," as well as "a sense of civic responsibility,"

> stayed on quietly, maintaining their houses, gardens and church memberships and keeping for themselves a sense of continuity. Then, when reinforcements came, so to speak, they were encouraged to burnish and furbish as never before. The results are good and getting better.[54]

During the period from 1960 to 1965, therefore, the story of revival and renewal was tempered by a clear acknowledgement of continuity. The so-called pioneers who saw themselves as carving out new communities were encouraged to recognize existing communities of people interested in improving their properties and highlighting the architectural qualities of their neighborhood.

This specific concern to mediate between pioneers and incumbents of taste in the Capitol Hill neighborhoods reflected a wider effort within the restoration movement to strike the correct balance between local identification and stronger community ties on the one hand and heightened social prominence and cultural distinction on the other. Yet despite this concern with balancing different objectives and agendas, there were several notable shifts in the audience, tone, and content of the promotional brochures and press coverage of the house and garden tours during these years. The military flavor certainly disappeared from the Capitol Hill tours in the 1970s and 1980s, though members of Congress remained fairly prominent, and the ideal of diversity became a major marker of the shifting tastes and social values of the restoration and preservation movement.

From an architectural viewpoint the embrace of Victorian-era buildings was noticeable as the years passed and as the house and garden tours spread from Georgetown to Capitol Hill and on to other intown neighborhoods. The DCCA inaugurated a house tour in 1968 highlighting Gilded Age mansions such as that built for Christian Heurich and at that time occupied by the Columbia Historical Society (later the Historical Society of Washington, D.C.). It was one of the best-known Victorian landmarks in Washington and signaled the growing architectural and historical credibility of the Victorian era. Just a few years later CHRS president Thomas B. Simmons noted with satisfaction that Victorian architecture now enjoyed widespread "acceptability," which covered the spectrum from "real estate parlance to the serious and scholarly attention being paid it by the Victorian Society."[55] Washington restorationists joined the Victorian Society of America and forged links with restoration groups working in Victorian-era neighborhoods in other American cities such as the Brooklyn-based Brownstone Revival Committee.

The Victorian theme became most explicit in Washington's house and garden tours when the Logan Circle Community Association began its own tour in 1978. Held in December, the tour was called "A Victorian Christmas," a theme the organizers maintained in subsequent years. They focused, as the other tours did, on restored houses, as well as antique furnishings, and on the decorative Victoriana used in Christmas displays.[56]

The changes in taste that led to a more widespread acceptance of the architecture and urban patterns of the late nineteenth century accorded with the broader cultural atmosphere in the 1960s and 1970s in which older hierarchies of taste and canons of value were persistently questioned. Opposition to the apparent rigidity and homogeneity of expert-driven modernism in architecture and planning also crystallized in these decades and became a standard position for both progressive and conservative cultural critics. House and garden tour materials reflected the trend toward the valorization of personal taste, something that was also widely promoted as an ideal in the consumer marketplace. Expert arbiters of taste and the idea of universally accepted standards quickly lost ground as a consequence. Housing remodelers did not abandon the idea that some places and some periods of building were intrinsically more worthy than others. The rapid destruction of older buildings and environments, however, both real and perceived, promoted a broadening of existing assumptions about cultural and historical value.[57]

THE TASTE FOR DIVERSITY

Perhaps the most noticeable shift in the social tone of the restoration movement and its promotional apparatus related to the emerging prominence of diversity as a structuring value and model for good citizenship. This emphasis paralleled the breakdown in existing canons of aesthetic value. The 1968 Capitol Hill house and garden tour brochure articulated this emerging ideal. "Hill residents are fascinating in their variety of backgrounds, skills and attainments: rich and poor, the highly educated and the straightforward working man, some who have returned from far corners of the earth and some who have been right here all their lives."[58] The author of the brochure went on to say that the built environment of the Capitol Hill neighborhoods—which was described as intimate, varied, and human in scale—provided an apt context for this social variety. The Capitol Hill real estate agent most closely aligned with restoration, Barbara Held, distributed a newsletter promoting the restoration trend in the late 1960s and early 1970s. Her Thanksgiving edition from 1970 included the following characterization of the Capitol Hill residential community:

> It is FRIENDLY, it is a YOUNG community, it is a WALKING or better still a BICYCLING community. It is DIVERSIFIED—Groups and cultures mingle and mix and the result is a livable, vibrant, URBAN experience. The "Hill" offers the opportunity of really CARING—of GETTING INVOLVED so deeply in community groups, in projects—that the "Hill" becomes you and "you" an integral part of the community.[59]

In an introduction to a CHRS tour brochure from 1964, historian of Washington Constance McLaughlin Green, herself a resident of Capitol Hill, touched upon similar themes. She asserted: "The rigid conformity that critics of modern America attribute to suburban living does not exist on the Hill."[60] According to this idea, the choice to live in an "intown" neighborhood distinguished one as an individual and at the same time involved such residents in a more authentic form of social life and a more robust form of citizenship. Indeed, such promotional material in this period emphasized the authenticity of place again and again. It was contrasted with an image of suburban conformity and inauthenticity that was roundly criticized by William H. Whyte, Jane Jacobs, and Betty Friedan in influential books published in the late 1950s and early 1960s. According to such popular sociology of the American city, the putatively atomized suburbs diminished civic life and thus weakened citizenship.[61]

A tendency to erase overt expressions of class privilege from the promotional material associated with the house and garden tours accompanied the restoration movement's diversity theme. By the late 1960s restoration advocates eschewed the "society page" image in Washington and cultivated a far more democratic idea of its representatives. If domestic arrangements like those of the McCain family, which still presumed maid service as a norm, remained prevalent in the late 1960s, evidence of them was carefully excised from the promotional literature for the house and garden tours. This change reflected the social character of organized housing restoration with the entry of many young, liberal pioneers who moved into houses in areas previously considered marginal to the restoration effort. It was a shift that also mirrored the changing tone of the small local newspapers in the Capitol Hill area in the period. While the jauntiness of *Roll Call* and the *Capitol Hill Spectator* had set the tone for the local papers in the early 1960s, new papers with a different outlook appeared during the late 1960s, including the *East Capitol Examiner*, with its more earnest and politically committed tone. Neighborhood politics and cultural identity thus underwent a shift that placed social diversity and cultural inclusiveness at its center.[62]

Yet the house and garden tours in Capitol Hill and other parts of intown Washington continued to highlight the expenditure of substantial sums of money on the remodeling of houses and to promote the social change that was required to further that process. The rhetoric of urban revival in the late 1960s and 1970s focused on community, authenticity of place, and liberal social values. But the activity of remodeling houses that underpinned one major aspect of that revival was premised on a set of hierarchically structured social distinctions. Those distinctions clearly privileged the choice to live in the city's central area neighborhoods over simply being there, and the capacity to marshal the physical resources needed to first purchase a house and then undertake the labor of remodeling.

CONCLUSION

Neighborhood restoration was an activity structured by social class, driven by cultural distinctions, and marked by judgments of taste. Nevertheless, the expansion of the organized restoration movement during the 1960s promised a more universal and inclusive attitude to the past. Advocates and activists increasingly linked housing and neighborhood restoration to the self-conscious liberal project of neighborhood diversity, not just to civic vigilance and citizen responsibility as they had since the 1920s. This new dispensation, connected to wider social and cultural changes underway in the decade, provided historic preservation with a dramatically widened sphere of action.

But notwithstanding this conscious inclusiveness and embrace of diverse forms and participants, restoration and preservation groups still needed a negative example against which they could sharpen their message. In Washington they had two symbolic and geographical counterpoints. On the outside, the suburbs provided the example of a putatively anodyne, lifeless environment against which to contrast the supposed richness of urban life. On the inside, there was the federal government with its tradition of insensitivity to the local population and disregard for the places they valued. But even though it proved useful as a straw man, the federal government in the 1960s was in turns both an implacable opponent and a source of great strength and policy innovation for Washington's neighborhood preservationists.

CHAPTER 3

The White House and Its Neighborhood

Federal City Making and Local Preservation, 1960–1975

Planners and policy makers in the early and mid-twentieth century regarded the decay of residential and commercial areas of Washington, D.C., such as the old Southwest, as inimical to the dignity of the developing National Mall. By the early 1960s, however, urbanists and inhabitants in Washington identified a converse threat. The scale, function, and questionable architectural character of much federal development threatened to enervate the surrounding urban environment, diminishing the vitality of the public realm by undermining its permeability and social variety. Questions about how to deal with the physical relationships between the federal city and the constituent city were thus vital considerations in the 1960s and 1970s. Moreover, the terms of the urban debate shifted sharply as a consequence of the growing prominence of historic preservation in the city's intown areas.

While citizen advocacy was vital to the way the major redevelopment issues played out, and to the preservation agenda as it rapidly evolved in this period, it would be inaccurate to characterize the period as a battle between insensitive planners and policy makers on the one hand and an insurgent local citizenry on the other. Urban experts and decision makers in government led and shaped the discussion about the appropriate form of the city and about the nature of historical monuments and their proper relationship to questions of formal monumentality.

Looking at the influence of urban experts in this period also invites a reassessment of the relationship between preservation and modernism. The idea that the historic preservation enterprise was somehow a visceral, popular reaction against modernism is undermined by events in Washington in this period. Among the group of expert leaders who repositioned the debate many were explicitly modernist in orientation and few, if any, could be regarded as outright traditionalists. The modernist proclivities of urban renewal by the 1950s and of some of the government's own redevelopment efforts in Washington in the 1960s certainly had a catalytic effect on opponents of large-scale urban transformation. But it is equally true that many who were active in the promotion of preservation objectives were sympathetic to modernist architecture. Certainly architectural traditionalists had a waning impact in debates about the city in Washington by 1960. And with the election of John F. Kennedy as president in that year, the executive branch of government began to show how modernism and preservation might be compatible.

Under the influence of tastemakers, journalists, planners, consultants, and design professionals such as David Finley (bureaucrat, museum director, and preservationist), Carl Feiss (architect and planning consultant), Frederick Gutheim (planning consultant, architectural critic, historian, and preservationist), Elizabeth Rowe (planner and chair of the National Capital Planning Commission [NCPC] in the early 1960s), Wolf von Eckardt (*Washington Post* architecture critic), Francis Lethbridge (architect), and John Carl Warnecke (architect and landscape architect), decision makers in Washington in the early 1960s began to question older assumptions about how to manage the expansion of government functions and the points of collision and connection between the federal and local cities. This group of urban experts, whose influence on the form of Washington emerged during the Kennedy administration, was very conscious of how the retention of older buildings shaped the character of the city. They stressed the fragility of the existing environmental and urban order, the importance of the relationships between buildings and open spaces, and the richness of older places. Frederick Gutheim, for example, frequently referred to the need to recognize "the total fabric" of an area or town, and the importance of the historical layout of towns. He also highlighted the unintended consequences and detrimental impact of removing apparently insignificant buildings that shape the character of places. Such concerns were central to the rapid development of preservation powers and procedures in the two decades beginning around 1960 (Figure 14).[1]

Figure 14. Frederick Gutheim with his folding bicycle in Washington, D.C., circa 1962. Source: American Heritage Center, University of Wyoming.

The core concern of this group of designers and urbanists was the relationship or tension between the architectural monument and the more everyday historic environment. How should the two be balanced and related in Washington, D.C.? Where should the former be privileged and when the latter? How should the two be connected and defined? Adjudicating and balancing between these competing priorities also implied the reassessment of what should be preserved. In the end, of course, these were not only formal considerations. Confronting these questions inevitably also raised the problem of how, and in whose interests, the city should be governed.

NOT A NEW MONUMENTALITY

In the decade following World War II leading voices in modern architecture and urbanism internationally exhibited a growing concern with the question of monuments and monumentality. They were not primarily worried about the fate of historic landmarks and the historic environment. Rather they were interested in the formal and physical qualities associated with monumental buildings—especially the sense of permanence and of magnitude that they conveyed. Historians and critics such as Sigfried Giedion, Lewis Mumford, and Henry-Russell Hitchcock were all concerned with the apparent failure of modernism to find an authentic, monumental mode. Emerging leaders of postwar architectural practice in the United States such as Louis Kahn and Paul Rudolph were likewise vitally concerned with this problem. The strong concern of modernists up to the 1940s with grasping the underlying forces of an industrial world and of connecting people with the technological apparatus of modern life seemed to have implied a parallel forsaking of images and forms that transcended the needs and concerns of the present. As observers of the modern movement began to reflect upon the evolution and nature of that movement they recognized that the durability of monumental buildings—their capacity to inspire awe and humility—was a quality largely absent from "the new architecture." This apparent weakness in modern architecture up until 1940 inspired a "search for a new monumentality." While the term "monumentality" was vexatious, the issue was widely acknowledged as real. Machine aesthetics, functionalism, and programmatic rationality did not in themselves provide an obvious pathway to the expression of deep communal aspirations. Moreover, this apparent

failure had seemingly left the way open for a continuing traditionalism in major public buildings, despite the taint of totalitarianism that
lingered around such architecture in the wake of the Third Reich's architectural program.[2]

In traditionalist Washington, D.C., in the 1950s and 1960s the debate
about modern architecture and monumentality was particularly reso-
nant. The question of how to be both modern and monumental was a
central concern. Advocates of modernism believed it was a matter of
great urgency that the new architecture should be capable of expressing
institutional, civic, and national ideals, not just handling commercial, industrial, and residential functions. In this context, traditional monumentality was subject to sharp criticism. Even very accomplished examples of
traditionalism, such as John Russell Pope's National Gallery of Art (1937–
41), were not immune. Henry-Russell Hitchcock, for example, described
the building as "pseudo-monumentality."[3] Indeed most of the commentators that contributed to a 1948 symposium on the search for a new monumentality, organized and subsequently published by the British journal
Architectural Review, regarded the ongoing use of "traditional idioms" to
achieve monumental effects in public buildings as a kind of forgery or lie.[4]

Among the influential group of international experts who engaged
in this debate in the late 1940s and early 1950s, the Swedish art historian
Gregor Paulsson was alone in arguing against the need for a "new monumentality." But far from advocating traditionalism, he suggested that
"intimacy, not monumentality should be the emotional goal."[5] While
he was alone in the context of the 1948 *Architectural Review* symposium,
the *Review*'s advocacy of townscape in subsequent years via the drawings
and commentary of Gordon Cullen, in particular, helped to promote a
less heroic, more intimate conception of architecture and the urban environment. The "Townscape" campaign, as it has been described, highlighted the relationships between new and old buildings, between open
space and built fabric, and stressed the ways in which these relationships
affected the visual, and indeed corporeal, experience of individuals in
cities and towns. If there was to be a new monumentality, townscape
suggested, then it would be unintentional, historical, and picturesque,
even surreal, but certainly not singular and heroic.[6]

Townscape thinking and its focus on complexity and intimacy of scale
did not seem to be an obvious fit for Washington. In 1955 even Jane

Jacobs, who would later be known as a great advocate for small blocks, aged buildings, and physical diversity, and a fierce opponent of excessive formality and of the singular statement in architecture, regarded modernist monumentality as inevitable, even desirable, in Washington. But townscape thinking and related variants concerned with intimacy of scale and variety of urban experience rapidly gained momentum in the capital in subsequent years among planning experts as well as among the growing cohort of neighborhood preservationists.[7]

References to humanism in the built environment, as well as to the human scale, were pervasive by the early 1960s. While humanism was an unstable term in the period with a variety of applications, advocates in Washington typically invoked it as a way of contrasting their ambitions for the city with those of the federal government. That is, the human scale was clearly defined in opposition to intentional monumentality.

The terms of this discussion about monumentality and intimacy are important, as the stress on scale, contextual propriety, and historical meaning would shape expert and popular opinion about building ensembles and neighborhoods in Washington during the 1960s and beyond. Large programs of traditionalistic architectural redevelopment, such as the creation of the Federal Triangle (1926–47) and the expansion of the U.S. Capitol's auxiliary buildings, fueled disenchantment with the federal attitude to D.C. in the 1950s and into the 1960s. While considerable attention in the postwar years was focused on when and how Washington might embrace architectural modernism, the focus of architectural and urban design commentary quickly shifted onto this separate but related issue: Could Washington find or create an urban mood in anything other than the "grand manner"?

Both axes of the postwar debate—modernism/traditionalism and monumentality/intimacy—were vigorously debated in relation to the redevelopment of Lafayette Square, directly in front of the White House, and the renewal of Pennsylvania Avenue between the U.S. Capitol and the Treasury Building. Both projects were in zones of transition between the city's monumental core and its workaday residential and commercial fabric. The workaday city and the monumental city were tricky to relate to one another because, as Richard Guy Wilson has noted, Washington's monumental core around the National Mall "is not an urban space; its connection with the city is not stressed; it sits as a self-contained entity."[8]

The redevelopment of Lafayette Square, therefore, was something of a litmus test.

THE KENNEDYS AND LAFAYETTE SQUARE

John F. Kennedy once observed that Lafayette Square may be the "only monument" his administration would leave. But what kind of monument was this? Between 1961 and 1963 John and Jacqueline Kennedy played an active role in the Lafayette Square redevelopment, ensuring that the chosen scheme emphasized the retention of older buildings and the predominant character of its nineteenth-century row houses. Their only monument ended up, therefore, as an adaptive use preservation project and, formally at least, the scheme was antimonumental. For the Kennedys the unintentional aspect of Lafayette Square's historicity and its intimate, residential quality were precisely what made it a powerful link to the past. The Kennedys recognized that intentional monuments had a diminishing grip on public attention and that it would be the architectural and material cultures of earlier periods that would become the more powerful reminders and embodiments of the past: understated monuments (Map 5).[9]

In a 1962 television documentary Jacqueline Kennedy invited the American public to tour the White House with her to observe recent efforts to restore the official residence. At the end of that documentary—which attracted a very large viewing audience—John F. Kennedy joins his wife and describes his own view of the importance of history and its relationship to historic buildings. He notes that the White House "should be the center of a sense of American historical life" and argues that the restoration of the house had brought them "much more intimately in contact with all the men who lived here."[10] The liveliness and closeness of the past was most real, he suggested, in the actual rooms where events had taken place and among the furnishings and objects his predecessors and their families had purchased and used. In other words, it was the intimacy and affection for the architectural fabric and the objects that belonged to that place and were marked by age that shaped the Kennedy vision of how the past should be represented. Deliberate monumentality was not rejected outright by the Kennedys, but under their influence preservation took on new prominence in the evocation of the past and the enactment of citizenship.

In a period when U.S. historiography moved away from its traditional focus on statecraft, political events, and war and was transformed by new approaches to social history that investigated slavery, migration, and labor movements, Kennedy's vision of White House history sounds fairly conventional, even conservative. But as a way of addressing history in the built environment, the attitudes expressed by the Kennedys were something of a departure for official Washington and an important aspect of

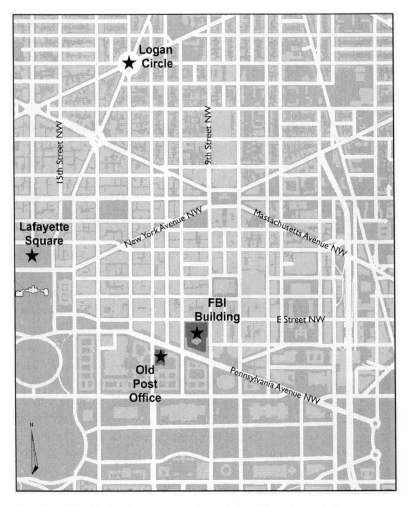

Map 5. Areas where federal government activity in the 1960s had a significant impact on local preservation activity: Lafayette Square, Logan Circle, and Pennsylvania Avenue. Created by and copyright Matthew B. Gilmore.

the Kennedys' wider effort to renew interest in American culture, history, and the environment—the national estate. Their extension of preservation and restoration efforts beyond their front gate into the wider environs of the White House neighborhood—Lafayette Square—made their period in the White House a bellwether for preservation in Washington and the United States as a whole.

Around 1960 the housing restoration culture in the capital, formerly confined to Georgetown and Alexandria, spread to a series of other neighborhoods, including Capitol Hill and the White House's own neighbors in Foggy Bottom. In the form of the Lafayette Square redevelopment, the Kennedys offered Washington's neighborhood restoration and preservation groups a powerful endorsement for their activities that signaled to them that they were taking the correct approach to the urban environment and to the past.

At the beginning of the century, the Senate Park Commission Plan for Washington (1901–2) had envisaged that Lafayette Square would be absorbed into the federal enclave as the setting for a group of executive office buildings (Figure 15). Charles Moore and Frederick Law Olmstead Jr., authors of the report that accompanied the plan, stated their view very clearly. "The proper solution of the problem of the grouping of the executive departments undoubtedly is to be found in the construction of a series of edifices facing Lafayette Square."[11] Lafayette Square should be to the executive branch what the Capitol environs would be for the legislative and judicial branches—an area for auxiliary functions and office accommodation. In the detailed aerial perspective of the plan, sometimes referred to as "Central Composition," the buildings around the square are clearly rendered in white, distinguishing them from the background buildings of the constituent city, which are red. In plan the buildings are shown as occupying whole blocks. Redeveloping the square in this way would have required the removal of all the existing buildings fronting the square. This plan to bring Lafayette Square into the federal city, both functionally and architecturally, by demolishing the existing group of mid-Victorian brick row houses, the St. Johns Church, and a scattering of other early twentieth-century office buildings went through several iterations. The most notable was a Cass Gilbert scheme (1918–19) that followed the spirit of the McMillan Plan and involved a series of colonnaded classical buildings fronting the east, west, and north sides of the

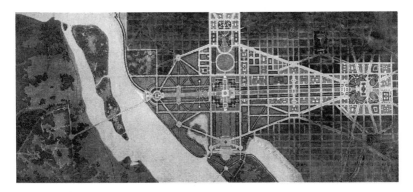

Figure 15. The National Mall, Washington, D.C. Plan showing building development to 1915 in accordance with the recommendations of the Park Commission, 1901. The plan showed both existing buildings and planned changes, including a monumental group around Lafayette Square (top center). Source: Library of Congress.

square. A Gilbert-designed annex for the Treasury Department on Madison Place—the eastern side of the square—was ultimately realized. But the remainder of the redevelopment plan was put on hold as the Federal Triangle was constructed south of Pennsylvania Avenue during the late 1920s and 1930s.[12]

After World War II, during the Truman presidency, the issue of what to do with Lafayette Square arose again. The growth in size of the federal government in this period and the desire to remove temporary accommodation from the National Mall precipitated a new set of proposals. Members of the Commission of Fine Arts (CFA) assumed at that time that the building program would involve the kind of formality and monumentality that was central to Washington's identity as a capital. However, in 1949 the chair of the National Capital Parks and Planning Commission, the accomplished Californian regionalist architect and chair of architecture at MIT William Wilson Wurster, urged the CFA to consider something more low key and more preservationist for Lafayette Square:

> Let us keep the Cosmos Club and the buildings on the west corner near the Blair House as well as St. John's and Decatur House. Let us keep the old Corcoran Building. . . . Washington has enough grandeur, and I hope we can stress the treasuring of the trees, planting more of them, and rehabilitating the city, very much as Georgetown has been done.[13]

Like Paulsson, Wurster was not concerned about whether a modern, monumental language could be found. He was clearly concerned instead with the question of intimacy and ambience. Nothing direct emerged from Wurster's intervention in the debate, and the Truman administration did not really carry the project forward in any meaningful way. But the existence of such sentiment, even if it was a minority view, presaged the shift in thinking that emerged strongly after 1960.

It was almost a decade before the issue was seriously considered again. In 1958 the General Services Administration (GSA) appointed the venerable Boston architectural firm of Shepley Bulfinch Richardson and Abbott to develop a scheme in partnership with Perry, Shaw, Hepburn & Dean, the firm responsible for much of the restoration work at Colonial Williamsburg in the 1920s and 1930s. Their involvement signaled growing sympathy with a more preservationist approach to the square. But in 1958 there was nothing preventing the demolition of all the existing buildings, and the architects presented two schemes: one that retained two recognized historic houses on the site—the Decatur and Blair-Lee houses—and another that removed them. In 1960, John F. Kennedy, still a senator, introduced a bill to designate the Decatur House and three other buildings on the square as National Historic Sites. The bill failed but again moved the project closer to the preservationist solution eventually agreed upon. The sentiments expressed in that bill prompted a press release from President Eisenhower requesting that GSA-appointed architects consider retaining the buildings around Lafayette Square as "an architectural symbol of the simplicity, beauty and clean lines traditional to the American style."[14]

The Kennedys finally determined the direction for the redevelopment of the square during their time in the White House, a direction that is not fully captured by Eisenhower's idea of the square as a stylistic exemplar. Indeed, the path they chose involved the retention of a whole series of stylistically disparate buildings, including the old Corcoran Gallery (now the Smithsonian's Renwick Gallery) as Wurster had urged a decade or so earlier. This was an exuberant Second Empire–style building that could hardly be described as having the "clean lines traditional to the American style."

Jacqueline Kennedy's evolving understanding of preservation practice via her experience of the White House restoration was probably the decisive factor in this outcome for Lafayette Square. In a profile of the White House restoration published in *Life* magazine in 1961 she explained:

> everything in the White House must have a reason for being there. It would be sacrilege merely to redecorate it—a word I hate. It must be *restored*, and that has nothing to do with decoration. That is a question of scholarship.[15]

The redeveloped Lafayette Square ultimately reflected this ideal of elevating historical authenticity and scholarship over current fashion or taste. The committee that Jacqueline Kennedy put together to assist with making decisions about the White House restoration undoubtedly informed her evolving view. The industrialist Henry Du Pont chaired the committee. Du Pont was the leading collector of American furniture and decorative arts and was at that time transforming the image of his Winterthur Collection from a tasteful expression of antiquarianism into a serious scholarly enterprise focused on design history.[16]

The strongest influence on both the Kennedys in these matters, however, was David Finley. As curator and historian Kurt Helfrich has noted, Finley and Jacqueline Kennedy "conspired together discretely to alter the plans for the square."[17] Finley had been the first director of the National Gallery of Art and when he joined Jacqueline Kennedy's restoration committee in 1961 was chairman of both the CFA and of the National Trust for Historic Preservation, which he had been instrumental in founding in the late 1940s. He was also an influential voice on the Committee of 100 on the Federal City, a civic body founded in the 1920s to champion comprehensive planning ideals and civic improvement. He therefore enjoyed wide-ranging influence and authority in the matter. That authority was strengthened by his personal connection to the Kennedys.

Banker and philanthropist Charles C. Glover Jr. was also a Committee of 100 member and was seemingly the first to suggest retaining the streetscape on Jackson Place rather than just two or three significant individual buildings. But it was not until John F. Kennedy consulted Californian architect John Carl Warnecke (1919–2010) during an informal discussion that an architectural and functional solution was found to the redevelopment problem. Warnecke was from the San Francisco Bay area, and his earlier work, such as the Mira Vista Elementary School in

Richmond, California (1951), and additions to the White Oaks Elementary School, showed a sensitivity to site and landscape that characterized much of the most engaging work that emerged from the area in the 1930s, 1940s, and 1950s. Warnecke's perspective on the project was not circumscribed by the ongoing debate between traditionalists and modernists in Washington at the time. Instead it demonstrated a clear affinity with the vision articulated by his fellow Californian W. W. Wurster a decade earlier. The plan Warnecke developed, which was ultimately adopted, fully expressed the desire of Jacqueline Kennedy, Finley, and Glover to preserve as many of the buildings fronting the square as possible, and to maintain its prevailing scale. Warnecke's plan subjugated the imagery of the new structures to the expressive character of the old buildings, using new buildings on both the Madison Place and Jackson Place sides of the square as backdrops, even though they were to be the functional loci of the redevelopment scheme.[18]

Such an overt uncoupling of the functional program from the architectural identity of the square did not sit well with some members of the CFA, especially veteran architect Ralph T. Walker. But by this time the Kennedys and David Finley—who won the debate within the CFA, based on the Kennedys' support—were thoroughly committed to Warnecke's contextualist approach to the problem, in which two self-effacing main buildings deferred to the established historical pattern (Figure 16).[19]

The ultimate implementation of the Lafayette Square preservation project was testimony not only to the personal influence of the Kennedys but to the growing support within the architectural profession and among the public for the retention of elements of the built environment in the midst of changing functional requirements and urbanistic contexts. A *Washington Post* editorial from October 1962 acknowledged the growing manpower needs of the executive branch of government but decried the efforts of the GSA to turn the area into what it called "another government beehive." It welcomed what it described as Warnecke's compromise proposal and noted the strong public support for a plan that, it said, "promises the preservation of a charming enclave of greenery and good taste at the heart of the city, and provides a precedent for intelligent conservation throughout Washington."[20]

John F. Kennedy provided explicit endorsement for the idea that Lafayette Square might be exemplary. He wrote to the GSA director

Figure 16.   Architect John Carl Warnecke and Jacqueline Kennedy with the model of Warnecke's scheme for Lafayette Square. Source: John F. Kennedy Presidential Library.

Bernard Boutin in October 1962 expressing his satisfaction with the War-necke scheme and his conviction that

> the importance of Lafayette Square lies in the fact that we were not willing to destroy our cultural and historic heritage but that we were willing to find the means of preserving it while still meeting the requirements of growth in government. I hope the same can be done in other parts of the country.[21]

Kennedy's comments encapsulated the new preparedness to consider the ways in which federal projects might serve the interests of preservation where possible, rather than asserting the obsolescence of older urban environments.

A handful of buildings were demolished as part of the project, and several new "nineteenth-century style" buildings constructed as infill. Large-scale preservation efforts such as this tend to involve a selective montage of historic places to support particular stories and images of the past, and questions remain about the merit of creating this particular historical tableau and about the new architecture that formed its background. But there is no question that the positive reception of the project within the emerging preservation profession, by much of the architectural press, and by the public at large made it a signal project for the period.

While rarely referred to today, the discussion of contextualism became very prominent in the North American architecture discourse in following decades. That discussion was prompted in part at least by the success of adaptive use projects such as Lafayette Square and other widely publicized reuse projects in commercial and industrial settings such as the highly regarded Ghirardelli Square project (1962–68) in San Francisco by Lawrence Halprin. The Lafayette Square project also marked a shift in direction that would have significant implications for how historic buildings were treated in a wide expanse of intown neighborhoods in Washington.[22]

JOINT COMMITTEE ON LANDMARKS

As historian Zachary Schrag has noted, "the Kennedys considered Washington their hometown" by the time they moved into the White House in 1961.[23] Their involvement in the Lafayette Square redevelopment over the next two years highlighted their concern with both protecting and improving the physical environment of their city. Perhaps their most important legacy to the city though, Schrag suggests, was to appoint "local liberals" to key District posts, many of whom had been vociferous critics of federal insensitivity to Washington during the Eisenhower years. The appointment of Elizabeth Rowe to the NCPC in 1961 was particularly significant for the future of preservation in Washington. The wife of James Rowe, who was an adviser to successive Democratic administrations in the 1930s and 1940s, Libby Rowe, as she was known, had grown up in Washington's Adams Morgan neighborhood and was a longtime resident of the Cleveland Park neighborhood. Her historical attachment to Washington inclined her toward what Frederick Gutheim suggested was an "idyllic image of the city as a collection of neighborhoods defined by tree-lined streets and handsome buildings."[24]

Rowe chaired the NCPC from 1962 to 1968, and under her influence the commission took a much more skeptical approach to major modernization projects. She opposed highway development where it threatened to destroy existing residential areas and was responsible for establishing the

Joint Committee on Landmarks (JCL), a body dedicated to identifying and preserving culturally significant places in the District of Columbia.[25] The JCL was the instrument for achieving preservation controls in Washington between 1964 and 1982. As such, it was a vital link that connected to the community-driven efforts of citizens' groups in Georgetown and elsewhere between the 1920s and 1960s to the era of widespread preservation protections and expanding historic district designation in the late 1970s and 1980s.

Under Rowe's leadership preservation became an obvious priority for the NCPC in a way that it had not been in earlier decades. The decision made to create the JCL in May 1964 followed a major study by planning and preservation consultant Carl Feiss, who was the leading preservationist voice in the planning field nationally in the period. Congress did not grant the JCL the wide powers to acquire and manage property that Feiss recommended in his report, but the JCL was asked to identify and categorize Washington's historic places. The JCL's subsequent report and list was the most extensively researched effort of its kind in Washington to date.[26]

Prominent local architect Francis Lethbridge headed the committee, and other members were drawn from the CFA and the NCPC. Lethbridge's identity as a designer and his clear vision of what historic preservation could achieve for cities highlights why it is erroneous to assume that preservationists were motivated primarily by their hostility to modernist architecture and planning. The work of Lethbridge and that of his architectural partnership, Keyes, Lethbridge & Condon, focused on the creation of small, modern houses possessing the informality and site sensitivity that also characterized the work of highly regarded West Coast designers such as Warnecke and Wurster. Along with other locally active designers of modern, suburban houses such as Charles Goodman, Lethbridge worked on a number of large-scale, integrated community developments. For example, the low-key "developer's modern" used in the Holmes Run Acres community in Fairfax County, Virginia, just outside D.C. was based around a series of designs developed by Lethbridge and Nicholas Saterlee, another member of the original JCL. The preservation of the natural scene in such developments was a vital aspect of Lethbridge's work and something that clearly informed his approach to historic preservation.[27]

In a 1964 address to the American Institute of Architects (AIA) conference with the title "Seeing the City in Time" Lethbridge illustrated one of
his own modern designs and observed that "preservation of landmarks
and places calls for the same point of view, the same frame of mind, that
causes one to work very hard to preserve the natural topography and
amenities of the site in the simplest or most modest kinds of architectural development."[28] Lethbridge's disposition toward clear planning and
preservation controls to provide meaningful contexts for the expression
of historic values in the built environment was clearly connected to his
convictions about what constituted good quality in contemporary design.
The site of an individual architectural project and indeed the city itself,
he argued, must be viewed in its temporal dimension. Architects need
this synoptic, historical perspective, he suggested, in order to avoid the
"myopic vision of the drafting board" and the "petty distractions of competitive practice."[29]

But Lethbridge rejected the implication that a historical perspective
was necessarily culturally regressive, arguing in fact that viewing the city
"in time" was the best way to avoid reactionary architecture and dreary
clichés because it would provide architects with a genuinely shared basis
on which to proceed, and a kind of productive prejudice in favor of their
own cities. It is worth quoting this passage in full:

It may be felt by some that a plea for a return to the applied principles
of historic perspective is an argument of ultra-conservatism, a nostalgic
preoccupation with the past, or an unwillingness to apply contemporary means to our present problems of city planning. This is not so. The
synoptic point of view and the development of rational forms of urban
design from a base of common understanding and common purpose
on the part of architects, engineers, administrators, businessmen, citizens
alike offer the only hope for us to break away from the narrowminded
domination of hand-me-down architectural attitudes and styles, bureau-
cratically entrenched muddleheadedness and simple, unembarrassed private greed. We must take the time, all of us, to develop a full view of the
Visible City; to find out where we have been, where we are and where we
seem to be going, for without some intelligent recharting of our present
course I fear we shall end up precisely where we deserve to be—either
here or hereafter.[30]

The architect, planner, or city designer, he asserted, "must be able to judge the importance and the value of those elements of the city that have come down to him through time and must be able to relate them successfully to the new requirements of life in the city today."[31] The emphasis Lethbridge placed on "relationships" (a broadly spatial question) and "continuities" (the temporal dimension) did not necessarily imply stylistic or formal harmony. He insisted rather on perceiving a complex whole and the temporal layers from which that whole is formed. He pointed sympathetically to Cullen's townscape approach in this address along with other emerging perspectives on urban form and perception proposed by Kevin Lynch and Lawrence Halprin among others.

One architectural historian, reading against the conventional interpretation of townscape, has described it not only as picturesque—which he says it was in a deep historical not merely shallowly aesthetic sense—but surrealistic and genuinely modern in its embrace of fragmentation.[32] Lethbridge and his colleagues in Washington on the JCL in this period did not necessarily embrace the more radical implications of townscape thinking. But while stopping short of advocating the role of the fragment as the authentic expression of the past, Lethbridge nevertheless embraced the idea that all periods in the cities provided enriching elements in the townscape and the most characteristic and interesting places in Washington, such as the area of the canal in Georgetown, were "made up of many different kinds of building from different times."[33]

In November 1964, as part of National Landmarks Week, an event sponsored by the National Trust, the JCL published its preliminary list and map of "Landmarks of the National Capital" and publicized them through an accompanying photographic exhibition (Map 6). The list was composed mostly of federal buildings, structures housing national cultural institutions, embassies, and substantial private residences, the latter mostly chosen from among those built in the late eighteenth and early nineteenth centuries. But it also included important topographical landmarks and preserves of open space in the city as well as significant elements of the townscape. For example, under the heading of *places* and listed as a Category I landmark were "The Squares, Circles and Vistas Created by the Plan of the Federal City—The Mall; The Ellipse; Lafayette Square; The Capitol Grounds." Most significantly for the subsequent creation of historic districts in Washington's intown areas, and most radically for a document that was created for the purposes of planning review, the list also identified a dozen or so primarily residential districts that were not controlled by the government. Georgetown and a substantial part of Capitol Hill were classified as Category II landmarks, "to be preserved where possible." A larger group that included the Lincoln Square area and East Capitol Street, further east from the Capitol complex, the Logan Circle area, the Dupont Circle area, the Kalorama area,

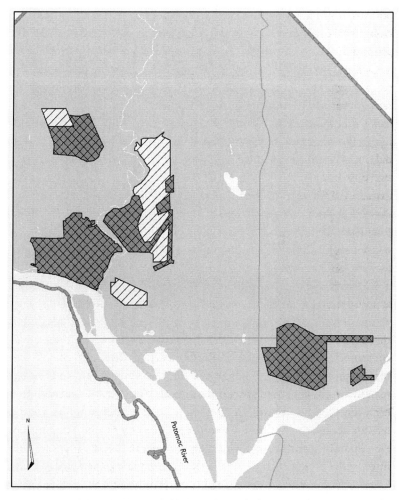

Map 6. "Districts of historic or monumental merit" (dark) and "areas for further study" (light), from Joint Committee on Landmarks, 1964. Map redrawn and copyright by Matthew B. Gilmore.

and Cleveland Park were identified as Category III landmarks, "to be preserved if practicable."[34]

The landmarks list carried only symbolic authority as there was no legislative or regulatory framework to provide enforceable protections for places listed by the JCL. But the landmarks committee was also explicitly charged with "the development of suitable legislation for the District of Columbia, to help carry out a program of effective preservation."[35] Such legislation was not achieved until 1978, and issues and ideas associated with preservation evolved considerably by the time it came into force. However, the suggestions of the JCL in 1964 foreshadowed many of the historic districts that neighborhood groups actively worked to create in later years and that subsequently received the protection of the local preservation law after 1978. Moreover, the effort that led to the 1964 list brought together several individuals who would go on to drive the push for federal historic preservation legislation, successfully enacted in 1966. In addition to Carl Feiss, the JCL called upon the advice of Helen Duprey Bullock of the National Trust and Richard Howland of the Smithsonian. All three would play a significant part in advocating for a more comprehensive system of protections nationally in subsequent years.[36]

ENSEMBLES, SQUARES, AND CIRCLES

While really only a guide at this point, the creation of a D.C. landmarks list provided impetus for highlighting architectural and physical qualities in the landscape that had previously been taken for granted. During the same landmarks week in 1964, architects Donald Jackson and Stephen Kloss from the NCPC led a walking tour around Logan Circle to draw attention to the historic qualities of that distinctively Victorian residential circle. The landmarks list identified the circle itself as a Category I landmark along with other prominent squares, circles, and triangles that were part of the L'Enfant Plan for Washington and also listed the surrounding residential area as a Category III landmark. In at least two respects the NCPC approach to preserving Logan Circle reflected ideas that underlay the Lafayette Square plan. It was an attempt to give definition to the circle as a key element of the city's distinctive street pattern and to amplify the historic character of the L'Enfant city. Moreover, the NCPC interest in the historical significance of the houses around the circle underlined an interest in the residential architecture and character of the whole ensemble.[37]

Their comments indicated that they believed the visual and physical qualities of the buildings at this key intersection would act as a fulcrum for strengthening the identity and renewing the physical fabric of the whole surrounding district. In other words, it was not just a two-dimensional area on a plan that they wanted to protect, but the qualities of a fully realized three-dimensional environment marked by a special architectural character developed over time. It was, as Donald Jackson noted, the "architectural integrity" of the whole ensemble that mattered.[38] Richard Howland underlined the point noting that it was not the charm of the individual elements as much as its quality when viewed as a totality—the fact that it was all "pretty much of a piece"—that mattered.[39] What was also important in terms of future direction for preservation was that the NCPC architects exhibited a preparedness to preserve and promote the qualities of neighborhoods widely perceived by the city's middle class as blighted and possibly dangerous.

The tendency to see the value of such ensembles and view "the city in time" quickly gathered strength among specialists in the period. In 1963 the *AIA Journal* produced a special issue on Washington to mark the occasion of the institute's annual meeting being held in the national capital. The issue reflected a diversity of opinion about urbanism in Washington. But a surprising amount of space was given to commentators who were interested primarily in the more vernacular elements of the city and sympathetic to historic preservation. Robert J. Kerr, director of Historic Annapolis, and Frederick Gutheim both focused on the efficacy and desirability of historic districts, or area preservation plans. Gutheim noted that "in déclassé parts of the city—the area just east of the now abandoned baseball park, for example (Shaw/LeDroit Park)—whole blocks of structurally sound houses nearly a hundred years old form distinctive and attractive parts of the city with a valid claim to preservation."[40] Kerr suggested that places such as Dupont Circle, Logan Circle, and Cleveland Park, while they contained very different mixtures of functions and stylistic tendencies, shared with Georgetown, Alexandria, and Annapolis a visual coherency and "'sense of place' that made them appealing and their preservation economically viable."[41]

Kerr argued for the wider application of ideas pursued in Georgetown, which in his opinion achieved a "unity of general feeling and atmosphere" out of a great diversity of architectural, urban, and human elements. His

article foreshadowed the preservation ideas reflected in the JCL's landmarks list, which contained a number places not previously recognized as
historically significant. He cited the Capitol Hill neighborhood, Embassy
Row, Cleveland Park, and Sixteenth Street as places worthy of further
study and possible incorporation into historic districts. Gutheim's article
argued for recognition of the strong determining influence of areas by
highlighting the city's vernacular traditions and pointing to the interesting contrasts they made with the monumental city. For Gutheim the
overall effect created by the city's distinct places was much more valuable than the design of particular dwellings, which were in most cases
characteristic rather than outstanding works of architecture. For both of
these commentators the metaphor of urban mosaic was a guiding idea.
The city's value as a built environment, they both suggested, was formed
in the contrasts and patterns that emerged from viewing strongly indi-
viduated neighborhoods and districts in the context of the urban whole.[42]

In the wake of the AIA meeting, and of the JCL surveys of the city's
historic landmarks, the local chapter of the AIA produced a guide to
Washington architecture that also underlined urbanistic and historical
qualities that belonged to groups of buildings and places rather than just
individual landmark buildings. The guidebook was put together by Francis Lethbridge and Hugh Newell Jacobsen, an architect whose infill houses
in Georgetown were a model of how to build modern but contextually
sensitive houses in historic areas. The publication included a number
of groups of houses in Alexandria, Capitol Hill, and Georgetown among
the architectural highlights of those areas, and the editors referred more
than once to places where the effect of the whole was greater than the
sum of its parts. The guidebook did not embrace ordinary patterns in
the built environment in an unqualified way, nor did it specifically champion overtly Victorian elements in the landscape. But those elements
were not persistently derided and excluded in this publication as they had
been in earlier works of a similar kind.[43]

In the first half of the 1960s, therefore, Washington's architects, planners, and some of its most powerful political figures all paid much more
attention to the value of the city's existing buildings and neighborhoods
as monuments and historic places. The significance of this was that the
city's historically valued architectural past, at least in a formal sense,

expanded widely to include large parts of the original City of Washington as well as some select areas just outside its original borders. Changing attitudes to nationally significant places such as Lafayette Square provided a highly visible example of the possibility of preserving an architectural context, not just a few historically significant buildings. Most of the newly identified landmarks in Washington were unintentional historic monuments, not monumental buildings. Moreover, the emerging sense that the historical city was a healthy habitat and vital civic arena earned growing support.

In 1963 John F. Kennedy articulated his belief that cities were more than the systems and buildings of which they were made; they are also, he asserted, the "setting in which men and women can live up to their responsibilities as free citizens."[44] This overtly liberal and humanist vision was one that clearly resonated with the expanding restoration movement in Washington. As we saw in the previous chapter, prominent restoration advocates nationally equated the revitalization of intown neighborhoods with an ideal of renewed citizenship. Nevertheless, the effects of this widening embrace of the historic city remained uncertain. There was now increased architectural, planning, and political support for a broadened idea of historically significant places, as well as social, cultural, and economic forces that all militated against their outright destruction. But, as Wolf von Eckardt remarked in a 1963 *Washington Post* column, Americans were still more likely to expend energy and money lining up to shake hands with a "robot Lincoln at Disneyland" than they were in protecting worthy historic buildings.[45] Francis Lethbridge had warned, meanwhile, that despite the strides that had been made, there were equally powerful forces encouraging the continued decay and destruction of old buildings and urban areas.

One of the forces that continued to cause such destruction was the federal government's own improvement and expansion plans. While architects and planners associated with government agencies and projects helped to knit together an intellectually coherent approach to preservation in the early and mid-1960s, major efforts to improve the capital continued to ignore or misapprehend the desires of Washington's inhabitants. Perhaps nowhere was this more evident than in the redevelopment of Pennsylvania Avenue.[46]

AMERICA'S MAIN STREET

The idea that Pennsylvania Avenue is America's Main Street is a corny notion adopted and promoted by the National Park Service in its interpretation of the area. But it nevertheless resonates with the ambivalence of Washington's dual identity as national symbol and local environment. It suggests that the Avenue is a familiar place to most Americans, a place "of comfortable tradition and sure faith" as Sinclair Lewis once wrote of an archetypal Main Street.[47] But just as Washington is a "very strange home town," as *Architectural Forum* observed in 1963, so is Pennsylvania Avenue a highly unusual, even disconcerting Main Street. It has much less in common with a classic small town Main Street than State Street in Chicago or even New York's Broadway.[48]

By the middle of the twentieth century Pennsylvania Avenue was lined on one side by the most coherent group of classical buildings in the country and on the other by what one architect described as "an incredible mixture of old and new, large and small, government and private sector" buildings.[49] The Avenue's duality, as with the city itself, could hardly have been more pronounced. Described by its chroniclers as "monumental and miniscule . . . a compact American morality play, a slice of its good and bad life," the Avenue hovers uncertainly between federal pageant and the workaday life of Washington.[50]

The source of that uncertainty is in the multiple historical roles of the Avenue as a boundary, ceremonial boulevard, and place of pleasure and commerce. The inarticulacy of the relationship between the National Mall and the city of Washington that Richard Guy Wilson has remarked upon is nowhere more evident than along the mile or so of Pennsylvania Avenue that links the symbolic centers of the executive and legislative branches of government.

Starting life as a barely discernible quagmire marking the most direct path between Congress and the White House, it grew to become the heart of the city's most vibrant commercial district. It also became one edge of the city's vice district during the Civil War and subsequently home to Washington's Chinatown. In the 1920s the federal government seized on an opportunity to "dignify" the area and provide accommodation for its expanding departments by acquiring a large parcel of land between the National Mall and Pennsylvania Avenue from Sixth Street to Fifteenth Street Northwest. The Federal Triangle was thus chosen for development ahead of Lafayette Square, which had previously been considered the natural locality in which to develop accommodation for the executive branch.[51]

The Federal Triangle development fundamentally changed the character of Pennsylvania Avenue and its environs by the time the original phase of the project was completed in 1947. In the postwar years Washington's old downtown in the blocks to the north of the Avenue were facing commercial challenges that would see land values compromised and the viability of its key department stores threatened.[52] When John F. Kennedy rode along the Avenue in his inaugural parade in January 1961 and reportedly remarked that "it's a disgrace—fix it," the absence of significant new investment on the north side of the Avenue during the preceding decades strongly marked the parade route's appearance.[53] Whether or not Kennedy's remarks are apocryphal, there is no question that the condition of the northern side of the Avenue in the 1960s provided impetus for the master-planning and redevelopment process that unfolded over the next quarter of a century.[54]

The Pennsylvania Avenue redevelopment process had significant implications for preservation in Washington. It brought into sharp relief questions about who had "a right to the city": that is, it encouraged interest in the question of the meaning and limits of place-based citizenship in Washington. Did inhabitants of the city have a role in determining how this important street should look? Or was it a matter primarily for the federal government? The project provoked the question of how to represent the Avenue's historical experience and meanings in three dimensions.

In 1963 Kennedy appointed an Advisory Council on Pennsylvania Avenue headed by Nathaniel Owings, founding partner of the storied New York architectural firm Skidmore, Owings & Merrill. The following year the advisory council presented a master plan for the area, guided by the following list of principles and objectives:

1. Pennsylvania Avenue is inseparable from adjoining areas.
2. The Avenue, as the nation's ceremonial way, should have a special character.
3. The Avenue should do honor to its lofty destinations.
4. The Avenue should be harmonious in itself and linked with the city around it in both its architecture and its planning.

5. The Avenue should be pleasant to traverse either on foot or by vehicle.

6. The Avenue should be reclaimed and developed as a unified whole.[55]

These ambitious objectives implied that a redeveloped Avenue would possess strong links to the existing city as well as a clear monumental character of its own. This was a major challenge. As planner Albert Peets noted as early as 1937, the Avenue was off balance and the sequence of openness and enclosure along it was inadequately controlled: "Constitution Avenue crashes through it; the plaza at Eighth Street is maimed; vast walls of stone down one side of the Avenue while parking lots cut gaps in the other."[56]

The Owings master plan attempted to address these problems, but it did so by diminishing the importance of the Avenue's links with the existing city. As Frederick Gutheim noted, this was "grand-scale planning," and the existing urban fabric within the old downtown was clearly to be subjugated to the cohesive, monumental vision. The plan envisioned the demolition of the Washington Hotel at Fifteenth Street and Pennsylvania Avenue, the Willard Hotel at Fourteenth Street and Pennsylvania Avenue, and the Old Post Office, though its tower was to be retained. Gutheim subsequently described these buildings as three "venerable historic buildings," and over time it became evident that they were places that many Washingtonians cared about and wanted to keep.[57]

Some new development on the Avenue in the late 1960s, including the new FBI building (1967–72), followed Owings's framework, though the early plans were not formally adopted. A 1969 update of the plan carried this momentum forward with the emphasis on robust monumental public buildings over the qualities and character of the fine-grained, downtown commercial district (Map 5). Even with recognition of Pennsylvania Avenue as a National Historic Site in 1965 under the 1935 Historic Sites Act, and growing preservation sentiment during the period, the 1969 version of the plan still recommended the demolition of the Old Post Office and other Avenue landmarks. This continuing commitment to demolishing key landmark buildings along the Avenue ignited opposition in the early 1970s. In March 1970 Wolf von Eckardt suggested to readers of his Cityscape column in the *Washington Post* that the Old Post Office "should not be wrecked but resurrected." Drawing on what was by that time an established critique of the federal architectural image in Washington, he said "now is not the time for more establishment monumentality and monotony."[58]

Von Eckardt's opposition to the Pennsylvania Avenue plan echoed concerns expressed by other experts in the period—Gutheim, Lethbridge, Rowe—about the potential for federal redevelopment projects to have a destructive and blighting influence on the city. But von Eckardt's critique, forcefully articulated and publicized in the *Washington Post*, also mobilized preservationist sentiment among a vital segment of the city's permanent population. Opposition to the destruction of the Old Post Office became the key event in the formation of Washington's first citywide preservation advocacy group.

DON'T TEAR IT DOWN!

In October 1971, a small group of people that Wolf von Eckardt described as "middle-class intellectuals," led by the television news writer Allison Owings, formed the group Don't Tear It Down! (DTID!) to protest federal government plans to demolish the Old Post Office.[59] A nucleus of civic-minded women, Owings, Leila Smith, Carol Bickley, and Terry B. Moreton, built a successful campaign based around the idea that D.C. inhabitants, not just the government, were entitled to have a say in the shape and appearance of Pennsylvania Avenue, and indeed the wider urban environment. They formed the group not just to express a preference for this old building over that new one, but, as with most popular preservation campaigns, as an expression of citizenship.

Allison Owings articulated the need to defend the city and to build a sense of shared cultural ownership of it. "There's so little sense of community in this town," she told a reporter at one of the early rallies in support of protecting the post office.[60] Carol Bickley, the first president of the organization, affirmed this mission of identifying with Washington and defending the city. She proclaimed a populist, democratic bias to the group, arguing that "people is what this is all about. We don't want the technocrats and the bureaucrats to tear down Washington's livability and destroy neighborhoods that let you know who you are."[61] For Bickley the values to be treasured in the city were opposed to the federal government's favored monumental mode. "Variety and vitality," Bickley suggested, were the basis of pride in the city. "When we tear down old buildings," she asserted, "we destroy some of our own roots."[62]

Through a mixture of legal challenges and political maneuvering DTID! established a formidable record of success in their first three years. Apart from shifting the terms of the discussion about the Old Post Office, which ultimately led to its preservation, they also played an instrumental role in two other prominent, successful preservation battles of the period: the nearby Willard Hotel, also on Pennsylvania Avenue, and the former Franklin School, on Franklin Square, just north of downtown. In both cases DTID! framed the battle as a defense of the city's heritage and the familiar character of its built environment against "federal monumentality" and/or "commercial banality."[63]

Despite the ultimate success of these campaigns, it was by no means inevitable that the momentum they created for historic preservation in Washington would be translated into an ongoing citywide preservation movement. The fact that it did was partly due to the influence of Terry B. Moreton. Moreton was one of the key organizers of the original protest against the demolition of the Old Post Office and was working at the time in the publications division of the National Trust for Historic Preservation. In 1972 she helped put together the Washington Preservation Conference, where leading experts nationally, such as James Marston Fitch and Antoinette Downing, spoke to, mingled with, and listened to local preservation advocates and neighborhood representatives from groups such as the Capitol Hill Restoration Society, Citizens' Association of Georgetown, and Dupont Circle Citizens' Association.[64]

Two clear themes emerged from the conference. First, speakers affirmed that if the city was to become a really satisfying place to live then the interests of its inhabitants could not be mistaken for the interests of the federal government, despite the fact that the government was its reason for being and its economic engine. Unsurprisingly participants agreed that historic preservation would be a vital means for achieving a more balanced planning regime. The Old Post Office campaign and the Pennsylvania Avenue redevelopment more generally were emblematic of this tension and the need to consider the views of inhabitants. The second theme was that such intensive campaigning could not be the ongoing basis for preservation and that a more systematic approach was needed.[65]

Just over twelve months later, the D.C. City Council indicated its support for a more systematic preservation regime. In September 1973, on the advice of the JCL and at the urging of DTID!, they passed regulation 73-25. The regulation mandated a six-month delay of any proposed demolition of a building on the JCL's landmark list or contained within a listed historic district. The intention was to buy time and allow communities and preservation groups to enter into negotiations with property owners about alternatives to demolition. The regulation was a significant step, but preservationists regarded it as just that. The ultimate goal was the passage of meaningful local preservation legislation.[66]

The passage of D.C's Home Rule Act through Congress at the end of 1973 dramatically improved the prospects of successfully passing preservation legislation. The Home Rule Act set in train the process that led to limited but meaningful municipal self-government for Washington, D.C., and brought together several distinct political blocs. One of those blocs was represented by DTID! activists. Their vision and milieu were quite different from most African American leaders in Washington. While black leaders were not primarily focused on the historic qualities of the built environment, they did share with white preservation advocates a desire to empower the local population and give the inhabitants of D.C. a much greater stake in its government. Walter Fauntroy, Sterling Tucker, Julius Hobson, Ivanhoe Donaldson, and Marion Barry, among others, envisaged the basis of local community and authority not as shared symbols of civility and stability such as the Old Post Office building, but as the transformative potential of an enfranchised African American majority. Despite these important differences, opposition to unfettered federal authority in the city provided a shared rallying point that eased the transition to home rule in the following years and provided, at least in the short term, a sense of common purpose among Washingtonians of different races and class sympathies.[67]

Despite the fact that events such as the Washington Preservation Conference largely articulated the views of white-dominated preservation groups and the citizens' associations (which were historically white organizations), African American leaders and community groups came out in support of the new preservation regulations. At the city council hearing about the delay of demolition regulation Watha T. Daniel, a Shaw activist and former president of community-based urban-regeneration organization Model Inner City Community Organization (see chapters 4 and 5), encouraged the council to pass the regulation and use it as a means to identify and preserve more sites of historic interest and significance for African Americans. Polly Shackleton, long-time Democratic Party activist and member of the D.C. Bicentennial Commission, saw the regulation as a mechanism to encourage citizen involvement and community pride that would in turn help to stabilize and improve urban neighborhoods. The following year DTID! worked together with the D.C. Bicentennial Commission to establish a legislative framework for preservation in Washington.[68]

It took several more years to draft and enact the effective legislation that was widely anticipated in the mid-1970s. During that period DTID! and other preservationists had mixed results utilizing the delay-in-demolition regulation. But the momentum that came from the Old Post Office campaign and the formation of DTID!, the mounting pressure from neighborhood associations, and the sense of local control enabled by home rule local government eventually led to the passage of the Historic Landmark and Historic District Protection Act in June 1978.

CONCLUSION

In the years between 1960 and 1978, the scope and meaning of historic preservation in Washington underwent a fundamental transformation. The very notion of the monument was revised and traditional monumentality in architecture and planning strongly criticized. Accompanying that shift in thinking was a shift in the character of those who saw themselves as responsible for the city's historical forms and places. Where architects, planners, and federal decision-making bodies had been at the heart of the process in the 1960s, neighborhood groups and local political concerns emerged as the driving forces during the early 1970s.

It was a period of steadily expanding preservation powers and one of growing political self-confidence for the city's permanent inhabitants. National expertise and leadership informed and overlapped with local advocacy, reinforcing the strength of preservation activity as a whole. As a consequence, campaigns to protect valued places became part of a wider effort to achieve a greater voice for inhabitants in local affairs. At the social level, this enabled a certain amount of cross-racial solidarity and cooperation.

But this whiggish story conceals the disenchantment, suspicion, and resistance that manifested as a result of the increased influence of housing restoration and historic preservation on the city in the 1960s and 1970s. The experts discussed in this chapter did not address the full implications of that resistance and critique. But at the neighborhood level such disenchantment was audible.

CHAPTER 4

Race and Resistance

Gentrification and the
Critique of Historic Preservation

Nationally, perceptions of neighborhood restoration and historic preservation changed markedly during the early 1960s, a result in significant part of the impact of bulldozer-driven urban renewal. Consequently preservation moved toward the economic and policy mainstream. Explicit support from the White House and subsequently from Congress, in the form of the 1966 Historic Preservation Act, reinforced this perception and had a very pronounced effect in Washington, where locals were especially sensitized to shifts in national policy. This new political, cultural, and economic credibility for the preservation field did not entirely cast aside the perception of its advocates as sentimental, nostalgic, and antiquarian. But it did give preservation a new modus operandi and a much wider sphere of action. The promise of historic preservation as a tool of progressive planning—so evident to John Ihlder in Georgetown and to others around the United States in the 1920s and 1930s—would now be realized across a very wide terrain in Washington, D.C. As the most ambitious, future-oriented plans for renewal faced growing hostility and criticism, preservation and restoration established a strong foothold as a cheaper and potentially more humane way of renewing the economic value, social health, and cultural vitality of urban space.

But the widened purview of preservation in this period also brought the field much more forcefully into debates about social justice, which, in the wake of civil rights, was more often than not framed as racial justice. Historic preservation advocates pitted preservation against slum clearance strategies, suggesting that restoration and preservation of existing buildings was a more just and subtle means of improving living conditions. Yet this also raised questions about how this could be done without breaking up established communities or forcing incumbent residents out of the properties that were to be restored or upgraded. With a growing concentration of poorer blacks in many of Washington's central area neighborhoods in the 1960s, where such preservation strategies might be desirable or prove fruitful, the contention that preservation was just another form of "negro removal" in Washington was a serious proposition.

Briann Greenfield has described the organized neighborhood restoration effort on North Benefit Street in Providence in the 1960s as a "program of planned gentrification."[1] While this is a somewhat anachronistic application of the term "gentrification"—which did not really come into wide usage in the United States until the late 1970s—Greenfield's meaning is clear. Renewal by restoration and preservation promised something more organic and less disruptive than large-scale clearance. But it was urban renewal nevertheless, which in essence was a set of policies focused on increasing the value of urban land. However comforting the image of preservation, and however pleasant the language associated with that image, organized restoration in big cities like Washington, D.C., has tended, in most instances, to produce a filtering up of the housing stock from lower- to middle- and higher-income residents—the common definition of gentrification. Naturally enough, in Washington the filtering up of properties produced a corollary change in the inhabitants of restoration areas as a whole and, therefore, a change in the social, and usually the racial, composition of those neighborhoods. The supercharged gentrification of the inner areas of D.C. in the twenty-first century and the outflow of African Americans of modest means to cheaper housing in Prince George's County, Maryland, and elsewhere have sometimes been interpreted as a consequence of the success of the housing restoration movement. It is hardly surprising, therefore, that at various times in the evolution of the restoration culture, the organizations and individuals who promoted restoration and historic preservation were the target of political criticism. The racial aspect of this was particularly powerful in Washington and emerged strongly even as policy makers and advocates argued that historic area protections and piecemeal neighborhood renewal could be a powerful tool of self-determination and economic empowerment.[2]

THE WHITE OCTOPUS

From 1960 onward the group of neighborhoods to the east of the U.S. Capitol became Washington's most active restoration area. But the class and racial implications of the restoration trend in the area were deeply contested. Local newspaper editor and chronicler of the changing neighborhood Sam Smith noted that between 1965 and 1968 Capitol Hill's Emergency Committee on Recreation (ECR) was "constantly at loggerheads with the Capitol Hill Restoration Society" (CHRS).[3] The ECR, a racially integrated organization led in the period by retired African American John Anthony, consistently argued that neighborhood amenities for the area's poorest residents were a more urgent priority than the restoration of houses in the area. In 1968 another group circulated an antirestoration flyer in the area that deployed the old populist image of the octopus in racial terms, identifying the presence of a "White Octopus" in the Capitol Hill neighborhoods.[4] The idea of the "concrete octopus" had been deployed widely in the fight against highway construction earlier in the decade, and so the idea of the strangling octopus already enjoyed currency in debates about the built environment in Capitol Hill. The "White Octopus" flyer drew on a black vernacular of race and real estate in Washington that had been around since at least the 1940s and perceived a concerted effort of established white power to remove blacks from key central places in the city. In later decades this idea was known as "the plan," or "the master plan," suggesting that urban planning, housing, and other civic and governmental efforts to reshape Washington were covert strategies for displacing and dispossessing poor blacks.[5]

During the late 1960s African Americans of limited means in Washington's Southeast quadrant, which included a substantial section of the restoration area on Capitol Hill, were concerned about displacement caused by the housing restoration trend. Local government officials were aggressively enforcing housing code violations in the area, a policy that led to the eviction of a number of residents. Some community leaders interpreted this as a deliberate effort to assist in the transfer of properties to white restorationists.[6]

A racially salient critique of housing restoration, mobilized in response to both the organized restoration groups and the government programs designed to assist the restoration process, took aim at an apparent misappropriation of the economic value and amenity of intown property in

Washington. In the late 1960s a group called the Capitol East Community Organization (CECO), an umbrella group that advocated for the needs and interests of the area's African Americans, garnered national attention for its sustained attack on the restoration movement. The director, Linwood Chatman, described the agents of the restoration movement in the real estate business as "scavengers" and claimed that black renters had already been "flushed out" of restoration areas.[7] Sam Smith, the activist editor of the *East Capitol Gazette* was quoted as saying that the restoration movement was "strip mining" the area and that the CHRS was, in effect, a major impediment to social justice aims. "Exploiters moved in quickly," he said, "made a fast buck, and drove out blacks in an attempt to fashion another Georgetown."[8]

Some recognition of the displacement problem was evident in local newspaper reports as early as 1965, and the CHRS openly acknowledged its dangers in 1967. That year they contributed to a report entitled "Capitol Hill Prospectus," which noted that one "effect of restoration has been to induce or force low-income people to move out of neighborhoods being restored."[9] Nevertheless, some middle-class, liberal whites who had moved to Capitol Hill and restored houses there in the 1950s and 1960s felt slandered by the idea that they were benefiting from a deliberate displacement of poor African Americans. For example, in February 1968 resident Josephine Turner defended the CHRS in the *Capitol Hill News*, arguing that CHRS members consistently promoted the good of the whole neighborhood. They fought, she noted, to protect the Capitol Hill residential population from slum conditions and inappropriate proposals such as the inner-loop freeway, a plan that had been defeated by a wave of resident opposition in the early 1960s. She mocked the idea that the CHRS was an exploitative force in the neighborhood, remarking that the author of the "White Octopus" flyer had selected, with no substantiating evidence, "one of the older, established combines of the Hill" (the CHRS) for the role of "White Octopus."[10]

Another CHRS supporter, Phillip Ridgely, pursued a similar theme in a letter to the editor of the national magazine *City*, where an in-depth article on the conflict between CECO and the CHRS was published in its August–September issue of 1970. Ridgley described CECO and Sam Smith as "bomb-throwers" who "have accomplished nothing for the community, black or white." He went on to describe his own position in the following terms:

> I have been resident on the Hill since 1964 and find that it is probably the most liberal group in the metropolitan area. That's why I get so disgusted when I read articles about those who have done so much to renew this urban area, depicted as some sort of white conspiracy.[11]

The difficulty for self-conscious liberals such as Ridgely was in accepting that their good intentions might have bad consequences, foreseeable or not. On the other hand, activists in groups such as CECO often focused on the individual agents of property investment rather than the wider structural forces at work in the property market and the housing system.

What was fundamentally at stake was the scope of collective entitlements in urban places. Going back to the 1920s, historic preservation activism had promoted regulatory and reforming approaches to private land tenure. Reforms such as historic area zoning were intended to serve a public good and depended on the sacrifice of some aspects of the individual property right. Nevertheless, as Ihlder's Georgetown restoration campaign from the early 1920s made very clear, zoning measures intended to guard against careless redevelopment were also designed to protect and promote the value of private property. The CHRS relied upon that model to explain and promote its activities in the late 1960s. However, new experiments in advocacy planning and community redevelopment that were underway in Washington and elsewhere in the late 1960s emphasized instead the collective aims and entitlements of area inhabitants over property values and the rights of property owners.[12]

The Model Inner City Community Organization (MICCO), a coalition of 150 community organizations, churches, and civic groups founded to guide a program of physical and human renewal in the Shaw area of Washington, was the organization that really publicized this new, democratic, and collectivist approach in D.C. Led by Walter Fauntroy and drawing on the expertise and authority of influential Boston planner Edward Logue and the first director of the federal Department of Housing and Urban Development, Robert C. Weaver, MICCO was established to enable a model of community-led urban regeneration that would avoid the problems of displacement caused by the Southwest urban renewal project. In Southwest, the great majority of previous inhabitants—people who had been part of what the District of Columbia Redevelopment Land Agency described in 1964 as "a functioning social system"—were de-housed by the renewal project and had their social system "destroyed or seriously disrupted by urban renewal."[13] MICCO efforts were explicitly arrayed against such an outcome, as its theme song made clear:

Shameful Shaw will be no more, Hallelujah!
Our old homes we'll fix like new, Hallelujah!
We will train for more new skills, Hallelujah!
All our streets are old and worn, Hallelujah!
Old Southwest it lost its fight, Hallelujah!
Old Southwest did one thing wrong, Hallelujah!
Shaw will work as one big team, Hallelujah!
Tenants, owners, workers, all, Hallelujah!
We'll unite our Shaw to plan, Hallelujah![14]

MICCO defined a form of capital in the community itself, stressing that the value of the area was in the established relationships of its inhabitants and the cultural, religious, and commercial institutions that mediated those relationships. The organization's articles of incorporation asserted that "this is our area. We not only live, work or serve in it, but we also pray and play within these boundaries. . . . We are not wholly without assets. We have ourselves and high hopes."[15] It was those assets, backed by a commitment to community involvement, that conferred the authority to make decisions about their neighborhood, MICCO asserted, not the ownership of the parcels of land within its boundaries.

Large-scale urban renewal in Southwest was the immediate memory that motivated Shaw residents and other black activists in Washington to proclaim their collective entitlements, their right to the city. But the central theme of their wider critique, one taken up by a range of groups in the period immediately before and after the April 1968 riots in D.C., was that urban space was being misappropriated by well-resourced and politically powerful whites. In the immediate aftermath of the clearance projects in Southwest, the argument was usually mobilized in support of strategies to retain and preserve much more of the urban fabric than bulldozer renewal allowed. Increasingly, however, as large-scale clearance projects moved into the policy background, CECO and other groups based in Washington's inner-city restoration areas adopted such arguments to contest the goals of restoration societies and historic preservation groups.

THE VALUE OF DIVERSITY

Generally speaking, while Washington's neighborhood preservationists were willing and able to defend their good intentions in the 1960s and early 1970s, they were ill-prepared to address criticism that they were benefiting financially from a systematic, racially specific appropriation of inner-city neighborhoods. Throughout the period from the late 1950s until 1978, when the U.S. Supreme Court confirmed the validity of historic preservation laws, preservationists nationally worked to rebut the arguments of property rights fundamentalists. To do so they focused on the ways in which the protection of historic districts encouraged a rising tide of property value that prevented disproportionate gains by a few individual property owners at the cost of the surrounding district. Historic area zoning or historic districting was, they argued, both a weapon against blight and a way of protecting against uneven urban development. The defense of historic area height limits by the secretary of the New York City Landmarks Preservation Commission, Frank Gilbert, in a 1970 conference address was typical of the way preservationists addressed the question of historic areas and their impact on property value. He asserted that a provision that limits "the height of new construction in a neighborhood is a reasonable response to the pressure to exploit and destroy the area" and pointed to the example of the Brooklyn Heights Historic District where new buildings were limited to fifty feet. "The provision," he suggested, "encourages the rehabilitation and maintenance of existing 19th Century houses, and real estate values remain high."[16] A series of advocates and experts in the period argued that as long as urban preservation programs were administered through a robust legal framework, backed by clear principles, and explained carefully to those affected there should be no reason that value could not be retained and enhanced in such areas. Criticism of preservation as a taking of property was thus rejected with a fairly coherent voice during the 1960s and 1970s.[17]

On the other hand, until the late 1960s most preservationists hardly considered that the activity most of them regarded as public-spirited advocacy for the protection of historical qualities in the environment could be viewed as a racially loaded land grab, akin to the hated large-scale urban renewal projects. The idea that restoration groups such as CHRS were echoes and agents of persistent Jim Crow norms in the built environment was anathema to most participants. Hence their defensive reaction to such criticism. But gradually advocates began to draw on several different strategies to address the criticism that preservation was a deliberate upscaling of neighborhoods and thus, implicitly at least, an attack on the poor. In particular neighborhood preservationists highlighted the ideal of social diversity. Over time this became one of the orthodox justifications for middle-class whites participating in restoration activity in areas with high concentrations of poor people, especially blacks and Latino migrants.

While it did not amount to an explicit response to the grievances of the poor, the idea that preservationists were *for* diversity galvanized their organizations against criticism. The momentum of the diversity argument was driven in part by the presence of younger, overtly liberal pioneers in the restoration culture by the late 1960s as well as by the realtors who sought to capitalize on the presence of those pioneers. The new orthodoxy depended on a subtle but noticeable shift in the social tone of the restoration movement and its promotional apparatus. That shift, which gathered momentum in the late 1960s and early 1970s, encouraged the prominence of diversity as a structuring value for inhabitants who professed their preference for the cultural richness and urbanity of intown areas.

In Washington during the 1970s the invocation of diversity was standard practice in the defense of preservation efforts. Addressing a historic preservation conference held in Washington in 1972, Capitol Hill resident and activist Noel Kane noted that "many of our members originally came to live on the Hill for the very reasons that they continue to live on the Hill—Diversity."[18] In a 1977 statement before a Joint Committee on Landmarks (JCL) hearing, the president of the North Dupont Community Association argued in support of an expanded historic district, explicitly invoking the protection of diversity. "By approving this particular historic district, you'll be saying that you're affirming what Dupont

Circle is, what it has been, and what it should be and that's an in-town diverse neighborhood and I think that's what historic preservation is all about."[19] According to many advocates of inner-city living, who were also supporters of restoration and historic preservation, the intown residential areas possessed a form of value derived from their diversity, a quality not easily obtained in other areas of the city and actively discouraged in the suburbs.

For advocates of restoration, diversity was both a politically potent ideal and a commonplace that they used to attribute value to their project. As such it had no definitive grounding or measurability. In the Capitol Hill neighborhoods the presence of a growing white middle class in Southeast sections in the 1960s and then in the Northeast sections after about 1970 was, in statistical terms, creating greater racial and economic diversity. Dupont Circle and neighborhoods to its north, especially Adams Morgan and Mount Pleasant, were also economically and racially diverse in those decades. But it is difficult to say if diversity was increasing or if the idea of diversity was simply earning more adherents. It certainly seems, as social scientist Frank H. Wilson has argued, that a self-conscious and specifically middle-class idea of urban diversity became much more prominent in public discussions about inner-city life.[20]

Research based on census data for the Capitol Hill area in the 1970s has problematized the picture of diversity promoted by restoration advocates and preservation-oriented organizations in the period. It suggested that, at least according to some measures, the composition of the Capitol Hill neighborhoods became less diverse as the project of restoring the properties in the area advanced further. While the ideal of the intown area as socially diverse and physically authentic was widespread by the early 1970s, there is also evidence that at least some "back to the city" advocates were alarmed by the process of displacement and social homogenization that accompanied the neighborhood restoration process. Noel Kane was so concerned with this seemingly perverse process that he founded the Capitol Hill Action Group, an organization dedicated to preserving "Capitol Hill as an area where people with different economic and racial backgrounds can live together." He expressed his concern that the aspirations of black residents may not always be served by preservation "if preservation means turning the Hill into an enclave of expensive single family units. This kind of preservation will not only hasten the exit of black home-owners and renters from the area but also would push out low-income whites and students."[21] His concern, in other words, was with both racial and income diversity.

Despite the efforts of people such as Kane and the Capitol East Housing Council, which arranged the rehabilitation of houses for people on low incomes in the area, during the 1970s a pattern emerged that turned out to be more or less inexorable. That process, commonly called gentrification by 1980, affected a dozen or so census tracts in neighborhoods that are now collectively known as Capitol Hill, as well as a handful more in the city's inner Northwest between Dupont Circle and Mount Pleasant. Comparative analysis of the 1970 and 1980 censuses and direct interviews with recent arrivals in the area carried out by social researchers revealed fundamental changes in the social character of central Washington in this period. The most significant measurable changes were (1) a higher rate of growth of housing costs by comparison with wider metropolitan trends, (2) significant racial change from black to white, (3) a noticeable decrease in the average household size, and (4) a noticeable transfer of rental to homeowner housing units. In very general terms small households of white homeowners were obtaining properties formerly inhabited by larger households of mostly black renters.[22]

It does not necessarily follow from this that restoration areas such as Capitol Hill and Dupont Circle all of a sudden became homogeneous neighborhoods of well-to-do whites, what journalist and advocate George Frain criticized as "lily-white enclaves."[23] While local critics of the restoration movement such as Frain, Sam Smith, and Keith Melder believed that private market restoration entailed many of the same negative effects as demolition-driven urban renewal, where poor blacks would be replaced by middle-class whites in key central-city locations, most advocates of remodeling and restoration saw it as the opposite of large-scale urban renewal. Instead of wholesale destruction and the dispersal of natural communities, private market restoration promised targeted interventions into the built environment and support for existing cultural patterns. The CHRS claimed, for example, that "today's restored Capitol Hill was not done by government or corporate developers, but by the industry and enterprise of individuals."[24] The statement highlights the belief of preservationists that the restoration movement was diametrically opposed to government-initiated bulldozer renewal. But it also points up the difference in outlook that existed between the restoration movement and its critics. The value that was created in the restoration neighborhoods was, according to the CHRS, the outcome of individual initiative and so was rightfully appropriated by those who had undertaken the personal and financial risks associated with it. This individual initiative would then lead to the strengthening of the community at large. This contrasted with the racial and community entitlements espoused by black community groups such as MICCO.[25]

While in many ways a matter of political conviction, opinion about the process also depended on social and geographical vantage point. Inside the established restoration neighborhoods, and for hopeful believers at their fringes, the money and energy being invested in old houses suggested a flowering of new hope in the inner city. But for poor blacks in particular, who lived in the areas defined by earlier waves of experts as negro ghettos and slums and adjacent to the restoration zones, the in-migration of mostly white, middle-class inhabitants was not necessarily a source of hope but of indifference or even resentment. Where pioneers spoke hopefully of diversity, others saw only inequality.

Restorationists' new investment and the physical changes it produced in central area neighborhoods in Washington and parallel activity in other large cities, especially New York and San Francisco, led observers in the late 1960s and early 1970s to proclaim an urban revival and a "back-to-the-city trend." This happened even as city populations declined and as the fiscal situations of the governments of these cities remained grim. With the benefit of hindsight, what was really taking place was the great expansion of a vocal political constituency committed to what it saw as the values of urban life, including its apparent diversity when compared to the suburbs. Amplifying the perception of change were small-scale real estate brokers such as Capitol Hill's Barbara Held, who saw that a substantial amount of money could be made from the turnover of property. Some of these agents, no doubt, were also genuinely committed to a broader idea of social diversity and the community vitality and economic growth that they believed went together with it. While it is difficult to say with certainty which groups benefited most from this process, what is clear is that by 1980 there was a predominantly white, middle-class constituency in Washington large enough to rehabilitate much of the terrain of the intown areas.[26]

The apparent contradiction between the belief in the value of diversity and the structural impetus toward class homogeneity, a contradiction highlighted by scholarly critics of gentrification from the late 1970s onward, does not preclude the possibility that private market revitalization encouraged some other forms of social diversity. Deviation from prevailing household types was certainly a significant feature of restoration neighborhoods. The image of the urban pioneer most often depicted in Washington's mainstream press and restoration literature in the late 1960s and early 1970s was a well-educated, young, married couple with little capital but plenty of energy (Figure 17). But alongside those couples were unmarried straight couples, as well as single men and women, gay couples, and a variety of other household types. It seems fairly clear, however, that whatever the household configuration, the audience for the message about diversity was generally highly educated and middle class. Moreover, the beneficiaries of restoration-driven neighborhood revitalization and historic preservation were principally middle-class property owners and small-scale real estate brokers. Though, certainly, there were many property owners of modest means for whom the restoration trend and its accompanying rising property values was something of a windfall.

From the time the Georgetown Homeowners' Committee began to advocate for historic area zoning in the 1920s and 1930s, historic preservation in Washington, D.C., had been intimately linked with the success of the housing restoration trend. While such ideals waned somewhat during the heyday of large-scale urban renewal, the restoration of old houses in intown areas continued. The 1960s, punctuated by civil disorder and characterized by talk of the "urban crisis," are remembered in Washington for the rioting and conflagration of April 1968 following the assassination of Martin Luther King Jr. Yet the idea of renewing the cultural life and social conditions of central-city areas through housing restoration and preservation did not die. Indeed through the first half of the 1970s it was unquestionably a driver for increased property values in intown neighborhoods. Large-scale clearance was broadly discredited, and the restoration trend spread to several neighborhoods previously unaffected by the trend.

The spread of the neighborhood restoration ideal and the attempts to achieve very different goals using broadly preservationist methods underline its currency in the period. Growing numbers of policy makers as well as some community activists saw the potential for organized restoration

Figure 17. "Whites Moving in to Capitol Hill," circa 1969. The photograph was taken for a *U.S. News and World Report* story but did not appear in a published article. The contact sheet caption described the shoot as "Whites Moving in to Capitol Hill." Source: *U.S. News and World Report* picture collection, Prints and Photographs, Library of Congress.

and historic preservation controls even in black neighborhoods where there was little obvious prospect for in-migration of middle- and upper-income restorationists and white-led gentrification.

ANACOSTIA AND LEDROIT PARK

By 1973 Georgetown was almost completely populated by whites, and the deep historical ties of African Americans to the area had been largely severed by the high cost of housing. As we have seen, Capitol Hill experienced growing social tensions around the issue in the period, and the 1970s also saw growing concern about the displacement of lower-and middle-income people, both black and white, in the Dupont Circle area. But uneven patterns of race and real estate across the District of Columbia made any unified reading of the effects of restoration and preservation very difficult.[27]

Prominent preservationist voices in Washington evinced a growing awareness of the problem of restoration-fueled gentrification. In 1973 the *Washington Post* architecture critic, Wolf von Eckardt, vigorously supported the idea of a preservation scheme for the African American neighborhood around Logan Circle that would also be a publicly financed housing program for the existing inhabitants of the area. In fact, he explicitly posited the idea as a test case, an experiment in allying preservation with the welfare of the existing community. Arguing for a link between restoration and community justice, he attempted to short-circuit the inevitability of restoration and preservation being associated with displacement. Von Eckardt was almost certainly aware of the growing body of innovative planning and preservation activity underway in other cities that was directed toward disrupting that connection and promoting the interests of established urban communities. Among the most prolific and influential were the writer, teacher, and organizer Joan Maynard, who was active in Brooklyn, the urbanist and preservationist Arthur Ziegler from Pittsburgh, and Leopold Adler, an investment banker from Savannah, Georgia, who found his avocation in the preservation field and became one of its national leaders.[28]

In 1971 Ziegler wrote a short book describing how his organization, Pittsburgh History & Landmarks Foundation, had pioneered methods of retaining existing residents of moderate income while restoring a historically valued but physically deteriorating area of the city, the Mexican

War Streets. It was a guidebook for how preservationists in inner-city areas should proceed, but also contained an indictment of the social effects of historic preservation activity in preceding decades. He compared preservationists unfavorably with redevelopment authorities, noting:

> Historic preservation groups across the country from the 1930s up until today remorselessly removed neighborhood residents regardless of their longevity in the proposed historic district or their commitment to that area. They simply replaced them with well-to-do residents who could understand the value of the structures and who could afford to restore and maintain them.[29]

Ziegler proposed alternatives that would repair and restore dwelling units, preserving their historical qualities, but do so in a way that encouraged the retention of existing residents. Like advocacy planning, Ziegler's model presumed the participation of local residents, and like antiblockbusting strategies from the same period it was an attempt to circumvent the economic exploitation of physical and social change by real estate agents and investment capital.[30]

In Savannah, Adler recognized a very obvious threat to the physical qualities of the city's Victorian district. Urban restructuring and the reconfiguration of the geography of race and class in the 1960s led to problems of property decay and neglect and the erosion of the fabric of the area. Inspired by Ziegler's work in Pittsburgh, Adler decided to turn historic preservation in Savannah to the cause of neighborhood conservation. Seeing an opportunity to expand the work of the well-known Historic Savannah Foundation, Adler asked the organization to become involved with a project to restore a large group of houses in an area occupied mostly by poor African Americans. The foundation, however, refused to get involved, and Adler turned to other sources of help for the project. In a fairly subtle way Adler's subsequent initiation of the Savannah Landmark Rehabilitation Project was a historic preservationist critique of what had become conventional historic districting and restoration practices. The project, despite a number of political mistakes and legal setbacks, demonstrated ways that restoration could be used to promote inclusionary zoning or fair housing strategies instead of encouraging restrictive and exclusionary conditions in historic places.[31]

This same commitment to protecting and empowering existing inhabitants informed the designation of historic districts in LeDroit Park and Anacostia in 1973. In 1970 both areas were home to predominantly African American populations. On the face of it they were quite similar. Both neighborhoods were originally built as speculative developments beyond the boundaries of the L'Enfant city in the second half of the nineteenth century. And more importantly, both neighborhoods had struggled economically through the 1960s with various social transformations, leaving their physical resources vulnerable to decay and the inhabitants insecure about the future of their communities. But the histories of the two areas are otherwise quite different.

The Uniontown area of Anacostia had always been working class, but its inhabitants were predominantly white until the 1960s. In fact when the lots were sold in the 1860s and 1870s they had whites-only covenants. Following a period of quite intense racial hostility focused on the desegregation of the schools in the 1960s the white population quickly left the area. Many blacks displaced by urban renewal in the city's Southwest section had moved into new garden apartments and public housing projects such as the Sheridan Terrace in neighboring areas. As houses became available due to white flight, blacks also moved into the hundred-year-old Uniontown subdivision, which was the area eventually nominated as a historic district. As a consequence, in the early 1970s few people living in the area that would be designated as a historic district had historical ties to the neighborhood.[32]

LeDroit Park was very different. After starting life as an exclusively white, suburban subdivision in the 1870s it was briefly the site of an attempt at residential integration around the turn of the twentieth century before becoming a largely middle-class black enclave in the 1920s. However, as middle-class blacks established a number of other significant communities further from the center of the city in places such as Petworth, the number of prosperous inhabitants in LeDroit Park dwindled. By the early 1960s a core group of long-term residents remained, but newspaper reports from the period represented it as blighted and it was known for its organized gang activity.[33]

A feature-length newspaper report on the area, published in 1974, indicated that long-term residents held widely diverging opinions about the physical and social state of the LeDroit Park neighborhood. Francis

Williford told reporters that "the only reason I live here is because I own the property. Otherwise I'd be gone." On the other hand, Roland Brown spoke optimistically of the area's future, saying "it's a dream for me . . . to see the small neighborhood struggle back to the serenity and prestige it encompassed in the days before World War II."[34]

Having joined in the effort to create stronger preservation protections in Washington in 1973, the D.C. Bicentennial Commission, under the leadership of Polly Shackleton, urged the city's planners and its JCL to identify places of cultural and historical significance to African Americans. This led to the designation of the historic districts in LeDroit Park and Anacostia (Maps 7 and 8). The commission believed that such recognition could generate knowledge, build pride, and foster what is now sometimes referred to as social capital. It was part of a wider effort to increase awareness of black history at the time.[35]

Promoters of events such as Black History Month argued that increased understanding and community pride should be built not just on knowledge of historical oppression but also of black resistance to that oppression and the creation of alternative spaces for black culture and social life. In a February 1973 black history week supplement in the *Afro-American*, Dr. Benjamin Quarles of Baltimore's Morgan State University argued that "black history reveals the contributions of blacks, but it also reveals the deeply ingrained patterns of discrimination against blacks and the variety of ways in which they struck back." Yet he noted that this has generally "been omitted from textbooks."[36] Similarly, Ron Powell and Bill Cunningham, the authors of the *Black Guide to Washington*, published in 1975 and funded by the Afro-American Bicentennial Corporation, noted the omission of black history in American civic culture. "Yet, slowly and painfully the outline, traces and foundations of a black heritage are beginning to emerge. The black past, as its stands alone or is interwoven in the total picture of American history, is now being discovered."[37] Such commentary helped drive the ideal that the historic past, including the historic resources embodied in buildings and neighborhoods, could be part of an optimistic mission to build credible political representation and economic prosperity for African Americans in Washington. The theory was that fostering increased pride and awareness in the identity and historical legacy of neighborhoods through the historic districting process would have a positive impact on living conditions and real estate value. In this way existing inhabitants were the ones who would benefit, not those attracted by the potential financial gains.[38]

The idea of building community pride or social capital in historical assets was, however, somewhat compromised by relatively low levels of engagement in the process. Washington's Department of Housing and Community Development commissioned a report in 1978 that assessed the impact of the historic district designations on the LeDroit Park and Anacostia Historic districts. It found that only a small percentage of

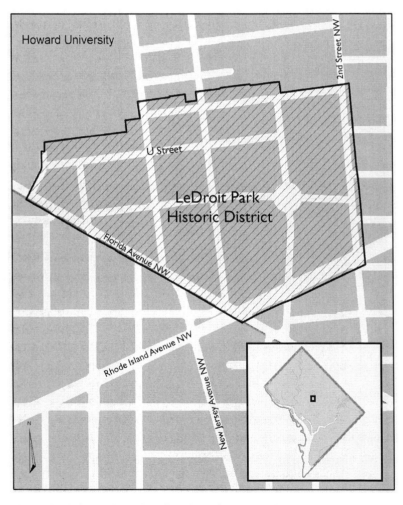

Map 7.   LeDroit Park Historic District. Created by and copyright Matthew B. Gilmore.

inhabitants in the areas knew about the designation of the historic districts, and fewer still knew what it meant legally or why they were considered significant. In LeDroit Park there was a small but committed group of residents, led by Theresa Brown, who were actively involved in the historic districting process and the fight against the expansion of Howard University. But neighborhood restoration and historic preservation did not engage the majority of people. The same was true in Anacostia. Despite the long-standing efforts of John Kinard to build pride

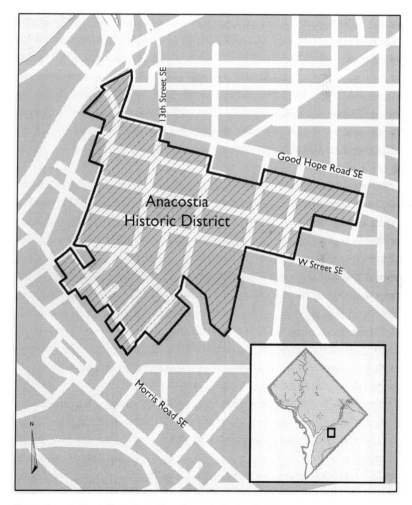

Map 8. Anacostia Historic District. Created by and copyright Matthew B. Gilmore.

and historical awareness through the Smithsonian's Anacostia Community Museum and his support of the historic districting and renewal process, the study found that it was difficult to locate overt supporters of historic districting within the community.[39]

The effort to reorient the social consequences of neighborhood restoration and historic preservation in the 1970s in Washington was consistent with a national tendency toward experimentation and expansion within the historic preservation field. Such experimentation was driven directly by local political currents—especially the gathering momentum of the home rule campaign—and those currents were also tied to a broader reconceptualization of history and neighborhood as loci of democratic entitlements. But despite the wide ambition and energy invested in the idea of neighborhood identity, preservation politics remained stubbornly connected with the efforts of a particular class fragment. That class fragment contained relatively few nonwhites. Consequently, the neighborhood preservation movement struggled to transcend its origins as an alliance of middle-class property owners.

1978

Three events that culminated in 1978 changed the way preservationists addressed criticism of their project to restore and preserve Washington's intown neighborhoods. In June the U.S. Supreme Court settled a decade-long dispute between New York City and Penn Central Transportation over the fate of the Grand Central Terminal. The majority opinion in the case found that New York City's Landmark Law was valid and did not enable the "taking" of property as the appellants suggested. The decision underlined the legitimacy of historic landmarks laws by confirming that such legislation could reasonably be expected to serve the public good. The decision also relieved some of the pressure on preservationists to justify their activity by reference to its positive impact on property value.[40]

Just two days after the vital Supreme Court ruling, local legislation was introduced into the D.C. Council that would become the D.C. Law 2-144, the Historic Landmark and Historic District Protection Act. When it came into effect at the beginning of 1979, it was one of the most robust local preservation laws anywhere in the nation. The young lawyer responsible for drafting the legislation, David Bonderman, was vice president of the citywide not-for-profit preservation organization Don't Tear

It Down! when he became involved. During the process of drafting the D.C. law Bonderman wrote an amicus brief for the Supreme Court case on behalf of the National Trust for Historic Preservation and looked to the arguments that were put in the Supreme Court case as a road map for the D.C. law. But the D.C. law was a difficult balancing act. It had to meet expectations of constituents in rapidly changing areas such as Dupont Circle that it could effectively slow and prevent wholesale demolition and redevelopment, while not discouraging new investment in other recognized historic districts such as Anacostia, which faced very different challenges connected with disinvestments and the decay of housing stock.[41]

The third key contextual factor that reshaped the preservationist response to criticism of restoration and preservation efforts was the election of Marion Barry as Washington's mayor in November 1978. Barry had carefully built political support in the city for more than a decade, but his supporters could not easily be characterized. He garnered votes from affluent, predominantly white, wards west of Rock Creek Park, as well as those of some of the city's poorest residents in areas with high concentrations of African Americans east of the Anacostia River. Most of the black elite stood behind either the incumbent, Walter Washington, or Sterling Tucker, a councilman, former head of the Urban League, and the man widely expected to succeed Washington. But Barry ran as a coalition-builder and reformer, winning sympathy from an unexpected cross section of poor blacks and more affluent intown whites.[42] As Howard Gillette Jr. has written, Barry's "victory sent a mixed message. Identified with the causes closest to the black power movement, he had nonetheless made himself acceptable to whites."[43] This left open the distinct possibility that the very different interests of his dual constituencies might not be easily resolved.

While the new preservation law was debated, black councilor William Spaulding described the proposed law as elitist and argued that it would accelerate the displacement of poor blacks.[44] On the other side of the debate, and responding to the new political context created by Barry's election, the locally based historic preservation group the Dupont Circle Conservancy promoted a new interpretation of the effects of historic districts on real estate value. That interpretation sought to decouple preservation from gentrification and evade the continuing criticism that restoration and preservation led to the displacement of the poor. Under concerted pressure from black activists in neighboring Shaw in the early 1980s, who strongly opposed a campaign to expand the Dupont Circle Historic District on the grounds that it would cause such displacement, conservancy president Charles Robertson argued that neighborhood re- development and restoration occurred irrespective of historic district boundaries.[45] Robertson argued that developers will go "where they think they will make a profit, regardless of historic district lines."[46] The Dupont Circle preservationists suggested, moreover, that historic districts could assist in the maintenance and improvement of the housing stock, while maintaining the area's viability as a neighborhood with a substantial population of low-income inhabitants. Pro-preservation developer John B. Ritch III, who was active in the Dupont Circle area, argued that the tax credit provided by federal law for properties in historic districts would make feasible the maintenance and repair of historic structures and the maintenance of rents affordable to the current residents. His argument was that the federal preservation tax credit would subsidize the D.C. tenancy laws, which had formerly had the effect of allowing people to stay in properties that were deteriorating around them.[47]

This reading of the effects of historic district protections on real estate could be interpreted simply as a cover for the real interests of preserva- tionists who were keen to legitimize their campaign and avoid politically sensitive criticism. But several years later the first significant piece of re- search dedicated to understanding the effects of historic district designa- tion on the displacement of incumbent residents provided some support for the view put by Ritch and the Dupont Circle preservationists. Den- nis E. Gale's 1989 report, *The Impact of Historic District Designation in Wash- ington, D.C.*, concluded that there is "no evidence to date that historic district designation affects property values."[48] Yet he remained guarded about the results, warning that the research had not been able to control for several factors, and it would be necessary to carry out further research to draw stronger conclusions. Subsequent research that surveyed evidence from around the United States was equivocal. Eric Allison's analysis of nine New York historic districts found that they made no appreciable dif- ference to real estate value.[49] On the other hand Akram M. Ijla's doctoral research on six cities in the early 1990s indicated that local historic dis- trict designation "is associated with higher property values."[50] Economist

Donovan Rypkema has conducted the most far-reaching research on this question, and on balance he concludes that there is evidence to argue that district designations push up the value of real estate. But, as one might expect, Rypkema also asserts that it very much depends on the individual instance. Listing, he suggests, "does not necessarily add economic value to a given piece of real estate . . . but it can be a catalytic tool."[51]

Rypkema's assessment of the impact of historic district designation reflects the perceptions held on both sides of the issue in Dupont Circle in the early 1980s. The preservationists argued that historic district designations and expansions did not necessarily mean anything for property value. But their opponents saw an effort to use preservation as a catalytic force to increase demand for property among so-called urban pioneers and restorationists and, therefore, enhance the overall value of the property within the historic district. African American neighborhood activist and local political entrepreneur Edna Frazier-Cromwell suggested as much when she remarked to preservationist Charles Robertson that "many people are concerned that an historic district designation may adversely impact property owners in our community who are on fixed incomes."[52] In other words, she was concerned that higher tax assessments would accompany rising real estate values and make remaining in the area unaffordable for many. Dupont Circle preservationists countered this by pointing to the experience of Anacostia and LeDroit Park, where historic district designation had not initiated significant growth in housing costs. Shaw community activists responded by noting that it was naive to think that realtors would not try to use the cachet associated with the Dupont Circle name to sell houses in the historic district to middle-class whites, especially in the more affordable parts of the district that had previously been considered part of Shaw.[53]

Real estate value in American cities during the twentieth century was deeply affected by perceptions of physical and social change, and in Washington, as in other American cities, these perceptions have been shaped by ideas about racial succession. Therefore, the mostly black and mostly low-income residents of midtown or Shaw were understandably anxious that a change in the name and in the racial composition of their area would lead to a marked increase in the cost of housing. The idea that the proposed Dupont Circle Historic District expansion, first proposed in 1977 and revived and resubmitted in 1982 (see chapter 5), would not affect the racial and class composition of the area was perhaps disingenuous. But in this particular battle preservationists in Washington found themselves on unfamiliar terrain. The default position for several decades had been to claim that restoring properties by private means and encouraging preservation through land-use planning and historic area zoning had the capacity to revive ailing property value and tax revenues in central-city locations. Dupont Circle preservationists now found themselves in the invidious position of having to deny that preservation controls were necessarily associated with increases in property value. They insisted that the right mix of regulatory incentives would ensure that property values did not rise in such a way that made the area unaffordable for low-income residents.

Intown black activists were not the only ones who objected to the booming growth in historic districts in the period. The American Institute of Architects saw a danger in the expansiveness of the preservation controls enabled by the new preservation law, arguing in 1978 that the proposed preservation "bill would freeze all progress in the city."[54] But it was the development industry that dedicated the most resources and embarked on the most concerted campaign to undermine the impact and legitimacy of preservation controls. In the late 1970s and the 1980s the Washington firm Wilkes Artis, led by the influential land-use lawyer Whayne Quin, represented a host of owners and lobby groups who saw a threat to their interests in the continued expansion of historic preservation activity. This coalition of highly motivated and well-resourced property owners had not accepted the legitimacy of the *Penn Central* decision or the provisions of the new D.C. preservation law, and they persistently challenged historic district applications on the grounds that they contravened the property rights of owners and arbitrarily closed off large segments of the city to new development. In particular, they objected to the idea that places enclosed within historic districts should be considered significant and worthy of protection by default, simply as a consequence of falling within such districts.

After 1978 real estate lawyers staked out and occupied the populist terrain that preservationists had carefully assumed in the aftermath of bulldozer urban renewal. Property interests accused preservationists of elitism and of ignoring the basic welfare of the city's inhabitants and of putting their own aestheticism and personal tastes ahead of the city's wider economic and social development. In a letter to the city's Historic Preservation Office and the statutory landmarks commission (JCL), Whayne Quin challenged preservationists' entitlement to see themselves as defenders of the city, asserting that "not infrequently, persons who are stalwarts of historic preservation overlook the more basic needs of a public welfare."[55]

Developers simply did not accept the idea that protecting the fabric of old buildings and neighborhoods was an unqualified public good, something that was presumed and promoted by preservationists. They seized upon preservationists' public interest claims, depicting them instead as particular and narrow. In 1979 developers tested the legality of the system of historic landmark designation. In an appeal case about the listing of the Demonet Building on Connecticut Avenue as a historic landmark, lawyers for the developer, Dominic Antonelli, took aim at the District of Columbia's preservation law. They questioned the constitutionality of statutes that delegated authority to executive commissions such as the JCL with broad guidelines to represent vaguely drawn concepts such as the "public interest" or "buildings of historical interest."[56] The developers also sought to undermine the legal standing of the JCL by questioning the idea that it could make legally binding decisions: that is, decisions that could be subject to the meaningful review of a higher court. In doing so, the developer's lawyers also questioned the validity of the idea that historic preservation protections were in the public interest at all.[57]

While the District of Columbia Court of Appeals declined to rule on the substance of the Demonet challenge and developers tended to accept the law in following years, the latter maintained their attack on the scope and legitimacy of preservation. Thereafter, developers focused on the political and economic context surrounding the law. That is, they fought the battle more at the level of public relations. In an article written for a real estate trade publication in 1981, Whayne Quin argued that there was a lack of balance between historic preservation and other public needs "such as a viable economy, and social needs such as housing, transportation and general health and prosperity."[58] He rehearsed a variation of the same argument in a letter to the JCL the following year. Referring to his client's property just north of Dupont Circle, Quin suggested that "the public welfare would be better served by the creation of affordable housing than the retention of a parking lot."[59] In a position paper with the title "A Comprehensive Preservation Plan for Washington," the Washington Board of Realtors and Greater Washington Board of Trade reiterated the point, questioning the breadth of public interest and support underpinning the rapid growth in preservation controls. The paper asserted that "Washington is too important to be frozen in a romantic past which exists only in the minds of a few."[60]

The developers acknowledged, therefore, that there were entitlements other than those belonging to private property. But they emphasized that these entitlements were multiple and sometimes competing. They also tried to associate their own efforts with the public welfare, especially as it related to housing. By so doing they attempted to draw the attention of the Marion Barry–led D.C. government away from qualitative concerns about environmental and cultural value—the principal concerns of preservationists. They asserted instead the importance of quantitative measures, such as the number of new dwelling units under construction and the number of jobs generated by new construction. Whether or not it was wholly cynical, the campaign by real estate capital to resist the growing influence of historic preservation did present Marion Barry's D.C. government with a means of constraining and undermining the goals of the preservation movement.

CONCLUSION

Across the period from the late 1960s through to the 1980s, preservationists encountered sustained attacks on the legitimacy of their project to restore and preserve inner-city neighborhoods. By the late 1970s this resistance derived from two quite different sources. The arguments mobilized by African American neighborhood groups on the one hand and by property interests on the other covered similar concerns about housing justice and affordability. But to successfully counter these related attacks, preservationists had to modulate their arguments for different audiences while not appearing to contradict themselves. Preservationists now had to convince politically potent low-income blacks, not just an entitled middle class, that historic preservation was a legitimate way of controlling change in urban areas. To do this they had to work against the assumption that restoration and historic districting were ways of initiating social change by conferring prestige on a district, and thereby encouraging growth in real estate values. At the same time they had to assuage the public impact of developer criticism, which was motivated primarily by a concern with property value.

Preservationists in the key intown areas where restoration and preservation efforts were at the center of neighborhood politics and neighborhood improvement argued that area preservation was neutral with respect to property value. It was, of course, difficult to uncouple historic district proposals from the restoration trend, which almost certainly did contribute to increases in housing costs. Nevertheless, were you to remove the restoration trend from the equation, as subsequent research has tended to show, there was nothing inevitable about the connection between designating historic districts and rising housing costs. Preservation advocates, therefore, increasingly focused their explanations for historic district proposals on their noneconomic implications. They talked, as they always had, about preserving neighborhood identity, but also about cultural and community resources and about the opportunities for communities to exercise greater control over decisions.

CHAPTER 5

Whose Neighborhood?
Whose History?

Expanding Dupont Circle, 1975–1985

Resistance to historic preservation and neighborhood restoration forces in Washington in the late 1960s grew more vociferous in the 1970s as the movement gathered momentum and exerted greater influence. Most participants in restoration and preservation groups, however, believed that forces of dilapidation, decay, and outright destruction were still the greatest threats to the traditional architectural patterns and social vitality of the city's intown areas. The riots that followed the assassination of Martin Luther King Jr. in April 1968 punctuated and accelerated the physical decay of the built environment in several key areas. But given the impact of the riots on perceptions of disorder in the inner city, and the centrality of those events in the narration of the city's recent history, the preservation and restoration effort resumed its confidence and regained its momentum with remarkable rapidity.

In 1976 John J. Schulter, editor and publisher of *The Intowner,* a monthly neighborhood newspaper, proclaimed the revival of urban life in Washington's inner Northwest. Schulter introduced the theme of urban revival by recounting his own experiences during the riots. Schulter went out into the streets around Nineteenth Street in the Dupont Circle neighborhood with two neighbors, Robert C. Weaver, secretary of the Department of Housing and Urban Development—probably the most powerful African American in Washington—and White House press photographer Ron Edmonds. Schulter was armed with a .32 caliber pistol—"long unused or thought about since my organizing days in the South when it was the Ku Klux Klan that might be coming to get me"—and sporting a red armband to indicate his role as a citizen volunteer.[1] He and his companions—one white, one black—were citizens on patrol, looking out for looting, arson, and other forms of property damage associated with the social unrest centered on the Fourteenth Street corridor, but which had spread as far west as Eighteenth Street. Schulter recounted the episode in his newspaper several years after the events to point to the contrast between the time of the riots and their aftermath, which were filled with apocalyptic sentiment about the fate of the city, and the time of his writing in 1976, with its buoyant inner-city property market, declining rates of crime, and evidence of a revival of its commercial and civic institutions.[2] Schulter recalled asking himself in 1968 if Washington could ever come back. "Would it ever again be a city where Americans white and black, young and old, rich and poor could walk the streets and make a living in peace and serenity."[3] By 1976 his answer was a resounding yes. This imagined state of grace that existed at some time in the past was again at hand, he suggested. He concluded his article by recounting a recent conversation with a major property developer about the intown neighborhoods in Northwest D.C. The developer remarked that "This is the new frontier. This is where I want to buy."[4]

In early 1977 *The Intowner* was again enthusing about conditions in the inner Northwest. It reported that crime was down in the third district, which covered much of Shaw, as well as Logan Circle and its environs and the eastern sections of the Dupont Circle neighborhood. The paper also reported a rapid rate of housing sales and growing house values in the area and generally championed the changes underway across the terrain of Washington's intown neighborhoods. In 1978 *The Intowner* ran a story proclaiming the "Nation's Cities Poised for Stunning Comeback."[5] Sick cities, it seemed, were getting better, the urban crisis abating. At least that's how it looked from the perspective of a white, liberal, self-conscious cosmopolitan in Dupont Circle.

Schulter's account of the riots—a parable of citizen vigilance and cross-racial cooperation—implied that his liberal vision of social and race mixing had triumphed over the militant identity politics and anomie of the late 1960s and early 1970s. There was, nevertheless, also a vaguely threatening note in the reported remarks of the anonymous real estate developer. Why was Dupont Circle the "new frontier" for capital investment in real estate and what did this mean? Schulter pointed to the seemingly positive social and economic climate in the Dupont Circle neighborhood as evidence of the urban revival in Washington. But the buoyancy in local real estate created a level of redevelopment energy that was causing considerable anxiety by the mid- to late 1970s. The atmosphere of reevaluation, ad hoc inhabitation, and renovation that had characterized many parts of the Dupont Circle area since the 1960s was giving way to a more thoroughgoing, real estate–driven redevelopment process. The northwestward extension of downtown via K Street and Connecticut and Massachusetts Avenues was pushing right up to the Circle and putting pressure on the surviving, if slightly jaded, historic mansions in the area as well as the overall pattern of row-house development that gave the area its prevailing atmosphere and identity. Restoration was going from strength to strength but also driving up real estate values and encouraging a more systematic booming of the area by investors and developers.[6]

In response, citizen groups agitated for downzoning to remove the economic incentive for demolition and redevelopment. They also argued that more of the district should be zoned residential to preserve its traditional identity as a predominantly residential area and invoked the negative example of the city's West End, which had been largely transformed into a business district in the decades since World War II. As in Georgetown a generation earlier, the residents of the inner Northwest ultimately turned to historic districting as the most effective mechanism for protecting the character of their area and ensuring that their economic and social investment was not misappropriated by real estate developers. The new class fragment that expressed itself through the reevaluation and restoration of intown neighborhoods now saw the potential for the erosion of the value that they were creating. They were poised, therefore, between the two great concerns of preservationists across the century— decay on the one hand and overdevelopment on the other. In leaving behind the sense of danger and decrepitude of the immediate post-riots era they were confronted with a development industry looking to boom the area and extract much greater value from its real estate.

Consequently, in the 1970s and early 1980s, citizen groups and restoration societies turned to historic districting as a means of controlling change, and the historic districts became a widely influential force determining patterns of growth as well as the rate and nature of change in much of the inner city. The innovations in urbanistic thinking and landuse regulation discussed in chapters 1 and 3 were the premise for a great expansion in the scope and ambition of historic preservation activity in this period. But most importantly, neighborhood organizations turned to preservation as a way to increase their control over the physical environment. Historic preservation activity and the laws that underpinned it were in turns both a reaction to and a catalyst for this trend in urban development. At different times preservationists could be cheerleaders or fierce opponents of private investment in the urban landscape. But whatever their view of a particular issue, neighborhood preservationists assumed a new level of entitlement in discussions about the appropriate intensity and type of building development. Historic districts more than anything were the key lever for this new sense of entitlement.[7]

This chapter discusses the conditions that motivated the designation and expansion of historic districts. It then examines the process of achieving the expanded districts and focuses in particular on the social conflict that arose around the process in Dupont Circle. As the influence of the historic districting mechanism widened in the late 1970s and the early 1980s, the idea that protecting historic, urban landscapes was a straightforward public good met with concerted opposition. The separate histories and entitlements that were connected to racial and class identities in particular became increasingly difficult to ignore in discussions about the shape of historic districts and the meaning of historical significance. The claims of neighborhood preservationists for the historical value of certain kinds of environments depended, to some extent, on an assumption of the universality of the relationship between individuals and those environments. These claims were challenged in Washington by large-scale real estate developers, who perceived a threat to their economic interests. But Dupont Circle area preservationists, who were among the most influential and energetic in the city, also faced a much less anticipated challenge from African American community leaders who rejected their legitimacy and expressed concern about the effects of historic districting on the identity of historically black neighborhoods. Such opposition did not undo the influence of historic preservation and historic districts. But it did change the character of historic preservation activity and subtly reformulated the neighborhood preservation movement in the 1980s.

PRESERVING A WIDER REALM

In the 1970s the historic preservation movement in the United States grew and evolved into a much more organized and formidable force.

Preservationists assumed a new level of responsibility for the steward-ship of the urban landscape in the decade strengthened by a profession-alized leadership, growing membership, and an exponentially greater resource base. Their most powerful tool was the identification and pro-tection of historic districts. The National Trust for Historic Preservation together with the new state and local historic preservation bureaucracies organized conferences and created a body of technical and promotional literature designed to foster community-level activity. One of the princi-pal ways that national preservation leaders encouraged a wider scope to preservation activity was by pointing to buildings and other items in the environment whose historical significance and physical qualities had been ignored in earlier years. By doing so they encouraged an appreciation of the significance of the everyday urban landscape. A growing number of Americans were evidently concerned about losing such everyday places, and the preservation movement, via its proliferating grassroots, articu-lated the value of those places, which had mostly gone unremarked in the past. Commercial, industrial, and modest residential buildings all re-ceived more attention as did the visual relationships among buildings and between buildings and topography. One National Trust publication from the period quoted Gordon Cullen's suggestion that "one building is architecture, but two buildings is townscape."[8] The author of a guide to *America's Forgotten Architecture* argued that the isolated building could no longer be regarded as the focus for preservation activity, and identi-fied townscapes as the proper domain of preservation practice.

> Building groups in combination with other constructed elements, land-scaping, and the street furniture—paving, fences, benches, lampposts, mailboxes, utility poles, chute covers, transit shelters, kiosks, street signs, and commercial signs—create a streetscape. Added to the natural environ-ment, these give us townscapes, the unique ensembles that mark an iden-tity for every place where humans have put their hands.[9]

Such appreciation for the historically determined value of the physical environment, and of the landscape as a cultural product, had enjoyed some currency in the late nineteenth and early twentieth centuries. But in the postwar decades such holistic conceptions of place and landscape history were more frequently missing from the preservation discussion.

The evolving civic interest in defending cities against destruction in the 1960s and early 1970s, and the development of a new legal and administrative infrastructure for preservation, inspired renewed interest among local preservation and citizen groups in protecting the whole scene, not just the landmark building. The evolving influence of ecological thought, which stressed the totality and fragility of environments, strengthened the reemergence of this wider sense of historical significance among preservation-oriented societies. Advocates used salient ecological concepts to point to the destructive influence of instrumental and analytically narrow renderings of the meaning and utility of land.[10]

Prominent preservation advocates in the 1970s underlined the value of cultural patterns in the urban environment, not simply the presence of important structures. In 1973, for example, William Murtagh, keeper of the National Register of Historic Places, described the fundamental importance of "anonymous structures—'anonymous' in their average aesthetic quality," for the identification and designation of historic districts.[11] This concern was already strongly evident before Herbert Gans accused New York preservationists of elitism in the *New York Times* in 1975 and of ignoring the historical significance of the everyday environment. In a reply to Gans's critique of the New York City Landmarks Preservation Commission, Ada Louise Huxtable rejected the accusation, noting that in New York, several large historic districts had recently been protected containing thirteen thousand buildings. These contained, she noted, a dense fabric of everyday residential and commercial structures without any connection to elite society, government, or high-style architecture.[12]

The growing interest in protecting such ordinary places in the urban fabric on the part of preservationists reflected an understanding of urban life and its value that Herbert Gans himself had helped foster in the 1960s with his widely influential study of the neighborhood life of Italian Americans in Boston. The "traditional" social patterns and physical spaces of urban life were something that scholars such as Gans, as well as sympathetic journalists and cultural critics, especially those who viewed suburbanization and bulldozer urban renewal negatively, had begun to view as a threatened value in this period. Partly in response to this perceived threat, preservationists expressed a growing desire in the 1970s to preserve the physical locus for this form of urban life, rather than see it as inevitably outmoded, unhealthy, and undesirable.[13]

In the "decade of the neighborhood," as historian Suleiman Osman has described the 1970s, the historic district became a powerful tool for delineating the boundaries of neighborhoods and for fostering their distinct identity within the wider urban landscape. In Washington, D.C., National Capital Planning Commission (NCPC) planners identified new historic districts in LeDroit Park and Anacostia to strengthen interest in, and protect, their individual character. Both were also understood as historically African American neighborhoods. Recognizing that as a positive tradition, rather than as a negative factor in housing conditions or real estate value, was also part of the motivation of planners.[14]

In addition to highlighting the value of neighborhood identity, preservation publications from the period encouraged interested local groups to identify historic districts themselves. Such publications provided very specific guidance on how to conduct research directed toward identifying the scope and edges of historic districts. One such publication from the mid-1970s warned against simply conducting a survey of architecturally significant buildings. The authors counseled preservationists to consider "topographical factors" that define a district, social facets of the neighborhood's history, as well as political and economic factors that might influence the creation of the district. They outlined, in other words, a whole strategy for recognizing the salient qualities and interpreting the meaning of cultural landscapes as well as for using the mechanisms available to control changes in them. In so doing, the authors sought to redefine and expand the meaning of "historical significance," the core concept in preservation listing. This recasting of what should be regarded as significant was in line with evolving international trends in the field.[15]

Particularly noticeable was the way National Trust and National Park Service publications in the 1970s encouraged local preservationists to recognize social meanings that attached to their area and link them to physical qualities. In effect they introduced the question of cultural heritage to the historic preservation field in the United States by encouraging professional preservationists and local activists to go beyond the identifiable architectural and building history of their districts and to ask who and what forces adapted those buildings and places to everyday patterns of dwelling, work, and consumption. Some preservation and neighborhood groups embraced this idea without hesitation, while others, as in

Dupont Circle, had to be pushed toward greater acknowledgment of the social and associational significance of places.[16]

ALL PRESERVATION IS LOCAL

The development of a national preservation profession in the United States involved a significant concentration of expertise in Washington, D.C., in the 1970s. The emerging preservation profession discussed and promoted the expanded realm of preservation policy and practical activity extensively. But this did not automatically translate into successful preservation action in the city itself. Being Washington, local events were inevitably shaped by federal politics, institutions, and law. But as with preservation in other parts of the country, local circumstances underpinned particular place protection efforts. The historic district designations and expansions that were so pronounced after 1975 in Washington's intown areas were a case in point.

Three main forces influenced the historic districting efforts after 1975. First and foremost was the destruction of buildings and neighborhoods caused by the continued expansion of the government and the related expansion of the government-influencing sector. Second was the animation of the home rule movement that saw the development of municipal politics in the District of Columbia in the 1970s. The third, encouraged and influenced by the first two, was the development of meaningful citywide historic preservation protections.

The U.S. Capitol is a fundamental symbol of stability and continuity for the United States. But the building and its grounds have nevertheless been in an almost constant state of development and change over the course of their life. The period between the end of World War II and 1980 saw the greatest expansion of the Capitol's footprint. The Senate approved new office accommodation for itself on Capitol Hill in the early 1940s and specific plans for the building later in the decade. This new office building was intended to do double duty, providing much-needed space for Senators and their staff as well as eliminating housing that was designated as slums in the near sections of Northeast. The Dirksen Senate Office Building was designed and constructed between 1949 and 1958 and involved the demolition of dozens of houses. As it turned out it was just the first of a string of projects that affected the blocks around the Capitol in the years to come. The NCPC abandoned the long-discussed eastern extension of the National Mall, which would have expanded the government presence along East Capitol Street, in 1962. But a series of buildings were constructed in an "L" formation from Union Station to the area immediately south of the Capitol grounds on Independence Avenue. The completion of the Dirksen Building was followed by construction of a new congressional parking garage, then the massive Rayburn Building—the third House office building—and planning and construction of the Madison Building, an annex to the Library of Congress. The Architect of the Capitol, J. George Stewart, also embarked on a controversial renovation of the east front of the Capitol itself, and finally Congress added a major extension to the Dirksen Building, which became known as the Hart Senate Office Building.[17]

As one might expect, the inhabitants of the surrounding areas, many of whom were active in the Capitol Hill Restoration Society (CHRS) and had purchased and restored houses in the area, were not happy about this. They used a range of arguments to protest against the ongoing expansion program, which some journalists criticized at the time as not only a consequence of expanding responsibilities of the federal government but also of the proliferation of the congressional committees and its self-serving patronage system.[18]

Capitol Hill residents had no legal mechanism to prevent Congress from using eminent domain powers to acquire land for its expansion program. But they were constitutionally entitled to just compensation. Beginning in 1961 the CHRS loudly protested the sums of money offered to residents who lived on the blocks that were to be condemned for the new House office building (the Rayburn Building) (Figure 18) and other nearby congressional expansion projects. They asserted that J. George Stewart had not recognized the real value of many of the properties in overseeing real estate evaluations and compensation offers. The CHRS focused, in particular, on restored dwellings and highlighted the amount of money spent by owners to bring the houses up to their present condition. They accused Stewart of "bargain hunting" and rushing the project, causing unnecessary economic pain and disruption to the lives of those affected.[19]

The wider community supported this set of protests about congressional expansion. The Rayburn Building project came in for the most sustained criticism. It was pilloried by the architecture press and mocked

Figure 18. Rayburn House Office Building under construction, Independence Avenue, Washington, D.C. Architect: Harbeson, Hough, Livingstone and Larson. Source: Prints and Photographs, Library of Congress.

in the metropolitan dailies for its lavishness. It was a huge and expensive building that also went well over budget, ultimately costing $100 million (a project that would probably cost between $1.5 and $2 billion in today's terms) and providing preservationist critics with an easy target. But the lobbying of Congress and campaigning against further encroachment of the neighborhood persisted through much of the 1970s.[20]

In 1971, the *Washington Post* editorialized about the poorly coordinated and ill-disciplined expansion of congressional facilities on Capitol Hill.[21] In 1977, in the midst of an ongoing debate about a proposed third Library of Congress building, the president of the CHRS, Thomas B. Simmons, chastised Congress in the *Washington Star* for its "erratic expansionist tendencies" and thoughtless approach to its neighbors. He questioned the need for its rapid expansion but also argued that if it must expand, "it need not rape the Hill."[22] In evoking this emotive sense of neighborhood violation Simmons drew directly on William Worthy's 1976 critique of institutional, governmental, and commercial expansion, *The Rape of Our Neighborhoods*.[23] Simmons demurred what he called "militant negativism"—the stop-it-at-all-costs attitude among some preservationists—and encouraged

Congress to find a way toward creative coexistence. "Our suggestions," he urged, "come from the vantage point of an exciting community actively restoring not only homes, but the necessary support of business growth, faith in the school system and personal safety."[24] In other words, Simmons suggested, through restoration and preservation the CHRS was not merely stopping things, it was reviving urban life, creating new energy, and renewing the neighborhood. The CHRS viewed their historic district expansion effort during this period as only one part of that wider project of urban revival, but also the key mechanism by which they could define the terrain of that revival and place-making project. Congress, he suggested, should respect the integrity of that terrain and that project and direct its expansion efforts away from it.

Over in Northwest, residents did not claim that their area was being raped, but they shared many of the anxieties about violation that Capitol Hill residents expressed in the 1970s. In the postwar decades, real estate developers perceived the old sections of Washington's downtown as largely off-limits for new commercial projects. Instead of assembling sites in the old downtown, developers increasingly looked to the north and west of the White House around Farragut Square and along Connecticut Avenue and K Street. In the decades since, K Street has become synonymous with Washington lobbyists in much the same way Wall Street stands in for the financial markets in New York. The new landscape that emerged along K Street west of Fourteenth Street, and in the block to the north, was an outward physical expression of the expansion of the government-influencing sector. As congressional activities expanded, and as its committees and the staff required to inform and administer them grew too, a parallel process emerged. Trade associations, unions, and other peak industry bodies, think tanks, and eventually a growing army of lobbyists themselves, moved into K Street and surrounds, dramatically changing land-use patterns and the urban character of those blocks.[25]

Dupont Circle's real estate and its urban character were inevitably influenced by the growth of this sector in the economy. The National Association of Homebuilders, one of Washington's largest trade associations, was a fairly typical case. They built a new national headquarters in the 1600 block of L Street Northwest in the mid-1950s, which they outgrew by the early 1970s, when they built another on Massachusetts Avenue. Meanwhile their local Washington metropolitan affiliate established itself a few blocks to the west in the 1960s. The Brookings Institution developed its headquarters on Massachusetts Avenue near Dupont Circle in the early 1960s, which they expanded several years later. In the early 1980s they attempted to redevelop and expand their accommodation still further, provoking a prolonged battle with Dupont Circle preservationists.[26]

Speculative office buildings on a much larger scale than had been common in Washington in earlier decades also had a significant impact on this part of the city in the 1970s. The prominent developer Oliver T. Carr Jr. opened International Square in 1977. It was the largest private office building constructed in the metro area in the 1970s, occupying an entire block between Eighteenth and Nineteenth and I and K Streets, Northwest. It was part of a much larger wave of new office accommodation in this section of the city and, if not already obvious, the scale of International Square underlined this was now the core of Washington's new office district.[27]

Joseph Passonneau's detailed figure-ground mapping of downtown Washington, also color-coded by function, vividly illustrates the changes that affected this part of the city across the second half of the twentieth century. While downtown commercial activity had bled into these blocks north and west of the White House by 1940, it was only in the decades after World War II that the area was rebuilt predominantly for office accommodation. The pressure on the Dupont Circle neighborhood was palpable. Where the battles along Pennsylvania Avenue, at the vexed edge between federal and local, were symbolic points of resistance against the monolithic architectural image of the federal government, Dupont Circle became the frontline of the battle between resident groups against the commercial priorities of the expanding office district (Figure 19).[28]

Preservationists in the ranks of the Dupont Circle Citizens' Association (DCCA) such as Ronald Alvarez and Anne Sellin would have been conscious of the growing, citywide sentiment in favor of preservation, and of the progress made by the citywide not-for-profit advocacy group Don't Tear It Down! in initiating a regulatory framework to prevent the demolition of historically significant places. The DCCA 1974 annual report contained a resolution in support of utilizing and strengthening the protections provided for National Register–listed buildings. By 1974 the DCCA had also established a historic district subgroup of their Residential Properties Committee. The work of the Residential Properties

Figure 19. Aerial view of Dupont Circle in Washington, D.C. The pattern of downtown development to the south of Dupont Circle is clearly evident in the lower section of the photograph. In the middle, the primarily residential section preserved within the historic district has a distinct morphology dominated by row housing and small apartment buildings. Photograph by Carol M. Highsmith, circa 1990s. Source: Carol M. Highsmith Archive, Prints and Photographs Division, Library of Congress.

Committee was focused on finding ways to protect against transformation and redevelopment of area properties for use as office space. Members clearly believed that preservation, and in particular a historic district, would be one of the strongest mechanisms available to them to prevent unwanted change in their area.[29]

This expectation of growing resident influence on planning and development decisions played a part in the mayoral election in 1978, D.C.'s first genuinely contested local election for over a century. As we have seen, the winner, Marion Barry, stitched together an unexpected constituency that crossed class and race lines. On one side were the liberal, (mostly) white, middle-class intowners, who formed the rump of the restoration culture and who voted for Barry in large numbers partly because of his express support for local decision-making and for historic preservation. On the other side were blacks of modest means, who looked to Barry for economic empowerment and political self-determination. Preservation politics in the period reflected these contradictions and tensions within Barry's constituency. The home rule campaign had brought disparate groups together to fight for common aims, which included greater control over decisions affecting the urban environment. Preservation promised a mechanism for grassroots control of decision making and a way to fight insensitive and impersonal forces, especially the federal government and private developers.

But the detail of designating historic districts, just like the priorities and preferences of local government itself, eroded the goodwill and sense of common purpose that underpinned earlier support for general principles. Representatives of the two main groups within Barry's constituency lined up against one another in the conflict that emerged about the proper extent of the Dupont Circle Historic District in the early 1980s.

HISTORIC DISTRICTS

Notwithstanding the racial tension in the Capitol Hill neighborhoods connected with restoration and code enforcement in the late 1960s, and the civil unrest in Washington in the wake of Martin Luther King Jr.'s assassination in April 1968, the restoration process continued strongly in the 1970s, resulting in increased efforts to designate and expand historic districts. Groups such as the CHRS and the DCCA wanted to ensure that aesthetic and economic investments made by pioneers in areas of restored housing would not be eroded by piecemeal redevelopment and urban intensification. Functional zoning and downzoning were planning tools deployed as part of this effort. But in both Capitol Hill and the inner areas of Northwest historic districting became the focus.[30]

The neighborhood groups did not have to begin from scratch with their historic district proposals. As we have seen, in 1964 the Joint Committee on Landmarks (JCL) defined the city's key historical resources and suggested a number of historic districts be designated (see Map 6, chapter 3). But the list and map of historic places that they created at that time remained indicative only, a guide for planning. In the mid-1970s, with the widespread expectation that a meaningful local preservation law would come into force, citizens' groups representing intown residential areas began to examine how they might utilize such legislation. For these groups, the obvious implication of a local preservation law was that it would give strong legal standing to historic district designations. In such districts, historic significance was designated by reference to the pattern and ensemble rather than by reference to individually significant buildings. A strong local law would thus enable neighborhood-scale protections, without the need to demonstrate the architectural or historic significance of each individual item within the district. Such historic district designations, backed up by the force of law, would place the burden on property owners to show why a building in such a district must be removed, rather than vice versa. District controls would thus give local citizens' groups and restoration societies greatly increased power to control the rate and character of change in their neighborhoods.[31]

The two areas where the most ambitious historic district expansions were proposed in Washington in the 1970s were the same two where restoration activity had been most prolific in the period immediately prior: Capitol Hill and Dupont Circle. The expansion proposals were led by the CHRS and the DCCA respectively and were viewed as a natural extension of earlier efforts to publicize restoration activity.

The process each area went through to delineate larger historic districts was contrasting. The Capitol Hill group worked closely with the District of Columbia's Historic Preservation Office (HPO), and the boundaries it proposed were accepted and designated without controversy. Their nomination reflected some sensitivity to the issues of race and class, an understandable reaction to lessons learned back in the 1960s, when the CHRS was publicly maligned for promoting forces that led to the displacement of poor, mostly black residents of the area. The district nomination evinced a confident and knowledgeable tone when it came to African American history. It acknowledged a substantial African American population living and worshiping in the area in the nineteenth century. The nomination form quoted local historian Letitia Brown, who observed that "by 1860, Negroes were scattered throughout the southeast quarter from South Capitol to 11th St East."[32] The historical description also highlighted the preponderance of "modest housing" in the area inhabited by "middle-class governmental workers" who formed "a solid community" that "supported a growing number of small commercial establishments."[33] In other words, the nomination made it very clear that the historic district bid was not an attempt to "fashion another Georgetown," as Sam Smith had accused in 1968, and signaled that it was not intended as an elite enclave of preserved magnificence.[34] Rather, the document explicitly argued for an idea of the Capitol Hill area as encompassing significant racial and class diversity and a generally modest pattern of residential buildings. The impression left by the nomination as a whole was that the area's history was characterized by an overall harmony, but one that encompassed a substantial variety, much as the built fabric achieved a harmony of scale and rhythm out of a variety of styles and types of facade expression.

While it included a clear sense of the different social segments in Washington that lived in the area and contributed to its development, the Capitol Hill nomination lacked any detailed discussion of how race influenced patterns of dwelling, or how restoration activity might have affected Capitol Hill's racial and class composition. Nowhere was reference made to racial tensions or the expression of racial hierarchy in the organization of space in the area. In this it was a quintessential document of its moment—1974–76—in which public productions of history underlined ideas of social consensus fostered by the bicentennial preparations and celebrations. Submitted in July 1976, the nomination reflected the sanctioned, multicultural narrative that informed the civic production of bicentennial history. It told a story of different peoples coming to share the same space and seemed to suggest the possibility that their interests could all be pursued and harmonized in that space.[35]

Preservationists in Dupont Circle embarked on a similar historic district expansion effort at the same time (Map 9). But the sense of control over the interpretation of the area's history was much less certain, and it lacked the ideological coherency reflected in the Capitol Hill nomination. The DCCA did not collaborate with the city's preservation office in preparing the nomination, and perhaps more importantly, they focused on a quite different sense of historical significance. Ronald Alvarez prepared their new historic district nomination, which would have trebled the area inside the district. Alvarez was a member of the Victorian Society of America and styled himself as an architectural connoisseur. While inclusive at the level of architectural taste, the Alvarez nomination focused mostly on physical qualities and architectural resources in the proposed district and made only a few halting references to social patterns in the life of the area (Figure 20). The Dupont Circle proponents seem to have viewed the absence of references to race in their historic district nomination as a way of avoiding seemingly arbitrary social distinctions. But it was a slightly anachronistic stance given the focus on African American

Figure 20. 1700 block of Q Street Northwest just a few blocks from Dupont Circle, as it looked in 2007. The well-maintained architectural detail, the consistency of scale, and the strength of urban character of row-house groups like this one made them highly prized by preservationists. Photograph by the author.

history and culture in the period and the recent example provided by Don't Tear It Down! in working with the D.C. Bicentennial Commission to identify sites of black history and significance. Moreover, despite the apparent high-mindedness of attempting to relegate racial distinctions to the past, the Dupont Circle nomination ignored the powerful historical influence of racially restrictive covenants that had shaped dwelling patterns in the areas to the east of Dupont Circle, even well after the *Shelley v. Kramer* Supreme Court decision had made it illegal to enforce such covenants.[36]

The DCCA succeeded in doubling the size of the existing historic district, but the city's planners in the HPO nevertheless recommended shearing substantial sections from the proposal in their report on the nomination. The HPO recommended that fewer blocks be included to the north, east, and south and that a separate historic district be created on Sixteenth Street. In so doing they recognized substantive justification for the expansion but disagreed with all of the boundaries suggested by the Alvarez-DCCA nomination except those drawn on the basis of topography. The largest section to be excluded was in the northeast corner of the proposed area. The city's planning and preservation officials explicitly rejected the implicit claim of the proposal that this part of the city belonged in Dupont Circle. The HPO staff pointed to a number of discordant elements in this section of the proposed district that made it heterogeneous with the rest of the historic district. But most importantly they argued that the blocks above Swann Street had never been considered to be part of Dupont Circle by local people.[37]

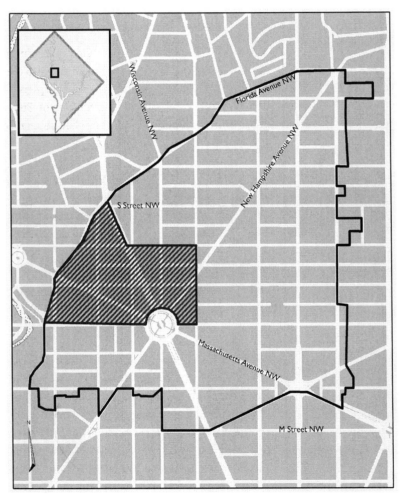

Map 9. Shaded area marks existing Dupont Circle Historic District in 1977, with proposed expansion area. Created by and copyright Matthew B. Gilmore.

The HPO's 1977 staff report noticeably changed the way the Dupont Circle preservationists addressed the issue of race and historical identity. In the twelve-month period between the release of the report and the JCL's final determination about the historic district, Dupont Circle preservationists attempted to influence the decision by arguing that the HPO report had ignored African American history. In a letter to the JCL the Dupont Circle applicants noted that inclusion of the area between Fifteenth and Seventeenth Streets, much of which had been excised from the designated district, would "assure landmark status for many black history sites."[38]

The following year the new head of the Dupont Circle preservation committee, Charles Robertson, renewed the campaign. In a letter to the chairman of the landmarks committee he mentioned a long list of significant individuals who had lived in the area, including members of Frederick Douglass's family, before turning his argument to what he saw as the principle at stake:

> The northern boundaries should be expanded to include the 1700 blocks of T Street, Willard Court, and U Street all of which were developed contemporaneously with the rest of the neighborhood, which conform architecturally, and which constituted one of the major black residential areas of the city at the close of the nineteenth and at the beginning of the twentieth centuries. We were particularly dismayed by the elimination of "Strivers Row" (1700 block of U Street), perhaps the most significant symbol of the assertion of black Washingtonians in the late Victorian period.[39]

Given that the DCCA had not used the term "black history" in their original application or given any detailed account of the role of African Americans in the history of the area, this represented a clear shift in strategy and a redefinition of the nature of the history supposed to be protected by the historic district. But their change of tack about the significance of social history to the historic district proposal did not sway the JCL. They agreed with the staff report that many parts of the expansion area simply could not be described as being in the Dupont Circle neighborhood and that, therefore, they should not be in the Dupont Circle Historic District. The expansion of the historic district, therefore, was much more limited than Dupont Circle preservationists had hoped.

EXPANSION REDUX

The Dupont Circle preservation committee—which incorporated separately from the DCCA under the name Dupont Circle Conservancy in 1982—began work on a new historic district nomination in 1980 and filed the application in 1982. Once again they sought to expand the district substantially to the north and east. In fact they basically reprised the boundaries identified in the earlier proposal but extended the boundary an additional block further east. It was a proposal that affected hundreds of properties, and real estate and business interests immediately objected (Map 10).[40]

The Dupont Circle preservationists were also confronted, however, with a less anticipated source of opposition, one that had not been evident during the 1977–78 expansion campaign. It came from a group called the 14th and U Street Coalition, which represented small business operators in the U Street area and was headed by a local political entrepreneur, Edna Frazier-Cromwell. Frazier-Cromwell protested that her organization and its members had not been consulted about the expansion proposal and that the Dupont Circle effort was a straightforward attempt to create for itself a wider zone of political and economic influence. This, she asserted, was completely unjustified by history, as she considered the area around Fourteenth and U Streets, which was to be included in the historic district expansion, to be in the heart of the historically African American district, known since the 1960s as Shaw. She also argued that the redevelopment or restoration of the area, widely assumed to be inevitable, should be controlled by the community and should minimize the displacement of existing residents and businesses. In a letter to Charles Robertson, Frazier-Cromwell made clear that her organization believed that the historic district expansion was a thinly veiled attempt to encourage further private market restoration in the area. The expansion of interest in restoration would lead inexorably to higher real estate prices, she suggested, thereby inflating property taxes, as well as rents, and initiating a process of rapid social change.[41]

In response, the Dupont Circle Conservancy launched a concerted effort to persuade the 14th and U Street Coalition that the historic district was not a tool of gentrification or an effort to "colonize" Shaw, but rather a means of enhancing community control of its historic assets and hopefully of fostering pride in them as a result. The conservancy pointed

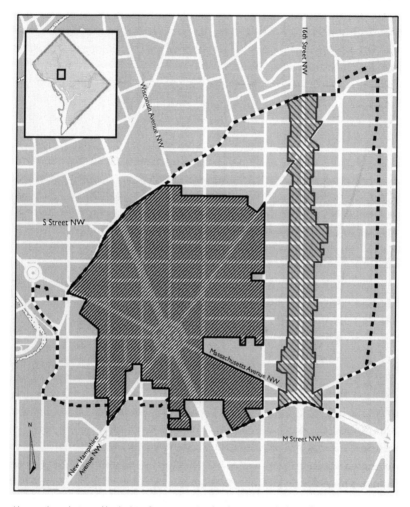

Map 10. Areas designated by the Joint Committee on Landmarks in 1977 on the basis of the D.C. Historic Preservation Office report. Note the expanded area of the Dupont Circle district (dark area) and the new historic district along Sixteenth Street Northwest (lighter area). The dotted line marks the extent of the second expansion nomination filed in 1982. Created by and copyright Matthew B. Gilmore.

to organizations in the area that were cosponsoring the historic district nomination, the Midway Civic Association and the T Street Block Council, that were both composed mostly of African American members. The Dupont Circle Conservancy was anxious to demonstrate its awareness of the issue of affordable housing, as well as the fact that proponents of an enlarged historic district represented a broad coalition of interests, not simply prosperous whites.[42]

Sensing, however, that they were making little progress and that the whole expansion effort might come undone as the result of the conflict with the 14th and U Street Coalition, the conservancy stepped up its campaign, working to influence *Washington Post* reporters Carole Schifrin and Anne Chase to write sympathetic articles about the proposal and offering to present their case to community groups.[43]

Chase did publish a piece about the conflict in the *Washington Post* in April 1983 and quoted Gladys Scott Roberts, an African American from the Midway Civic Association, who said that the Dupont Circle Conservancy "were doing a marvelous job. They discovered there was a great black history in this neighborhood."[44] Such commentary was deliberately mobilized to dispel the impression that the historic district expansion would enable racial succession from black to white in areas covered by the district. But the publicity did not go all one way. In fact, Chase's article led with critics of the expansion. Director of the Shaw Project Area Committee Ibrahim Mumin was unequivocal about what the historic district represented. "It's a land grab by the middle and upper middle class Caucasians who live around Dupont Circle to extend their political influence."[45] Even more tellingly, Edna Frazier-Cromwell remarked "I can just see the real estate brochures. 'Luxury condominiums in Dupont Circle East.'"[46] While it was relatively easy to deflect Mumin's comments, which implied an organized, racially motivated takeover, Frazier-Cromwell's suggestion that the historic district would be an agent of predominantly white gentrification was much harder to refute.

As Marion Barry's electoral defeat of Sterling Tucker in the Washington mayoral election of 1978 demonstrated, all was not black and white in D.C. politics, even if race was everywhere and in everything. The racial politics that attended the historic district dispute around Dupont Circle were also deeply embedded in the class dynamics that were very particular to that part of Washington. Many African Americans, such as

Maurice Thomas and Gladys Scott Roberts, who both lived in the contested area and participated in the effort to expand the historic district, embraced the idea that they were a part of a redefined Dupont Circle area. While not universally the case, many of these people associated themselves with the area's long-established African American elite, sometimes referred to as Washington's "black aristocracy." This group tended to support the pursuit of civil rights and de jure racial equality. They had historically distanced themselves from the idea that African Americans should build strong, separate racial institutions and businesses. In contrast race leaders and newspaper editors in Shaw tended to support strategies more attuned to economic autonomy and political empowerment. The most recent iteration of the latter perspective had emerged among black power advocates in the late 1960s and underpinned efforts to strengthen community control of the urban renewal process in Shaw and elsewhere. This racial and class dynamic remained relevant in the 1970s and early 1980s and shaped the conflict between the Dupont Circle preservationists and their opponents in the 14th and U Street Coalition.[47]

Even though the community-controlled redevelopment agenda had faltered in Washington in the 1970s, and in Shaw in particular, Edna Frazier-Cromwell and her supporters still saw the language associated with that phase of community mobilization as a legitimate and powerful tool. For example, a 14th and U Street Coalition flyer prominently asserted their determination to "promote community controlled redevelopment and, yes it's going to be difficult, but ultimately we will be the ones to determine what happens in our neighborhood."[48]

Skin tone also remained important at this intersection of race and class identities, something that was certainly not lost on white Dupont Circle preservationists. The surviving correspondence from this battle provides a glimpse of the complicated ways in which racially based claims could become sources of resentment and mobilize unexpected racial discourses. For example, a personal letter from Dupont Circle Conservancy member Katherine Eccles to its president, Charles Robertson, discussing ways of dealing with the ongoing opposition to the Dupont Circle Conservancy's historic district proposal, contained a particularly pointed reference to Frazier-Cromwell, describing her as a *"high yella bitch."*[49] The implication of this epithet was that Frazier-Cromwell was insincere in her opposition to the historic district proposal and politically opportunistic. Eccles insinuated that not only was Frazier-Cromwell using race as a rallying point for local political action (playing the race card), she was doing so "inauthentically" as her real social and racial identity should have aligned her with wealthier "strivers" who had traditionally been more closely associated with the Dupont Circle whites and who, in the historic district dispute, lined up behind the district expansion. Eccles here appropriated a black idiom for drawing social distinctions—that between ordinary, darker-skinned blacks and their lighter-skinned or "high yella" betters. This usage enabled Eccles to occupy an authentic position and set aside Frazier-Cromwell's position as self-serving and inauthentic. Eccles's own racial politics, as far as can be inferred from her public representations and correspondence with her fellow neighborhood preservationists, were explicitly liberal and integrationist. So it obviously galled her when Frazier-Cromwell opposed the historic district on the grounds that it was an assertion of white privilege. Eccles's use of the racially loaded expression "high yella" not only highlighted the personal animosities that the historic district expansion stirred up, it also underlined the complex coding of social space in that part of Washington and the obvious difficulties of establishing a multiethnic or multiracial consensus on issues connected to urban identity and space.

Charles Robertson, who led the Dupont Circle Conservancy campaign expansion, and Katherine Eccles, who was a tireless supporter, both lived in the historically black, disputed area. However, Robertson and Eccles never publicly contested the legitimacy of the goal of "community control." Instead they disagreed with the claims made by their opponents about the meaning and effects of the historic district expansion. As their frustration with the 14th and U Street Coalition opposition grew they became more and more agitated about the role played by Frazier-Cromwell. The conservancy archive indicates that for a time they assembled a negative dossier about Frazier-Cromwell's political activities that highlighted what they saw as her low regard for ethical standards.[50]

But by April 1983 they acknowledged the effectiveness of the opposition and the apparent inevitability of failure in the historic district expansion effort. Attorney for the coalition supporting the expansion, Richard Friedman, circulated a memorandum on April 19, 1983, that indicated a substantial shift in strategy. It noted that the historic district advocates now fully accepted the validity of the concerns of residents in the eastern and northern sections of the expansion area as represented by Advisory

Neighborhood Commission 1B, ShawPAC, 14th and U Street Coalition, and St. Augustine's parish. As a result, the Dupont Circle Conservancy now proposed to work with people of these communities to help them develop a separate historic district that would require substantial further research and that would likely have no direct association with Dupont Circle. Friedman recommended that "discussion should focus on developing an approach that avoids any inappropriate geographic or political incursion of 'Dupont Circle' into areas that have not been associated with Dupont Circle historically and are not currently identified with Dupont Circle."[51]

This effectively put an end to the Dupont Circle Conservancy's efforts to expand the Dupont Circle Historic District. However, with the designation of a separate Strivers Section Historic District (1983) in the northeast corner of the nominated area, following a recommendation from the city's preservation office, and later designations of Greater Fourteenth Street (1994) and Greater U Street (1998) Historic Districts, all of the area originally included in the Dupont Circle Historic District nominations created by neighborhood preservationists between 1977 and 1983—and much more besides—was given historic district protection (Map 11). Yet the circumstances by which this happened, the manner in which the historical significance of the areas was defined, and the individuals who controlled the process were completely altered: a consequence of the conflict that arose between Dupont Circle preservationists and the 14th and U Street Coalition.[52]

The assumption of responsibility for defining what was historically important in the surrounding district by Dupont Circle preservationists in the late 1970s was clearly a strategic error from their perspective as it consumed a great deal of energy and mobilized a potent form of opposition that had not previously been a factor in that part of the city. More important, it marks a significant moment in the whole history of how preservation operated in the District of Columbia. Over and above asserting their right to a basic welfare in housing and neighborhood accommodation, African Americans in this section of Washington emerged from this conflict with a clear sense that they were entitled to define and defend their own historical legacy in the environment: that they should play a part in defining the district's cultural and historical values. The growing interest in black history as a distinct and valuable tradition in the life of the city altered the stakes involved in preservation. Henceforth, it would not be possible for middle-class, white preservationists to assume that they could act on behalf of the wider community in these matters.

The conflict between the Dupont Circle Conservancy and the 14th and U Street Coalition marks a point at which the particularity of the entitlements of the past were disclosed as an explicit problem for historic preservationists. That is, the conflict underlined the problem not just of what should be saved and why, but who is entitled to decide. It also

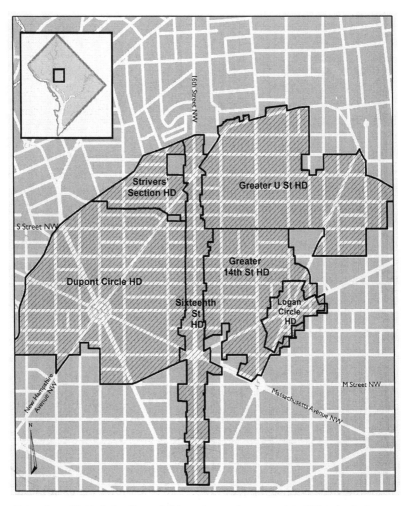

Map 11. Current historic districts. Almost all of the area between downtown and the old Boundary Road (Florida Avenue) in Northwest is now covered by historic districts. Created by and copyright Matthew B. Gilmore.

revealed the fragile nature of public interest claims for the significance of historic places. Dupont Circle neighborhood preservationists success-fully expanded their influence and promoted a widened sense of the significance of historic patterns in the urban environment. But in doing so they did not fully address the problem of how to link the historicity of space to social patterns.

The CHRS had made some attempt to do so in the 1970s and appealed to the idea of African American history in identifying the significance of that section of Washington. They were successful, at least rhetorically, in establishing the idea of the area's significance as multiple and inclu-sive. African Americans in the intown sections of Northwest, however, arguably had a much more powerful and distinct set of ideas about his-tory and heritage than the black community in the Capitol Hill neighbor-hoods. U Street–area African Americans mobilized a critique of historic preservation that not only questioned the legitimacy of those identifying historic and cultural value in the city's landscape, but also the very obvi-ous privileging of architecture and townscape over the social and memo-rial significance of neighborhood places.[53]

This criticism of white assumptions and entitlements in the realm of preservation had a noticeable impact in the period immediately after the disputed expansion proposal. Pat Press, a Washington preservationist, wrote a newspaper column toward the end of 1983 that demonstrated a growing awareness among historic preservation advocates that they could be perceived as too narrow in their rendering of the value of historic places. The title of Press's article, "New People for Old Houses?," indi-cated a growing anxiety in the ranks of Washington, D.C., preservation-ists that still not enough had been done to ensure social continuity within the framework of physical and architectural continuity that the preserva-tion laws enabled.[54]

The awareness of this problem, however, did not dampen the enthu-siasm for creating new historic districts in Washington. In the following years Kalorama Triangle, Cleveland Park, and Mount Pleasant all success-fully mounted neighborhood-based campaigns to designate substantial districts. The Mount Pleasant historic districting process faced some of the same challenges as Dupont Circle. An area with a complex racial, ethnic, and class mix in the 1980s, initial efforts to push forward a historic district nomination in 1982 met with significant opposition. Property interests, represented as usual in this period by attorney Whayne Quin, successfully exploited initial controversy and worked to magnify opposition to further historic districts, turning up at town hall meetings and addressing audiences by appealing to social justice aims and the needs of the poor. But a group calling itself Historic Mount Pleasant Inc. carried the campaign forward and put significant effort into building community support. They organized mail-outs about the historic district proposal and sponsored block parties to encourage discussion about it and support for it. In 1986 the Historic Preservation Review Board approved the district nomination, adding many more blocks to the growing terrain of historic districts in Washington's residential areas.[55]

CONCLUSION

The opposition that emerged to the Dupont Circle efforts in the early 1980s was not simply due to a failure by preservationists to make their movement inclusive or to agree on a shared set of aims for the neighborhood, though both these criticisms have some merit. The conflict was also a result of a wider group of people perceiving value in using historic preservation laws and ideas to promote their cultural identity and political aims. Political and cultural changes underway since the 1960s—especially the acceptance of the idea of multiple overlapping histories, structured around specific racial, ethnic, and class identities—as well as highly specific redevelopment issues made it difficult for participants to agree about what was valuable about the historic fabric of the city and which economic and social forces should be opposed. Embedded within those conflicts were implicit differences of values about the city and the uses of historic preservation. Was preservation about community defense or good city form? Was it to represent the historical identity of social groups in the urban fabric or to curate that fabric and protect its best buildings and streetscapes? In other words, was preservation for heritage or environmental enhancement?

It was, of course, used for both. But as the case of the Rhodes Tavern clearly shows, that dual identity could be the source of significant tensions and misunderstandings within the historic preservation movement. During the same period that intown neighborhood preservationists mounted campaigns to expand their historic districts, Washington experienced its most divisive preservation battle: the effort to preserve Rhodes Tavern.

CHAPTER 6

Rhodes Tavern and
the Problem with Preservation
in the 1980s

O n September 10, 1984, Washington's oldest commercial building, Rhodes Tavern (1799–1801), was demolished (Figure 21). Eulogizing the building in 1985, its erstwhile defenders, who called themselves the Citizens' Committee to Save Historic Rhodes Tavern, noted that "it straddled the two sides of the capital's character—the local city and the Federal seat."[1] This was important to them because it embodied the intertwined histories of national power and everyday life, reminding Washingtonians that they could be at home in the national capital, not mere onlookers. The Rhodes defenders described the demolition as "unnecessary" and "stupid" and depicted it as a case of elite interests and elite taste overwhelming popular sentiment and genuine historical significance.

On the first anniversary of the demolition the committee produced a broadside, the *Rhodes Record*, in which they described the demolition as having been "urged by the arrogant, sanctioned by the ignorant [and] executed by the avaricious."[2] The "avaricious" in this formulation were the development interests, and the "ignorant" were newspaper editors and city politicians who had not supported the preservation and restoration of the building. But the Rhodes campaigners evinced the greatest disappointment and sense of betrayal in relation to those they described as the "arrogant"—the official and unofficial guardians of the city's historically significant places. This included the citywide preservation group Don't Tear It Down! (DTID!), the architecture critic and prominent preservation advocate Wolf von Eckardt, and J. Carter Brown, scion of the Rhode Island Browns, director of the National Gallery of Art, and chair of the Commission of Fine Arts. All publicly sanctioned the destruction against what campaigners saw as the demonstrable will of Washington's citizenry. The Rhodes campaigners accused this group of experts of defending "what they found attractive"—uniform cornice lines and "architectural pomposity"—while enabling the destruction of the genuinely "historic."[3]

The prolonged legal wrangling and public discussion that surrounded the conflict over the Rhodes Tavern made it Washington's most prominent historic preservation battle since the campaign to save the Old Post Office on Pennsylvania Avenue in the early 1970s. That earlier battle

Rhodes Record

Published by the Citizen's Committee to Save Historic Rhodes Tavern

September 10, 1984: *Historic Rhodes Tavern is demolished.*

A Heritage Destroyed
185 Years of D.C., U.S. History End with Rhodes' Razing

Figure 21. Rhodes Tavern demolition, September 10, 1984. Originally published in the *Rhodes Record*. Source: Citizens Committee to Save Historic Rhodes Tavern papers, Special Collections Research Center, Estelle and Melvin Gelman Library, George Washington University.

coalesced locally based preservation forces into a more unified movement, propelling the home rule campaign and helping to build interracial alliances. Conversely, the Rhodes Tavern campaign exposed the conflicting priorities and interests within the expanded historic preservation movement in Washington. In doing so it brought to the fore basic questions about the nature and purpose of preservation. Should it simply be a way of keeping buildings and places that people care about, of protecting physical places as cultural heritage? Should it be a mode of environmental enhancement allied to the larger urban-planning and design process? Or should it be more political in nature, a means of mobilizing counterhegemonic forces against the regimes of land use and development that were tilted in favor of vested interests?

Each of these alternatives carried within it a vision of how historic preservation could foster place-based citizenship. But the ways in which the different historic preservation forces understood historicity—the volition of the past—and its manifestation in the physical environment and social life of the community diverged considerably. A sense of commonality about what was owed the past was elusive for those that identified themselves explicitly as preservationists. Using the Rhodes Tavern battle as a point of departure, this chapter explores the intersection of activism, expertise, and intellectual uncertainty that reconfigured preservation and the built environment in Washington in the 1980s. In doing so, what follows also reveals the ongoing challenges associated with creating a set of Washington-wide civic interests and institutions and a shared vision for the intown environment.

REDEVELOPING DOWNTOWN

In 1977 Washington, D.C.'s most prominent property developer, Oliver T. Carr Jr., announced plans for Metropolitan Square, a $40 million mixed-use commercial development incorporating most of the block bounded by F, Fourteenth, G, and Fifteenth streets, Northwest. Directly across the street from the U.S. Treasury Building, the proposed site incorporated the Keith-Albee Theater (1912), the Metropolitan Bank Building (1905–7), the Old Ebbitt Grill (ca. 1890), and the Rhodes Tavern, which were all on the District of Columbia's Historic Landmarks List and the National Register of Historic Places (Map 12).[4]

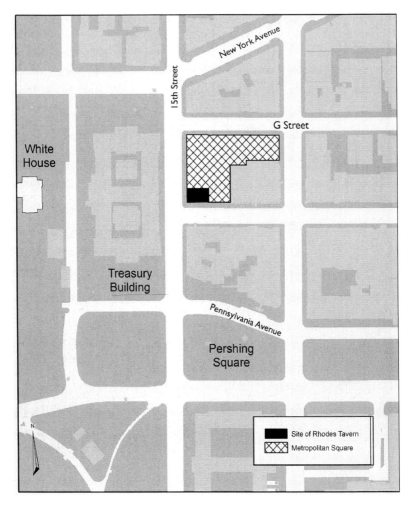

Map 12. Metropolitan Square redevelopment site and Rhodes Tavern. Created by and copyright Matthew B. Gilmore.

The Rhodes Tavern was a modest, three-story brick building, fairly typical of the federal period in Washington. During the twentieth century the street level in front of the building had been lowered, changing its proportions, entrances were reconfigured, stucco applied to the exterior, and finally a whole wing of the building removed. Its appearance was thus significantly altered from the building depicted in a number of early paintings and engravings (Figure 22). In contrast, the Keith-Albee

Figure 22. Watercolor by Anne Marguerite Henriette Hyde de Neuville depicting Rhodes Tavern when it was the Bank of the Metropolis, circa 1817. Source: New York Public Library.

Theater and Metropolitan Bank buildings were both much larger (eight to ten stories) and both very much intact (Figure 23). They were described in their historic landmark listings as being in the Beaux-Arts style. While strictly speaking the Beaux-Arts is not a style but an approach to architectural planning and design, what was meant by that in the 1970s was that they were both classical revival buildings with boldly articulated details and a metropolitan scale and presence in the cityscape. As such, they were a formally coherent pair, sometimes even mistaken for two parts of the same building.[5]

The project was subject to the delay of demolition regulation owing to the presence on the site of buildings listed on the National Register. This D.C. regulation, passed in 1973 in the wake of the battle over the Old Post Office, demanded that any proposed development that required the demolition of, or major alterations to, listed buildings would trigger a 180-day delay. During that delay, developers were required to enter into negotiations with the city and preservation groups about possible alternatives. The proximity of the site to the Treasury Building and the White House also meant that in this instance Oliver T. Carr needed to seek approval for his plans from the Commission of Fine Arts, which had the

Figure 23. Rhodes Tavern in its streetscape setting in the 1970s. To the left of the tavern are the Keith-Albee Theater and Metropolitan Bank buildings. Source: HABS/HAER Collection, Library of Congress.

task of design review for projects that would have a visual impact on the federal enclave, the National Mall, and the key landmark buildings within that zone.[6]

The size and value of the Metropolitan Square proposal was unusually large, and the project took on particular significance because it was within Washington's traditional downtown. This area, usually assumed to include the blocks between the White House and North Capitol Street, experienced a period of stagnation in the decades after World War II. But by the mid-1970s the construction of the Washington Metro was well underway, and by 1978 observers heralded the Metro's positive influence on amenity and land values in the old downtown area.[7] Oliver T. Carr used his position as the new president of the Greater Washington Board of Trade to promote the benefits of his Metropolitan Square project and its contribution to the incipient downtown revival. Downtown boosters in business, at the *Washington Post*, and in local government also heralded

its catalytic potential. W. C. Detwiler, president of Garfinckel's, a neighboring department store, remarked that "if this thing flies . . . it's going
to be very exciting for the downtown area."[8]

Along with the Washington Convention Center, which would be realized several blocks to the east between 1980 and 1982, and the Metro
Centre project, Metropolitan Square promised to kick-start a revival
both of large-scale development and of land value in Washington's old
downtown. This urban real estate dynamic gave Carr considerable lever-
age during the protracted battle over Rhodes Tavern, as it enabled him
to make public interest arguments about the positive economic impact
of his development project. In a 1983 op-ed, which was published in the
Washington Post under the heading "Save Metropolitan Square," Carr
noted that the partially completed project was already "one of the top
10 sources of real estate tax revenues for the District" and that delays in
completing the project were preventing construction crews and material
suppliers from doing their jobs.[9]

Carr did not, of course, invest in the Metropolitan Square site purely
because he wanted to improve the prospects of the old downtown area.
He saw an opportunity to make a profit on a real estate investment project. But the location had political significance and public relations implications. The allusion to saving his development project in the *Post* opinion
piece was a pointed attempt to upend the terms of the preservation campaign and occupy the moral high ground. His message was thus consistent with arguments put forward by real estate lawyer Whayne Quin in
the period, which highlighted the benefits accruing to the city and its
inhabitants from new development. Only in this instance Carr did not
oppose himself to preservation interests; instead he flagged his sympathy for preservation goals.[10]

In his initial announcements about the project Carr had declared his
willingness to preserve historically significant buildings on the site. In February 1978 his architect, David Childs of Skidmore, Owings & Merrill's
Washington office, unveiled nine different schemes for public comment.
They ranged from preservation in toto of all the listed buildings to complete demolition. It would ultimately become quite clear, however, that
both the developer and his architect favored something in the middle and
that their best chances of success, in terms of the politics, the economics,
and the aesthetics of the project, was with a solution that involved a

significant component of historic preservation. In fact, they anticipated using preservation as a bargaining chip that would enable them to argue successfully for greater height for their project and for the development rights over a laneway internal to the block that had always been a right-of-way.[11]

Rather than argue that the demolition of Rhodes or any of the building was inevitable, in May 1978 Carr said he would be happy to retain all the listed buildings on the site if money could be raised to do so—which he estimated would cost $5.9 million, later revised upward to $7.2 million. That is, he would not pay the cost of preserving and restoring the tavern, but he would facilitate a fund-raising effort through the auspices of the citywide preservation advocacy group DTID! Carr announced that he would use the six-month delay of demolition to facilitate a fund-raising effort that could then offset the costs of meaningfully preserving all of the listed buildings and incorporating them into Metropolitan Square. It was an unusual gesture at the time and one carefully calibrated to win sympathy. In effect Carr was saying that he was happy to support preservation and the public goods associated with it, but not to pay for them. So just as he reversed the terms of the debate about what needed to be preserved, he also put the onus back onto the community to support preservation financially at the site.[12]

By the end of 1978, however, it was obvious that the funds needed to support the retention of all listed buildings would not be raised, and in April 1979 Carr commenced demolition of rear portions of the Keith-Albee building. DTID! filed suit to prevent the demolition, but the court ruled that the demolition could proceed based on the fact that sufficient funds had not been raised to offset the cost of preservation. Nevertheless, negotiations between Carr, the city, and DTID! continued. A compromise agreement was reached whereby Carr could construct a complex that would (1) retain the Fifteenth Street facade and at least four bays of the G Street facade of the Keith-Albee building, (2) retain the Fifteenth Street facade of the bank building, (3) either donate Rhodes Tavern to a nonprofit organization for relocation or demolish it, and (4) relocate the interior of the Old Ebbitt Grill within the new commercial structure.[13]

Leila Smith of DTID! told *Washington Post* reporter Anne Oman that forced to choose between protecting Rhodes or the Keith-Albee Theater, DTID! chose the theater. "The popular support just isn't there for the tavern."[14] However, what became quite clear over the next few years was that the tavern enjoyed a surprisingly high level of public support. As it turned out Rhodes Tavern's persistent band of defenders impeded the execution of the deal that was agreed upon in 1979 and, as a consequence, the entire project for several years.[15]

While negotiations about the Metropolitan Square project were ongoing the city passed its new historic preservation statute, the Historic Landmark and Historic District Protection Act of 1978, which came into effect on March 3, 1979. When Carr applied for the raze permits to enact the terms of the compromise deal in the middle of 1979 the request was referred to the Joint Committee on Landmarks (JCL), a consequence of the new preservation law. The JCL found that a permit to demolish or move the Rhodes Tavern could not be issued unless the Metropolitan Square project could be shown to be a project of "special merit" for the District of Columbia. The special merit provision had been included in the new preservation law at the insistence of Mayor Walter Washington, who was concerned that the Washington Convention Center project—one of the other major downtown development projects underway in the period—might be delayed or derailed by the law in the absence of such a provision.[16] Special merit was defined in the law as follows: "special merit means a plan or building having significant benefits to the District of Columbia or to the community by virtue of exemplary architecture, specific features of land planning, or social or other benefits."[17] The decision about whether Metropolitan Square qualified for such a designation was to be made by the Mayor's Agent for historic preservation, Carol Thompson, following a public hearing.[18]

This set of delays, public hearings, and administrative reviews provided time for opponents of the demolition of Rhodes to expand their campaign. During that time their canny activism amplified the public debate about the building's significance. The longer the legal process went on the more likely it seemed that the building would be preserved.

THE CITIZENS' COMMITTEE

In May 1978, Joseph N. Grano, a Veteran's Administration attorney who had recently moved to Washington from New York, launched the Citizens' Committee to Save Historic Rhodes Tavern. Grano, who was active in the local branch of the Republican Party, was an abrasive contrarian.

But he succeeded in launching a campaign that not only garnered significant attention for Rhodes Tavern, it ultimately became a powerful means for furthering the D.C. statehood and voting rights campaign (Figure 24). Initially he drew on a small but committed core of Rhodes supporters, which included *National Geographic* photographic curator Geraldine Linder and artist and Rhodes tenant Richard Squires. The newly formed organization made its presence felt at National Preservation Week in May 1978. The *Washington Post* reported that Rhodes supporters gatecrashed official tours and encouraged participants to take tours of the Rhodes Tavern, which did not feature on the official program. From the very beginning the Citizens' Committee adopted a strategy of focusing on the building's historical associations and telling stories of the people who had occupied and passed through the building. In other words they were concerned not with how the building contributed to the architectural scene, but its role as witness to and locus of history.[19]

Richard Squires assembled a dossier of historical information, which was based on the work of Washington historian Constance McLaughlin Green. The Squires dossier was augmented significantly with further research by Nelson Rimensnyder who worked in the congressional research office and had been responsible for providing historical materials for the Committee on the District of Columbia in the years leading up to and following the implementation of home rule in the District. The Squires and Rimensnyder research became the basis of all the information that was provided to the newspapers and formed the basis of the public argument for retaining the building.[20]

The historical details that were deployed most frequently focused on the long life of the building relative to that of the city itself and its connection to a wide range of locally and nationally significant people and events. The building was constructed between 1799 and 1801, making it one of the city's oldest, and by the 1980s it was certainly the oldest commercial building in the old downtown area. In its early years it served a number of civic functions in addition to its role as a tavern. For example, the Orphans' Court met there, and it was used as a polling place in the city's first municipal elections in 1802. It was run as a boarding house after 1807 and featured in one of the more colorful published anecdotes about the burning of Washington by British troops in 1814. On August 24, General Cockburn and his men reportedly dined on fowl by the light

Figure 24.   Joe Grano showing the campaign materials produced by the Citizens' Committee to Save Historic Rhodes Tavern. Photograph by Linda Wheeler. Source: *Washington Post*/Getty Images.

of the fire that burned the neighboring "palace and Treasury."[21] Between 1814 and 1846 it was the home of Washington's earliest and most important private financial institution, the Bank of the Metropolis, and then to the Corcoran and Riggs Bank after that. It served a wide variety of commercial uses in the late nineteenth century before becoming the first home of the National Press Club in the early twentieth.[22]

The Citizens' Committee and other supporters emphasized the importance of the tavern as a place connected with municipal government in Washington. Supporters sometimes called it the first "Town Hall" and seized on its use as a polling place in 1802 with great enthusiasm despite the fact that this did not necessarily point to any wider political significance. The idea that Rhodes Tavern could be a symbol of the ongoing struggle for political self-determination in Washington, or home rule, gave the preservation campaign much of its fervor. However, campaigners saw more than a symbol of home rule in the building. They also promoted the idea that Rhodes was a marker of, and medium for, reconciliation between the federal government and the local city. In 1970 an NCPC study of downtown landmarks noted that "Rhodes Tavern has been associated with personages, institutions and events of both local and national significance."[23] The Citizen's Committee campaigned on the idea that the protection of the building would be recognition of shared traditions and places, an act of faith in the possibility that federal and local interests in Washington could be harmonized, or at least find some accommodation and mutual respect.

So, in addition to the building's connection to local events, the Citizens' Committee also stressed the seamless connections to national figures and the pageant of federal politics. For example, one of the more persistent themes noted by campaigners was that the building was a witness to presidential inauguration parades stretching from Jefferson in 1805 to Ronald Reagan, which occurred while the campaign to save Rhodes was still ongoing in 1981. The idea that the building had seen the whole panorama of Washington's history became a keynote of the campaign.[24]

HISTORIC WITNESS OR MISSING TOOTH?

On August 24, 1978, the Citizens' Committee to Save Historic Rhodes Tavern organized Conflagration Day, a reenactment of the burning of

Washington by British troops in 1814. Committee member Robert Gair dressed as British commander General Cockburn and was joined by a handful of others in a procession down Pennsylvania Avenue, with some members of the procession dressed as what the *Washington Post* described as "tavern wenches."[25] A couple of dozen more supporters marched behind the costumed reenactors carrying "Save Rhodes Tavern" signs. Designed to draw attention to the role of the tavern in a signal event in Washington's early history, the event also provides an insight into what the Rhodes campaigners believed its preservation could achieve.

Rhodes proponents promoted the idea that the building should be protected as a witness to history. Their campaign focused on the idea that its preservation would allow Washingtonians to connect imaginatively with the city's history. While the developer and others no doubt regarded the reenactment as little more than a theatrical publicity stunt, the event was in keeping with the wider public strategy pursued by the activists. From their point of view the reenactment was a way of transporting participants and observers to a moment in the past. The building was a medium by which the inhabitants of Washington in 1978 could come into close contact with the city's early history. The reenactment was staged to remind Washingtonians that even as the federal enclave succumbed to British invaders the young city endured and ultimately prospered. The Rhodes Tavern was a symbol and embodiment of that endurance and, as such, should be kept as a reminder of it.[26]

This way of imagining a historic building as a place that opens up vistas onto past events is akin to the way history painting traditionally functioned. Emanuel Leutze's depiction of George Washington crossing the Delaware (1851), to take just one very well-known American example, invites the viewer to become a witness to a vital historical moment, a moment of decisive military action and sovereign possession. For the Rhodes supporters, the Conflagration Day reenactment was supposed to work in a similar way.[27]

Randall Mason has shown that historic preservationists in New York in the early twentieth century were likewise motivated by the idea that closeness of association with the past and the capacity to see and imagine it could "refresh patriotism, civic virtue, piety and love." A historic building, according to one prominent architect and preservationist of that period, could be a "silent but effective preacher of virtue."[28] The

Save Rhodes campaigners inherited this tradition of civic patriotism and believed that the tavern could perform this role, allowing those who saw and used the building to imagine in a vivid, tangible sense the activities of the city in earlier decades and centuries. City councilor and former schoolteacher Hilda Mason struck exactly this note in her evocation of Rhodes Tavern's significance in 1979:

> As a former school teacher, I realize the importance of tangible reminders of the history of our city in the development of an understanding and appreciation of history in our children. Truly, history is not only to be found in textbooks; it resides in our historic places, particularly in buildings such as Rhodes Tavern.[29]

When the Rhodes campaigners wrote and spoke about preserving history above all else, they were referring to an affective connection to the past. They wanted to promote the kind of closeness to the past that we associate with depictions of history in cinema or painting, rather than the careful weighing and analysis of evidence typical of modern historiography. The Rhodes campaigners wanted D.C. inhabitants to be able to breathe in the subtle influences exhaled by the city's historic places. The Rhodes Tavern was, in their minds, an authentic artifact, but also a spur to personal and imaginative identification with the city at large and its history. In the view of the Save Rhodes committee, the building was a witness to past events. So by testifying on behalf of the building, bearing witness to its significance for the city, they were able to become—in an imaginative sense—witnesses to history themselves. The imaginary identification with the building in the moment, for example, when "Thomas Jefferson rode past on his chestnut mare" during his inaugural parade enabled a sense of custodianship over that event, that history, and the city in which it took place.[30]

While this kind of civic patriotism was an old-fashioned deployment of historic preservation sentiment, it did strike a chord in Washington in the late 1970s and early 1980s. The reasons for this were twofold. The preservation movement enjoyed unprecedented prominence in the city. But not everyone could own a substantial house in a well-regarded historic district. On the other hand, anybody could identify with shared symbols like the Rhodes Tavern. Second, in Washington connections to the city often had to be made rather than assumed. Most who participated in the events organized by the Save Rhodes campaigners were newcomers. They had been drawn to, rather than born to, the city. But the enthusiasm and determination of the campaign eventually succeeded in garnering great sympathy for the cause.

The Save Rhodes campaign's focus on historical associations was at odds with the emphasis on good city form championed by preservation professionals that engaged in the debate. Those who publicly sanctioned the demolition of the tavern—David Childs, Wolf von Eckardt, Leila Smith, J. Carter Brown—were seemingly unmoved by the idea that the building was a witness to history and redolent with the famous figures who frequented it. Responding to the growing campaign to protect the building, the architect of the Metropolitan Square Project, David Childs, called Rhodes Tavern "a pig" and suggested that it should be "put out of its misery."[31] *Washington Post* architecture critic Wolf von Eckardt, a steadfast supporter of preservation since the mid-1960s, described Rhodes as "amputated and badly misused," and agreed that it was not worthy of protection and restoration.[32] The city's most successful commercial architect, Shalom Baranes, wrote to a newspaper during the dispute and described the building as a "rubble pie of questionable historical value."[33] Most prominently, J. Carter Brown called Rhodes Tavern "a gaping tooth in the smile of 15th St."[34] In contrast to the steadfast witness to history evoked by the building's defenders—which implied a sort of moral fortitude—its detractors focused on its obvious physical failings. J. Carter Brown argued that so little of the original fabric was intact that a rebuilt Rhodes "would be fake, like a Hollywood set."[35]

This criticism of the architectural integrity of Rhodes Tavern and its apparent incompatibility with the surrounding streetscape, however, did not succeed in quieting opposition to its proposed demolition. The Save Rhodes campaigners now promoted the tavern as an underdog, something dismissed for its appearance and diminutive stature compared to its neighbors, but having intrinsic value because of its age and historical associations. As Joe Grano wrote in a 1980 opinion piece in the *Washington Star*, "the tavern should be preserved precisely because it *is* small in an age of 'big is better.'"[36] He went on to note that David Childs's preference for deleting Rhodes from the Metropolitan Square project was based on nothing more than "his personal aesthetic judgment that the development would look better without Rhodes Tavern."[37]

The apparent coziness of the deal struck between Carr, DTID!, and the city also galvanized the Save Rhodes campaign. They seized upon David Childs's role as a case in point. Not only was he a well-connected, establishment architect, he was the current chairman of the National Capital Planning Commission (NCPC). As such he had an unparalleled network of contacts and an unmatched sphere of influence in architecture and planning in Washington. In the view of Save Rhodes campaigners, DTID! was tainted by their association with Carr. Before the delay of demolition regulation triggered the formal negotiation process, Carr had engaged Betts Abel, DTID!'s recently appointed executive director, as an adviser to the project. These apparent conflicts of interest and the obvious irony of DTID! supporting the tearing down of a building provided Rhodes defenders with new ammunition in their campaign.[38]

PRESERVATION AS POPULAR POLITICAL EXPRESSION

In the events stirred up by the Rhodes controversy preservationists in Washington encountered a tension familiar in the wider urban development and planning system: that between legal process on the one hand and the sense of democratic entitlement and moral conviction on the other. Drawing on the experience of the antifreeway protests, campaigns against slum clearance policies, and the wider civil rights discourse, preservationists in the 1960s and 1970s sometimes departed from their older patterns of elite persuasion and incremental planning reform. Instead, they embraced direct protest and popular campaigning. During the campaign to save the Old Post Office on Pennsylvania Avenue, for example, planners, architects, and museum professionals joined with other citizens, taking to the streets in protest, writing letters to the newspapers, and joining advocacy groups. By these means they expressed misgivings about the demolition proposal, as well as about the wider direction of urban development and the changing character of the environment in Washington.

By the end of the 1970s, however, preservation had its own laws, review commissions, and regulations. A national legislative framework constrained federal government destruction while also underpinning and promoting state and municipal activity in the field. As we have seen, in

D.C., a strong, local law grounded in the 1978 *Penn Central* Supreme Court decision and enacted by the city's newly empowered and democratically elected municipal government gave preservationists a clear mandate to participate in the planning and redevelopment process. With this strong system to work within, moral influence and popular protest were arguably no longer as necessary as they had been in the preceding decades.

But not everybody saw it this way. For the Citizens' Committee to Save Historic Rhodes Tavern, the assurance that there was now a strong legal process around preservation did not ameliorate the sense of anxiety about the impending demolition of the Rhodes Tavern. For them the outcome of this particular battle was paramount, and the integrity of the evolving system, by comparison, was of little consequence. Whatever compromise was reached, Joe Grano's view was that the Rhodes Tavern's "historical significance mandates that it be preserved."[39] When accused of not playing by the rules during the dispute he welcomed the characterization, telling a journalist that "I didn't play by the rules. I had my own game."[40] For Grano and his supporters the sustaining mythology was much the same as for earlier preservation campaigns: the building's defenders were public-spirited, private citizens, vigilant protectors of the city's history, holding out against the barbarism and pecuniary interest of government and developers.

This conviction underpinned three more years of legal and political maneuvering. In February 1980 the Mayor's Agent for historic preservation determined that the Metropolitan Square Project was a project of "special merit," which effectively enabled the issuing of demolition permits. In response, the Citizens' Committee petitioned the District of Columbia Court of Appeals to set aside the decision. But in May 1981 the court affirmed the decision of the Mayor's Agent. The Citizens' Committee then attempted to take the issue to the Supreme Court, but the court refused to hear the case. In 1982 the focus of the fight moved to Capitol Hill, where D.C.'s nonvoting delegate to Congress, Walter Fauntroy, sponsored a resolution in support of preserving Rhodes, which was referred to the Committee on the District of Columbia. Nothing definitive emerged from any of these efforts, but the Rhodes defenders did succeed in delaying the demolition further.[41]

During that time the Rhodes campaigners garnered extensive national publicity and began to build their profile among constituencies in D.C.

that had heretofore not engaged in the issue, especially black Washingtonians. Walter Fauntroy's support for their efforts was significant in this
respect.[42] The first mention of the "save Rhodes" campaign in the *Washington Afro-American* in a June 1982 editorial coincided with Fauntroy's
congressional resolution. The newspaper concluded:

> only by restoring this physical reminder of the City's earliest days can a
> sense of community and local pride be engendered. Destroying Washing-
> ton's earliest roots and sense of place will demolish local confidence in
> ever achieving self-government.[43]

Fauntroy thus identified the campaign with the home-rule movement
and the statehood campaign that had grown from it.

In 1983 the Citizens' Committee collected more than twenty-three
thousand signatures in support of holding a ballot initiative on the issue
of preserving Rhodes Tavern, easily enough to trigger an initiative under
the D.C. rules. The proponents of Initiative 11 and the Citizens' Committee shared the conviction expressed in the *Afro-American* editorial that the
tavern fundamentally expressed the aspirations of Washingtonians for
greater self-determination in municipal affairs. Proponents of the ballot
initiative assumed that most Washingtonians agreed with this sentiment
and would support the preservation of the tavern at the ballot box. The
healthy turnout to the poll in November 1983 vindicated that conviction,
and more than 60 percent of them voted "to declare and implement
District of Columbia public policy of preserving the Historic Rhodes
Tavern on its present site."[44]

In the wake of the ballot Mayor Barry appointed a commission to
examine how and whether the outcome could be implemented as dic-
tated by the Home Rule Act. But the District of Columbia government
took the position that Initiative 11 was purely advisory and did not prevent it from issuing raze permits to the developer, Carr. Further challenges ensued, but the court ultimately found that the law implied by
Initiative 11 was in fact unconstitutional and, therefore, could not become
the policy of the District of Columbia. After more than six years of
heated legal and political contestation the tavern was finally demolished
in September 1984.

While the campaign to save the building failed, Initiative 11 suggested that preservation might thrive as a mode of popular, counterhegemonic politics mobilizing citizen participation amid highly fraught and contested redevelopment questions. However, the Rhodes campaign also revealed a level of instability and uncertainty around what preservation was for and who should speak in its name. In this sense, it paralleled the controversy about who could speak on behalf of the Dupont Circle neighborhood and surrounds in establishing historic districts there in the late 1970s and 1980s.

COLLABORATION, ETHICS, AND PROFESSIONALIZATION

The historic preservation movement in Washington splintered in the years following the Rhodes Tavern dispute. Opponents of the Save Rhodes campaign characterized Joe Grano as a divisive figure. His attacking style and populist posture built a very successful campaign with a high profile in D.C., and beyond, but alienated many of the established and effective preservation forces in the city. The local politics of Dupont Circle in the period highlight these tensions and the divisive impact of the Rhodes campaign. In 1981 Grano leveraged his public profile as the face of the Rhodes campaign to have himself elected president of the Dupont Circle Citizens' Association (DCCA). This almost immediately caused a split in the organization. Charles Robertson, a museum professional who worked for many years for the Smithsonian American Art Museum, led the DCCA's preservation committee at the time—a position he had already occupied for several years. But Robertson supported a very different kind of approach to preservation from Grano. So when Grano took over as president of the DCCA Robertson distanced himself and established a separate preservation organization, the Dupont Circle Conservancy. It was a reaction against the politics of the Rhodes Tavern campaign and the vicissitudes of the popular politics championed by Grano.[45]

The splintering of preservation forces in the 1980s, however, had deeper roots. The Rhodes campaign and Grano himself magnified differences and brought them to the surface. But the differences in values and outlook among key actors at the time went well beyond tensions aroused by the campaign to save the Rhodes Tavern. The experience of the city-wide nonprofit advocacy group DTID!, the concerns of the presidential historian and Art Deco Society of Washington (ADSW) founder Richard Striner, and the role played by the Dupont Circle Conservancy under the leadership of Charles Robertson point to some of the difficulties involved in maintaining a cohesive preservation movement in Washington in the 1980s.

The designation "preservationist" in fact obscured three distinct, though overlapping, objectives that came under that broad preservation umbrella in the 1980s. The Rhodes campaign revealed the potential for preservation to mobilize popular democratic participation on behalf of particular historic places and against powerful interests. But while some newly motivated preservation campaigners focused on the entitlements of the people or the citizenry, against the propertied or the political powerful, others focused on the entitlements of those not yet born to enjoy the places inherited from the past. For those, like Richard Striner, who viewed the preservation of historic places as an intergenerational obligation, this collaboration was an ethical responsibility. A third perspective saw effective preservation action more as a problem of the appropriate exercise of expertise in the service of protecting and improving the qualities of the physical environment. Events in the 1980s in the wake of the adoption of statutory powers and the formation of professional procedures for historic preservation saw these three closely connected missions—direct democratic expression, exercise of an ethical duty, and the building of the professional capacity of preservationists as urbanists—become more distinct. But the inability of actors at the time to articulate the conflicts and confluences between these different objectives caused ongoing misunderstanding in preservationist ranks.

The experience of DTID! highlights the quickly evolving nature of preservation at the time and the difficulties presented by its competing priorities. Formed as a spontaneous response to the threatened demolition of the Old Post Office building on Pennsylvania Avenue in 1971, the organization quickly became an important voice for preservation in central Washington (see chapter 3). During the 1970s DTID! filled a gap left by the vigilant neighborhood-level preservation groups, who operated almost entirely in their own bailiwicks. DTID! focused on downtown area landmarks and promoted the establishment of a historic district in the old downtown. But by the late 1980s the good name it had built in the 1970s was battered and its formerly ambitious agenda curtailed.[46]

A surge of international investment capital in the 1980s, much of it originating in Japan, introduced new redevelopment pressures in central Washington. DTID! shifted its course as new money began to flow into downtown Washington and the real estate industry began to work aggressively with Washington's local government to redevelop the blocks east of the White House.[47] But DTID! was under significant financial stress by the mid-1980s after expanding quickly in the 1970s and establishing an office with permanent staff in 1978. In 1984, just weeks before the Rhodes Tavern was razed, they opted to change their name to the less confrontational DC Preservation League (DCPL) and indicated that they would now work more collaboratively with developers. President Robert A. Peck announced that "while aggressive lawyering (to prevent demolitions) once was our chief means of living up to our name, we now find ourselves increasingly called upon by developers to participate in early discussions of rehabilitation schemes."[48]

For some observers the shift in emphasis was a natural evolution prompted by new conditions and a new maturity. Discussing DTID!'s adoption of a different name in 1986, *Washington Post* urban affairs columnist Roger Lewis linked the change to a broadening of the preservation agenda and a mainstreaming of what he described as a formerly "fringe movement."[49] Washington architect and preservation consultant Sibley Jennings likewise supported the move, seeing the shift "toward working more in drawing rooms and board rooms from a position of strength" as good for preservation.[50] This mode of elite networking and persuasion was, after all, not altogether alien to the field. This kind of advocacy had been a major part of preservation from the late nineteenth century onward.[51]

The popular campaigning of the 1960s and 1970s dramatically broadened the appeal and impact of preservation, but one of its mainsprings had been the exercise of influence among and between different sectors of the elite. Nevertheless, in the mid-1980s the oppositional tactics and publicity-oriented modus operandi that preservation had established in the 1970s were integral to its identity. When DTID! announced its new direction it caused some concern. As far away as New York observers remarked on the changing identity of the well-regarded Washington organization, with one newspaper report putting it down to the "gentle pressure of gentrification."[52] Advocates in Washington were also uneasy about the posture adopted by the rebadged DCPL. The Committee of 100 on the Federal City, which was, and is, a quintessential voice of elite influence and expertise, criticized the DCPL's willingness to work so closely with developers. Advisory Neighborhood Commissions involved in land-use disputes between residents and developers, former members of DTID!, and the neighborhood-based D.C. Alliance for Preservation all voiced concerns about the independence and authority of the DCPL.[53]

The Rhodes Tavern battle damaged DTID!/DCPL's reputation with the grassroots, and the organization faced ongoing criticism in the 1980s for its willingness to enter into deals with the property development industry. Their failure to oppose the planned demolition of the Woodward Building compounded the problem. The Woodward was a prominent early twentieth-century office building that was within the downtown historic district and noted as an important contributing building in the district nomination. Jon Gerstenfeld, the developer of the project, was listed as a corporate sponsor of the DCPL in 1986. DCPL also approved several other heavily compromised preservation deals in the period that further tarnished their reputation. In particular they endorsed a series of facade preservation projects: the old Penn Theatre at 650 Pennsylvania Avenue Southeast; the Army and Navy Club, Seventeenth Street Northwest (Figures 25 and 26); the Bond Building on New York Avenue; and the Homer Building on Thirteenth Street in the old downtown. In 1988, DCPL president Robert A. Peck, who had presided over the name change and shift in philosophy, accepted a position with the prominent land-use law firm Jones, Day, Revis & Pogue, further highlighting the close links between the DCPL and the real estate development industry.[54]

The historian and architectural enthusiast Richard Striner emerged as a prominent voice in preservation in Washington in the 1980s and became a trenchant critic of the DCPL. Striner was one of the founders of the ADSW in 1983, and soon after he championed a major effort to preserve the city's abused and abandoned Greyhound Bus Terminal. In the course of that battle he formed a dim view of the DCPL. Striner had become involved in preservation because he felt a strong emotional attachment to the city's fabric and especially its interwar architecture. This affective connection motivated his research as well as his advocacy. But he soon realized that while this combination of sentiment and understanding was a necessary precondition for effective preservation advocacy, it was

Figure 25. The Army and Navy Club at 901 Seventeenth Street Northwest (also known as 1627 I Street Northwest) on the east side of Farragut Square in Washington, D.C., soon after completion in 1911. Library of Congress, Prints and Photographs Division.

not sufficient to protect buildings. The strong financial incentives within the urban development system put the integrity of the preservation process at risk, he believed, because genuine expertise was too frequently undermined by money. Moreover, the traditions of elite networking that were seen as one of preservation's strengths by Silbey Jennings and others could equally result, Striner believed, in a "genteel weakness" that undermined the field as a whole.[55] Striner arrived at the view, therefore, that only a robust, even rigid, ethical framework could ensure preservation's integrity and its success as a major social movement.

As cochair of the D.C. Alliance for Preservation in the late 1980s Striner, along with Laura M. Richards of the Committee of 100, drafted a set of ethical guidelines intended to constrain the way that individuals and member organizations of the alliance could behave with respect to preservation testimony in particular. As in most other cities with a landmarks

Figure 26.   The Old Army and Navy Club building incorporated into a twelve-story office building, designed by Shalom Baranes Associates in 1986. Photograph by Agnostic Preachers' Kid. Source: Wikimedia Commons.

law, the decision-making process in historic preservation in Washington depended on paid experts delivering assessments of landmark and historic district proposals and of the impact of development proposals on recognized historic places. This meant that in many cases property owners and developers would pay recognized experts to undermine the case for listing a place or to suggest that the property in question did not contribute to a historic district. Striner wanted to find ways that the preservation movement could blackball certain paid experts as ethically unfit for the task of providing such testimony. Moreover, he believed that the preservation field was too dominated by architectural connoisseurship and taste and, therefore, insufficiently attentive to historical significance in the wider sense. The Rhodes Tavern case highlighted tensions between those who valued places primarily for their historical associations and others who focused more on architectural and urbanistic qualities. Similar tensions played out locally in many other cities around the world at the same time. Striner wanted to use his ethical framework to encourage a greater number of academic historians into the preservation field and limit the influence of architectural expertise. By doing so he aimed to move the field away from what he saw as its flawed adherence to a notion of architectural pedigree and integrity. In his view preservation had to rid itself of the tendency to operate as a beauty contest.[56]

For Striner, the adherence of preservationists to an ideal of aesthetic quality was the product of a persistent confusion that beset the field. In a 1993 essay on preservation and ethics, he noted that "a great many people in historic preservation routinely confuse two very different objectives: the preservation of our heritage and the enhancement of our physical environment."[57] He acknowledged that there was often a great area of overlap between these two objectives but that there are inevitably times when the two are at odds. In such situations, he argued, the preservationist should support heritage protection. This bias toward the protection of heritage would, he observed, be based on a natural inclination among preservationists toward a conservative social ethic that treats society, in the famous formulation of Edmund Burke, as a partnership "between those who are living, those who are dead and those yet to be born."[58]

While many Washington preservationists no doubt shared Striner's sense of obligation to both past and future, as well as his suspicion of forces that might corrupt preservation, they were not necessarily persuaded that the stricter provisions in his proposed ethical code would be workable. Striner suggested the exclusion from the ranks of preservation of anyone with a vested interest in real estate development, including architects. Dupont Circle Conservancy chair Charles Robertson was one of those who rejected key aspects of Striner's approach to the problem. In a letter to Striner and his D.C. Alliance for Preservation cochair, Anna Carter, Robertson noted that aspects of the proposed code "insist on an exclusivity of commitment to the cause of preservation that is not required to avoid conflicts of interest, does not serve the goals of the historic preservation movement and would severely handicap the activities of groups such as ours." He cited the probable exclusion of most architects, lawyers, builders, and developers from the preservation process as particularly harmful. Such exclusions, he concluded, went "so far beyond what is accepted by the community as necessary and appropriate, the proposed code fosters not the impression of ethical conduct, but rather the impression that members of subscribing organizations are cliquish, narrow-minded and intolerant of dissent."[59]

Like Striner, Robertson wanted to improve the standard of preservation advocacy and the standing of preservation in the Washington community at large. But he emphasized a different set of values from Striner and understood the objectives of the field in a quite different way. As the leader of preservation efforts in the Dupont Circle neighborhood since the late 1970s he encountered a range of opposition to preservation efforts: everything from straightforward developer pressure to neighborhood conflict around gentrification, fought along the lines of both race and class. But he maintained a fairly consistent commitment to the idea that preservation would only be effective if it professionalized its procedures and worked more closely with government, real estate interests, and architects. The conservancy itself had several architects as well as a handful of landscape architects among its members.[60]

Robertson wanted the Dupont Circle Conservancy to act not just as an advocate and publicist, but also as an informal review commission. The conservancy should be, he believed, a source of expertise on preservation methods and a broker for rehabilitation projects, advising on the limits of new construction before the projects arrived at the point of litigation. In this, the conservancy's ambition mirrored the stated objectives of the DCPL, but in practice the organization maintained a greater sense of distance from the development industry and a narrower focus on the intown sections of Northwest. The Dupont Circle Conservancy also actively lobbied the D.C. government on a range of issues related to the physical environment as it affected the nearby historic districts and local historic preservation law. Robertson carefully redrafted the procedures for the landmark designation review process, attempting to remove loopholes in the language. The conservancy persistently encouraged stronger enforcement of the building permit system and the enforcement of fines for code violations. In the absence of such enforcement conservancy members themselves policed and reported the installation of signs, awnings, satellite dishes, and sidewalk cafes that did not conform to the historic district regulations. They also tried to persuade property owners within historic districts to leave brickwork unpainted and follow other "best practice" guidelines for the stewardship of historic properties in the area where such things were not specifically covered by regulations.[61]

Taken in its entirety the conservancy's activity amounted to an effort to curate the physical environment around Dupont Circle and in other nearby historic districts. This curatorial emphasis was hardly surprising given the influential role of museum professionals in the organization. Robertson (Smithsonian American Art Museum), Alison Luchs (curator at the National Gallery), and Leo J. Kasun (art educator at the National Gallery), along with several architects and planners, formed the nucleus of the organization in the 1980s. The conservancy treated the historic districts in their area as collections that possessed distinct qualities and particular value. Their value in transmitting a deeper understanding of the city's past depended, they believed, upon proper care and presentation. Such districts could be expanded and changed, but only with judicious oversight. From Robertson's viewpoint this required cultural expertise. Property owners and inhabitants of the area could not be expected to possess such expertise. So presenting the conservancy's aesthetic and historical expertise in this way was a strategy aimed at winning respect and influence for the conservancy across the full range of interests involved in real estate and neighborhood politics.[62]

The ambition to work with other parties in the development process involved direct engagement with realtors and property developers. Richard Striner looked askance at such relationships and saw in them an outsized regard for property and its value, as well as a formalism that privileged environmental order over cultural heritage. Evidence from the debate about Rhodes and other preservation battles at the time indicates that journalists and the general public mostly believed that the purpose of preservation was to keep nice places, attractive buildings, and good architecture. Joe Grano's efforts, for example, were derided as a crusade to save "Washington's ugliest building."[63] Consequently, both Striner and

Grano worked in different ways to undermine prevailing ideas about what preservation was for. It was not that either was against keeping beautiful or smart-looking buildings—Striner, after all, founded an art deco appreciation society. But they believed these places represented something deeper. Striner and Grano both believed that the obligation to preserve significant places was a responsibility to protect history, something that belonged properly to the city and its people. What was less clear were the answers to the questions what history and which people.

WHO ARE THE PEOPLE? WHAT IS THE PAST?

Disagreements about the cultural value of the Rhodes Tavern and about the proper role of architectural and curatorial expertise in the preservation field delineated some of the ambiguities confronting preservationists in the period. The differing perspectives on the value of Rhodes Tavern and about why preservation was important cast doubt over who was a preservationist. The lack of consensus highlighted, moreover, the breakdown in coherency of what constituted the people's voice in a campaign such as Save Rhodes. In their influential 1978 book, *Collage City*, Colin Rowe and Fred Koetter highlighted the gap between "the people" as a rhetorical figure and the actual manifestations of social groups fighting to achieve particular ends in cities. For architectural and planning populists of the period, preservationists included, "the people" was an indispensable ideological armature. Rowe and Koetter, however, viewed "the people" in a skeptical light, depicting it as a trope:

> Suffused with generosity, they [populists] surrender to an abstract entity called "the people"; and while talking of pluralism . . . they are unwilling to recognize how manifold "the people" happens to be, and consequently whatever "its" will, how much in need of protection from each other its components happen to stand.[64]

Washington very obviously contained multiple communities within the same territory and several overlapping citizenries. As such, stable oppositions between community and government on the one hand or citizen interest and private pecuniary interest on the other were less clear than they had seemed in earlier years. DTID! rhetorically asked "Citizen? or Developers" in their first newsletter in 1971. Rhodes campaigners similarly asserted that there was a clear choice between vested interest and public good. But they could not isolate the interests of the citizenry from those of finance and real estate in 1981 with the same certainty that DTID! had in 1971. Real estate developers seized upon this apparent shift. It was not that they orchestrated in some total sense a situation where the power of such mobilizing invocations of *the people* and *the community* simply melted away. But they intervened and reframed the politics of development disputes very aggressively, responding to the evident attack on their direct interests.

Yet even as development interests attacked the scope of preservation efforts and derided preservationists as elitist, their projects evinced a new level of sympathy with the historic dimensions of the built environment in the late 1970s and early 1980s. A number of prominent developers in Washington, D.C., including Oliver T. Carr, seemed to embrace values that preservationists had long promoted: contextual sensitivity, the human scale, and the preservation of elements of the historic fabric. Carr's willingness to consider protecting several historic buildings as part of the Metropolitan Square project testified to this. Even before federal preservation tax credits came into effect in 1977—something that produced a boom in adaptive use and historic building rehabilitations nationally—there was growing interest in the commercial possibilities of the historic built environment.[65]

A vogue for historically derived forms and references in new architecture accompanied, and was perhaps spurred by, this growing commercial interest in and exploitation of historic places. The work of several architectural firms in Washington in the late 1970s and the 1980s, including Hartman and Cox, Swaney and Kerns, and Martin and Jones, testified to the interest and concern with historical forms and contextual sensitivity. Shalom Baranes established his firm in 1981 in the midst of this turn to history and has subsequently made a career out of overt historical reference and duplication. His historically inflected or inspired work is ubiquitous in Washington, D.C., and he remained a developer favorite even after many other architects had abandoned such an approach to design in the late 1990s and 2000s.[66]

But the expansion of historic preservation in the period and the pronounced turn toward historical reference in design was also a source of political and intellectual uncertainty. With developers now supporting the retention of some aspects of historic buildings and with governments now passing preservation laws and establishing landmark commissions, the established battle lines of the previous decade were blurred. Who exactly was for history and who sided with the city?

CONCLUSION

Property developers and commercial architects embraced "history" in this period in Washington. But on whose terms was history presented and preserved? The case of Rhodes Tavern highlights the absence of agreed objectives within the historic preservation movement and the absence of clear boundaries around the movement. The tavern was a highly significant place in the life of the city, but physically very much diminished. Should its high level of historic significance or its diminished architectural integrity have determined its fate? Such uncertainty and project-by-project particularity underlines the political nature of preservation. Each instance like the Rhodes Tavern has the potential to mobilize and empower constituencies in the city and build political movements that transcend the battle over a single building or place. They likewise have the power to reveal the very different values and aspirations that the inhabitants of a city bring to historic buildings and neighborhoods.

Nevertheless, the particular uncertainties and ambiguities encountered in the 1980s in Washington eased as the personalities involved changed, as new political issues and priorities arose, and as architectural and urbanistic fashions moved on. Preservation certainly lost some of its passion in the process, and the expansion of historic districts and the management of the overall system in the 1990s took on a smoother and more professional character. The city's preservation office worked with community representatives to establish new landmarks and districts during that decade. The formal systems established under the Historic Preservation Review Board after 1983 took on a more routine character. So a framework of protection and advocacy that emerged from the 1970s and that was tested and challenged in various ways in the 1980s settled into a functioning pattern that enjoyed some legitimacy in the 1990s.

During the 1990s Washington's intown area was poised between two eras. The preceding decades were characterized by a level of tumult and uncertainty about what the city would become: What would its streets and buildings look like in the future, and who would inhabit the intown neighborhoods? The restoration and preservation movement was a response to this uncertainty, a set of connected efforts to embrace a complex, diverse, aging city and to impose a level of environmental order and stability onto it. In the new century the uncertainty diminished. The trajectory of the intown areas seemed almost predictable. As in other major cities such as New York and San Francisco, where information workers huddled near high-status and high-paid work, the question was no longer whither the neighborhood. People simply wondered where the pattern of upscaling would go next. From the U Street area gentrification moved out along the Metro's green line to Columbia Heights; from Capitol Hill Southeast it gradually nudged northward, and city watchers and the real estate industry pronounced H Street Northeast was the next thing and so on. In this period the old riot corridors of Fourteenth Street Northwest, H Street Northeast, and Seventh Street Northwest, so badly damaged in 1968 and that had struggled so long for new investment and to regain a sense of commercial vitality, all of a sudden were booming, the key arteries in the gentrification of the central city.

But in the 1990s this air of inevitability had not yet settled on the intown areas. The old Soviet Safeway, as the main grocery store in the inner Northwest was colloquially known, did not yet compete with Wholefoods, which did not open their store on P Street, near Fourteenth Street, until 2000. The patterns of social change and the new real estate dynamics initiated in the 1960s and 1970s were not yet resolved decisively toward overwhelming and inevitable gentrification in the 1990s.

Prevailing beliefs about Washington's historical identity were also quite plainly the product of the previous three decades. In the 1990s inhabitants largely imagined Washington as a city of row-house neighborhoods. Many intown residents and most neighborhood organizations assumed, therefore, that the work of preservation would focus on protecting and preserving places built in the nineteenth century or according to similar patterns in the early decades of the twentieth.

In the new century a small but growing group of preservationists and neighborhood activists challenged that settled compact. In 2002 the Southwest urban renewal area was at the center of a fiercely contested battle about the nature of the city's past. It was much less covered at the time than the Rhodes Tavern battle had been in the late 1970s and early 1980s or the campaign to save the Old Post Office before that. But it was no less significant for what it said about the city's historical identity. At stake were the temporal boundaries of the historic. Where did the historic end and the modern begin? Was the modern, as represented by the modern movement in architecture and urbanism, now historic? And if so what did this mean for preservation and the image of the past?

CHAPTER 7

Modernist Urbanism as History

Preserving the Southwest Urban Renewal Area

In April 2003, the District of Columbia's Historic Preservation Review Board (HPRB) approved an application to register the Capitol Park residential development in Southwest Washington as a historic landmark. Completed in 1959, the complex was part of the first phase of the massive Southwest urban renewal project. A combination of large-slab apartment blocks and so-called town houses, the ensemble was situated on an expansive and carefully landscaped site—a superblock that consolidated several traditional city blocks. This was the first listing as a historic place for such a modernist project in Washington, a city that had assimilated the manifestations of the modern movement reluctantly. While specialists welcomed the move, there was obvious ambivalence about protecting Capitol Park in the wider community. After all, the original impact of the project on the city had been one of the things that propelled preservation activism and the wider milieu of intown activism and democratic planning several decades earlier. In the 1960s, 1970s, and beyond activists and neighborhood groups characterized the Southwest urban renewal area widely as an attack on the traditional form and character of the city, and an unjustifiable disruption of a cohesive, historically African American neighborhood. The landmark listing was thus something of an irony and a clear marker of changing ideas about the city's history and identity.[1]

A design collaboration between architect Chloethiel Woodard Smith (Figure 27), one of Washington's most committed urban and architectural reformers of the postwar period, and Daniel Urban Kiley, the outstanding figure in landscape design nationally, Capitol Park was also

Figure 27. Chloethiel Woodard Smith talks with young inhabitants of Capitol Park. Photograph by Phillip Harrington. Courtesy of Evan Harrington.

Washington's first realized example of the kind of modernist urban development envisaged by American progressive planners and architects
during World War II. In terms of urbanism, the new Southwest was Washington's Interbau, the contemporaneous development in the Hansa-
viertel section of West Berlin. The two projects both relied on the planned
destruction of an expansive area of nineteenth-century urban fabric, and
both were intended as model developments, orthodox essays in the new
spatial arrangements of modernist planning. Interbau included architectural contributions from Oscar Neimeyer, Walter Gropius, Le Corbusier,
Jacob Bakema, and a host of other leading international modernists.
Southwest would ultimately be home to buildings by a less well-known
group, but a group that nevertheless included Washington's leading modern architects alongside some of the best-known design talent nationally.
In addition to the Smith/Kiley collaboration, Southwest would eventually include work by Charles Goodman, Keyes, Lethbridge & Condon,
Morris Lapidus, Harry Weese, I. M. Pei, and landscape architect Hideo
Sasaki. Advocates of preserving Capitol Park based their claims about
its historical significance on its architectural pedigree. That significance
was also enhanced by the fact that it was the first residential project in
the urban renewal area. Smith's central theme, which set the course for
several of the other residential projects that followed, was the provision
of expansive and well-designed open space and the rejection of the street
as the fundamental element of the public realm.[2]

Capitol Park and the Southwest urban renewal area as a whole were
part of the response to the process of devaluation and decay that beset
many aging urban areas in the United States in the 1930s and 1940s. As
Andrew Shanken has argued, architects, planning experts, and policy makers developed and promoted a "sick cities" thesis in the period. According
to this thesis, a stagnant or "mature economy" undermined the health of
aging cities as real estate devaluation compromised the revenue streams
of city governments and, therefore, their ability to manage and maintain
the quality of the environment. In Washington, Louis Justement argued
that this process was a mortal threat to the city. The realized project in
Southwest was something of an essay in how to address that threat using
the tools of modern architecture and planning. The idea that a systemic
failure of the urban organism could be prevented by removing the old
buildings and creating entirely new urban and architectural patterns

motivated the ambitious conceptualization of Southwest. It was just one part of a much larger plan to remake much of the intown residential landscape of Washington in the postwar period. Most sections of that plan were radically revised or dropped in subsequent decades. But Southwest persisted, something of an orphan, a fragmentary record of an abandoned redevelopment agenda.[3]

Proponents of preserving Capitol Park and the wider setting in Southwest have argued that as one of the first local examples of this thoroughly modern planning model, the development is a major marker of a period of intensely optimistic and widely transformative urban and architectural thinking. Capitol Park's recognition as a historic place just forty-four years after its completion, however, was greeted with some skepticism and surprise by real estate developers as well as many preservationists in Washington. The redeveloped Southwest had, after all, long been regarded as an alien and unwelcome presence in central Washington. Journalist and activist Sam Smith described Southwest in the mid-1970s as "an assault on the city."[4] In the 1980s, the planner and geographer Dennis E. Gale asserted, "to wander through the southwest today is to be entirely exiled from the identifying legibility of Washington's inner town-house neighborhoods."[5] In some quarters that perspective persisted. Hence the bemusement expressed by some that parts of the urban renewal area might be considered for landmark listing. When the issue was before the HPRB in 2003, a newspaper article noted: "Who would have thought that a park created as part of an urban renewal project could be considered endangered—or that anyone would care?"[6] Sitting behind this question was the widely held assumption that urban renewal and historic preservation were somehow opposites.

This chapter examines that apparently ironic situation according to three historical phases: first, the key aspirations of Capitol Park and the wider Southwest project; second, the mixed reaction to its realization; and third, the landmark listing process and the complex legacy of the project. Chapter 1 provided a general picture of how a new environment was created from scratch in Southwest to revive the value of property in the city. This chapter looks in much greater detail at the nature of that environment. It also looks at how its explicit physical differences from the rest of the inner city have been reflected in a different pattern of social development and a different trajectory as real estate.

What the development of Southwest and the contest over its value and preservation reveal is not just the seemingly inexorable process of creation, cultural devaluation, and reevaluation. The battle to expand and include this section of modernist urbanism as part of Washington's valid past, something worthy of protection, reveals a willingness to challenge what had become a fixed image of Washington's urban identity. Identifying Capitol Park as a place worthy of keeping arguably altered the urban imaginary of Washington. The landmarking process helped to disrupt a cherished idea among preservationists and others that Washington is, in its essence, a monumental city surrounded by its distinct set of row-house neighborhoods.

"THE NEW TOWN IN THE CITY"

The transformation of the Southwest urban renewal area from the 1950s onward vividly illustrates that piecemeal rehabilitation and historic district preservation were not always regarded as realistic ways of regenerating the city's intown areas. The rehabilitation and preservation of Washington's historic residential fabric was a process that evolved across the whole century. Yet, as chapter 1 demonstrated, there was a period during the postwar years when influential city leaders and design professionals, prominent among them Louis Justement and Chloethiel Woodard Smith, envisaged a new norm for the city, an entirely different landscape based on principles derived from the modern movement via the Congrès internationaux d'architecture moderne (CIAM).[7]

In the view of influential midcentury urban thinkers, piecemeal remediation of decay and small-scale, privately driven interventions would, in most cases, not be adequate to the task of revitalization. CIAM leader Josep Lluís Sert, the German émigrés and Harvard Graduate School of Design leaders Walter Gropius and Martin Wagner, the Regional Plan Association's Henry Churchill, and Justement, who headed the American Institute of Architects (AIA)'s Committee on Urban Planning between 1946 and 1949, all believed that something much more radical was needed. To reverse the decay and remove the impediments to fulfilling family and community life in American cities required, they believed, government-led, centrally coordinated, large-scale intervention. In other words, bulldozer-driven slum clearance and complete rebuilding were necessary to reverse the negative trajectory. The champions of urban transformation found support for their convictions among Keynesian economists and bureaucrats. In the immediate postwar years the unanimity of purpose across a wide range of urban disciplines persuaded civic and business groups as well as metropolitan newspapers to join the coalition of renewal advocates. This coalition viewed large-scale urban renewal as a new model and norm for remaking urban space.[8]

Up until the early 1960s at least, promoters of this optimistic and expansive vision of urban change in Washington would have been happy with the response to their efforts. In 1962, the *Washington Post*'s architecture critic, Wolf von Eckardt, pronounced the Southwest project—and Capitol Park in particular—a success. The 1,500 families that had already moved to the area, he asserted, "are proof that it is possible to lure middle income people back into the city." His article echoed the underlying economic and physical planning rationales for the project. The inhabitants, he observed, "can now walk to work instead of cluttering up the highways. And they spend their money in town." He cited the prospects of increased tax revenues and the spur to private investment provided by the project. When completed, he concluded, providing a line for the real estate agents' advertising pitch, "it will be a new town in the city." Its most important contribution, von Eckardt insisted, expanding upon the "new town in the city" theme, was in the example it provided of "urban beauty and livability."[9]

Also writing in the *Post*, real estate editor John Willman reinforced von Eckardt's positive assessment of Southwest. He focused on the market for Capitol Park describing the new inhabitants that he observed as "cosmopolitans" and as "a broad cross-section of young careerists."[10] The *Washington Star* was similarly enthusiastic about the transformation. Its real estate and urban affairs commentator, Robert J. Lewis, joined the chorus of praise for the completed Capitol Park. Lewis found qualities that he also identified in the restoration areas in the early 1960s, especially "a human-scale," and even described the Town House section of the development as a "contemporary-style Georgetown."[11]

The national architecture press echoed the positive reception of Capitol Park in Washington, and the designers of the project received peer recognition from the AIA. The *Architectural Forum*'s editorial support for a vision of the Southwest project that attracted well-to-do white-collar workers was long-standing. The finished product, at least as it appeared in the Capitol Park development, seemingly justified this support, and in 1963 they described Southwest as the "finest urban renewal effort in the country."[12] The *Forum* judged the project to be a success in architectural, economic, and social terms and "one of the most unlikely and most helpful stories in Washington's history."[13]

Success in the architecture press was explicitly measured by reference to new forms. But it was clear from much of the commentary that new forms in this "new town in the city" were a proxy for new people, the real aim of the urban renewal project. The destruction of the old forms was, therefore, a destruction of established social connections and ultimately of memories just as it was the removal of substandard housing. For midcentury urban experts that destruction was of course the premise for effective transformation and the kind of successful new development that the journals and the mainstream press hailed in the early 1960s. The absence of cadastral constraints inherited from the past in the Southwest renewal area and the complete clearance of dwellings based on outmoded conceptions of lifestyle and transportation afforded the opportunity to plan and build along rational, modern lines. What Louis Justement called the "dead hand of the past" in 1946 was, in the view of many postwar planners, the primary impediment to improved living conditions.[14]

But the prosperous population that the project aimed to attract was not only interested in modern architecture and carefully landscaped open space. Southwest's proximity to key employment opportunities was vital to its success. Being in the city was ultimately more important than being a new town. In Southwest Washington, as the ads noted, one would enjoy the benefits of being situated at the heart of "this world center." It is located, they noted, "within walking distance to the federal building complex, the United States Capitol" as well as "shops and theatre."[15] To underline the cachet of the locality, real estate advertisements naturally pointed to the social cachet of its new inhabitants: "Capitol Park is already the residence of some of the nation's most important personalities in government, diplomatic, professional and business circles."[16] One source claimed that twenty congressmen resided there by 1963, and in 1966 Vice President Hubert Humphrey and his wife also moved to the area.[17]

Arriving at this conception of the ideal inhabitant for Southwest— ambitious, well educated, well connected, and at least reasonably well off—was, nevertheless, a circuitous and controversial process. In the late 1940s the *Washington Post* premised its support for a large-scale urban renewal project on the idea that the current residents of Southwest, including the poor, would be housed in the redeveloped area. Still fresh in the memory were the controversies that had accompanied some of the well-meaning activities of Washington's Alley Dwelling Authority in the 1930s and the rancor produced by attempts to relocate black residents in Foggy Bottom and the city's West End. By the early 1950s, however, as the overcrowding of the previous decades eased and whites began to leave the city for its surrounding suburbs in greater numbers, sentiment shifted toward a more business-oriented conception of what urban renewal should achieve. With this shift, the assumption that housing justice and rehousing of former inhabitants would be a central plank of the urban renewal process began to wane.[18]

Maintaining low costs and providing low-income housing did not necessarily fit well with the ambition to create a national showcase for new ideas in urban redevelopment. For the Southwest project to succeed in real estate and publicity terms, proponents of the scheme believed that it would have to possess a striking new architectural image. A more conventional format and architectural language would almost certainly have been cheaper to create. But for proponents much more was at stake than the housing options of the existing inhabitants of Southwest. The project also had to act as a model for how to remake a city, to preserve the prestige of the central area as well as the viability of its commercial property and businesses. Preserving a community and its neighborhood in other words might imply the destruction of significant quantities of capital. Historians have mostly agreed that the key event in coalescing opinion behind a bolder urban renewal scheme came in 1952, when the District of Columbia Redevelopment Land Agency (RLA) presented Louis Justement and Chloethiel Woodard Smith's superblock-planned, modernist-designed, and highway-oriented development scheme for the area. It was a visually compelling document that argued for large-scale action and for completely erasing and rethinking the conventional pattern of urban development in Washington.[19]

Two years later, a landmark Supreme Court case based on the grievance of a business owner in the Southwest redevelopment area, *Berman v. Parker*, further strengthened the argument for undertaking a project like the one imagined by Justement and Smith. In his 1954 judgment, Justice William O. Douglas asserted that "it is within the power of the legislature to determine that the community should be beautiful as well as healthy, spacious as well as clean." Widely quoted by redevelopment advocates both locally and nationally in following years, the judgment underpinned the legality of federal funding for urban renewal and the use of eminent domain powers to do more than was necessary to rid cities of the nuisances and "disbenefits" of slum housing. The judgment implied that governments could use condemnation powers and financing tools to actively improve the environment in the interests of citizens.[20]

In the years that followed preservationists also cited the *Berman v. Parker* decision to justify the expansion of historic preservation powers. Legal scholar Carol Rose has noted that this has sometimes been regarded as a great irony.[21] But when Southwest is examined alongside the incipient restoration movement in Washington's intown areas, it becomes clearer that large-scale urban renewal and piecemeal neighborhood restoration shared more than has usually been acknowledged. As architectural historian Richard Longstreth has noted, Southwest was developed according to "a new paradigm, one that would make the urban core a location of choice."[22] But by the time middle-class and well-to-do Washingtonians began making the choice to move to Southwest, other intown neighborhoods were already beginning the process of "upscaling." Georgetown was already an established "location of choice," and the Capitol Hill and Foggy Bottom restoration societies were promoting the opportunities to enjoy something similar in those neighborhoods. Even more than in Georgetown those neighborhoods offered very close proximity to the most desirable employment and recreational opportunities in the city. The new Southwest was promoted as a place with a high level of physical amenity in an environment that was urban in its densities and mix of uses and convenient to key places of employment. The restoration neighborhoods made similar claims in their house and garden tours. A key difference between Southwest and the flourishing restoration neighborhoods in the early 1960s, however, was the rate and visibility of change. For this reason Southwest attracted a chorus of criticism based in the growing civil rights discourse, while the restoration neighborhoods slowly evolved and largely evaded public criticism until much later in the decade.

DETRACTORS AND CRITIQUE

A growing body of commentary in the early 1960s began to undermine the federal urban renewal program's procedures, especially the slum-clearance approach, its products, which were built at a project scale, broadly modernist, and distinctly contrasting with existing urban patterns, as well as the wider set of claims about its social and economic efficacy. Direct morphological and typological criticism of projects was one part of this. The architectural and urban critic and community activist Jane Jacobs rose to national prominence with her influential 1961 critique of urban redevelopment, *The Death and Life of Great American Cities*. The book took aim at modernist urbanism and in particular Le Corbusier's influential promotion of what Jacobs described as "repetitive ranks of towers in a park."[23] She suggested, for example, that, among other things, tall residential buildings situated in superblocks and surrounded by expansive undifferentiated open space was a killer of the traditional functions of the street and sidewalk.

It was quite clear that at Capitol Park Chloethiel Smith and Dan Kiley revised the most unimaginative "tower in the park" approach. Writing in the *New Republic* Wolf von Eckardt acknowledged their more subtle approach to the overall layout of the project, overt recognition of the ramifying national critique of urban renewal in the 1960s. He wrote that in contrast to the "vast, useless and dull" spaces that have resulted from orthodox modernist, high-rise residential planning, at Capitol Park the "intimate feeling of neighborhood" was enhanced by its open spaces. This was due, he argued, to the fact that the spaces between high-rise buildings "are filled with town houses and the grounds are designed and landscaped so that people can and do use them."[24] This is a clear reference to Jane Jacobs's critique.

Nevertheless, for Jacobs and sociologist Herbert Gans, the two most prominent critics of slum clearance and urban redevelopment in the period, the problems could not be resolved so easily. More than just the formal emphasis on the individual slab block and its apron of grass, Jacobs saw the problems with superblock redevelopment as stemming from the hostility of planners to the conventional street, which contributed immeasurably, Jacobs believed, to the safety, functionality, and gregariousness of big cities. Gans and Jacobs both pointed to the complex social ecology that existed in places like Boston's contiguous North End and West End neighborhoods or for that matter Washington's Southwest. They emphasized that government officials and middle-class professionals in architecture and planning were generally incapable of detecting the richness of community association and cultural patterning that existed within such ethnic enclaves or in all-black neighborhoods. Jacobs and Gans argued that where proponents of dramatic transformation saw only squalor, chaos, and substandard dwellings, there was in fact an urban order, an economy, and a distinct set of cultural values. Jacobs's book became a bible for urban activists, and ultimately urban planners of many varieties in later years, and was certainly a touchstone for later critics of Southwest.[25]

Others, coming from very different political perspectives, also chimed into the debate. The young, conservative economist Martin Anderson, who was a fellow at the Harvard-MIT Joint Centre for Urban Studies in the early 1960s, questioned whether the claims of urban renewal promoters were really valid. In his dissertation, which was published as *The Federal Bulldozer* in 1964, Anderson argued that public investment was not stimulating the private economic activity that proponents of the urban renewal program claimed would ensue. In light of this lack of verifiable success, he argued, how could the state justify the broad swathe of destruction demanded by bulldozer renewal projects?[26]

The inhabitants of Southwest, of course, did not need to wait for nationally prominent critics to articulate such problems. Many perceived the dangers and possible injustices in project-scale urban renewal for themselves. Almost a decade before realtors Shannon & Luchs produced their glossy pitch for prospective inhabitants for the Capitol Park development, the Southwest Civic Association (the black residents' association) decried the lack of consideration given to poor blacks in the area. In a 1952 newspaper article one editorialist predicted that the Southwest urban renewal project would be oriented toward white, middle-class suburbanites who would be enticed by "attractive houses and lavish apartments close to government jobs."[27]

The D.C. RLA's rules strictly mandated that housing developments within Southwest could not discriminate on the grounds of race, and Capitol Park was one of the first, new housing developments in Washington in the period that was, technically speaking, integrated. However, as it turned out, the cost of renting rooms made certain that virtually none of the former inhabitants of that section of Southwest would return to their old area, at least in the short or medium term, and the great majority of new inhabitants were white. As the historian of urban renewal Francesca Ammon has noted, rents in the old Southwest were roughly half the D.C. average in 1950, whereas in the new Southwest of 1970, they were nearly double the average. Despite the prevalence of middle-income African Americans in Washington by comparison with most other cities, the correspondence between race and income level was, of course, very strong across the period.[28]

The young minister and civil rights leader Walter Fauntroy, later D.C.'s nonvoting delegate to the U.S. Congress, seized on this clear pattern of deliberate social restructuring in urban space to condemn Southwest. A range of different forces in Washington echoed Fauntroy's complaints that it was a deliberate dispersal of African Americans and an improper use of federal money and government authority. Congressional conservatives, who were opposed to the growth in federal expenditures on the urban renewal program and perhaps less concerned with the welfare of the inhabitants as such, nevertheless used arguments about social injustice to limit urban renewal spending.[29] Churches also raised objections. In 1961 the Catholic Church highlighted the obvious social injustices involved in such sweeping use of eminent domain powers. They were also concerned about the nature of what was built in the place of the old Southwest row houses. The preponderance of efficiencies in Capitol Park and the other new developments in the area, they argued, militated "against proper family life."[30]

Citizens' associations and preservation groups in other intown neighborhoods in Washington were likewise insistent in their descriptions of the troubles caused by Southwest. The new Southwest was physically proximate to, but culturally remote and morphologically other from, the rest of the intown landscape in the 1960s and 1970s. Over time Southwest became shorthand among citizen groups and columnists for misguided urban strategy. The Capitol Hill Citizens' Association described Southwest as a "catastrophe" in 1966. In the Adams Morgan neighborhood a planned bulldozer-renewal project stalled and was then rejected as community opposition mounted. Activists cited Southwest as a failed precedent for this form of redevelopment. Community-driven urban renewal in Shaw, under the aegis of the Model Inner City Community Organization, based its whole philosophy around avoiding the fate of Southwest.[31]

The mixture of local outrage and persistent national criticism of urban renewal ensured that Southwest would long evoke failure and loss. Pictorial depictions of the old area prior to demolition or in the midst of it tend to amplify that sense of loss. The Washington artist and illustrator Garnet W. Jex documented the urban-renewal process in an elegiac slide show preserved by the Historical Society of Washington, D.C. It mixes deep regret at the waste and destruction of the clearance project with a kind of aestheticization of the evanescence of transition. As with many journalistic accounts of places lost to urban renewal in the postwar years, Jex's document was a picturesque evocation of the rough and tumble character of the incumbent community—one that time and the rest of the city had largely forgotten. The slideshow and its commentary seemed to acknowledge the inevitability of change. But the redemptive possibility that underpinned modernist redevelopment ideology was completely absent from Jex's depiction.[32]

Within the space of less than a decade Capitol Park and the wider Southwest went from being a widely hailed success story to an unambiguous symbol of planning failure and social injustice. The fall from grace was rapid, but the negative impressions proved persistent. Genuine outrage at the assumptions that informed the project as well as conventional dismissals of modernist hubris and inhumanity persisted into the final years of the twentieth century. One journalist asserted as late as 1998 that the project was widely viewed "as a massive dreadful mistake."[33] While arguably still accurate at that time, it was a perception that would soon change.

RENEWING URBAN RENEWAL

In recent years the long-standing tendency to depict the Southwest urban renewal project as a dreadful mistake has been challenged by more careful consideration of its qualities and its long-term evolution. Scholars have argued that the project proved to be successful on its own terms and became the fulcrum of a stable, well-organized community. While its flaws are well recognized, its architectural and environmental qualities have become more evident to people as time has passed. Moreover, the promise of decent quality, racially integrated housing in Washington has, over the longer term, been realized to some extent in Southwest. The fact that the demolition of so many houses in the Southwest urban renewal area destroyed the physical locus of the existing community has not, of course, changed. Nor has the fact that blacks bore a disproportionate share of the disruption and dislocation associated with the project. What is clear, however, is that by the year 2000, although African Americans in Washington, D.C., continued to experience significant housing disadvantage, Southwest was not a major contributor to that disadvantage.[34]

In 1950 Southwest was one-third white and two-thirds black. By 1970 the urban renewal project had reversed those proportions, the changing racial mix mirroring the increase in rents. In the year 2000, however, it was once again a majority black area. Indeed the racial mix for the area as a whole had returned to the pre–urban renewal or 1950 levels.[35] A 1998 Urban Land Institute (ULI) report found that the "Southwest community enjoys a stability that results in part from being one of the most economically and racially integrated neighborhoods in the nation's capital."[36] While significant income and racial segregation continued to characterize the area internally, taken as a whole Southwest had become representative of the citywide population, a rare characteristic in Washington's intown neighborhoods. In contrast, in areas that had been redeveloped piecemeal, through restoration and infill development, the process of gentrification went from strength to strength. With a couple of notable exceptions, the populations of those areas skewed white. From the late 1990s onward the prospects of creating racially balanced and class-mixed communities seemed fairly remote in much of intown Washington.[37]

Despite Southwest's obvious stability and its desirable social mix, in the final years of the twentieth century many community members and property owners arrived at the view that the area needed investment and physical upgrading. In 1998 the impending departure of the biggest tenant in the Southwest Town Centre, the Environmental Protection Agency, heightened anxieties that the already meager commercial offerings in the area would be further diminished, robbing the area of amenity and initiating a blighting process. It was in this context that the Southwest Neighborhood Assembly (SWNA), the area's main neighborhood organization, invited the ULI to develop a strategy for renewing the urban renewal area. At the time the SWNA's president was Marc A. Weiss, an urban development specialist and scholarly expert on the urban renewal process and its history. Weiss initiated the involvement of the ULI, and the project ultimately involved thirty cosponsors who provided financial and in-kind support.[38]

When the ULI delivered its report in 1998, it focused attention on potential improvements to the Southwest Waterfront and the Town Centre. But the report also set out some broad strategic goals relevant to the area as a whole. Two of these had a direct bearing on the preservation battle that transpired at the site formerly known as Capitol Park in 2002 and 2003. The report suggested strengthening the identity of the area by highlighting and interpreting Southwest's history and heritage. They also suggested that there was scope for increasing the density of housing in a number of areas.[39]

In 2001 the Southwest neighborhood's History Taskforce, led by neighborhood activist Margaret Feldman, engaged the DC Heritage Tourism Alliance, who assisted the neighborhood in producing a heritage trail, River Farms to Urban Towers.[40] The trail documented key people, places, and historical changes that had shaped the area. In the panels that recounted the postwar history of Southwest, the text balanced regret at the loss of the old Southwest community with an enthusiastic interpretation of the significance of new developments, describing the urban renewal project as "a showcase of 20th Century architecture and planning."[41] Specific residential communities within Southwest had celebrated anniversaries of the new Southwest going back to the late 1980s recognizing the importance of its development. But the River Farms to Urban Towers heritage trail was a much more thorough assessment and interpretation of the area, and the first time that the wider cultural meaning of the new Southwest had been presented in a historical light. Its narration in this way underlined its wider significance to the city and the meaningful legacy embodied in its physical forms.

The contents of the heritage trail highlighted Southwest's modern architecture, including, in particular, the work of Chloethiel Smith. It also pointed to the historical significance of the wider urbanistic goals of what was attempted in Southwest in the 1950s and 1960s. But by the time the heritage trail came to fruition in 2004, providing this public recognition, redevelopment and intensification of part of the Capitol Park development was already underway. That redevelopment plan threatened to undermine some of Southwest's most distinguished environmental and design characteristics.

Critics of North American postwar housing developments such as Capitol Park have identified two main flaws in the performance of such developments over the longer term. These are poor energy efficiency and poor proximity and connectivity with transport and other urban amenities. Functional zoning in redeveloped areas like Southwest and their park-like settings diminished the urbanity of the surrounding environment. Recent research has argued that many of them can and should incorporate greater residential density as a way of addressing this weakness. The 1998 ULI report recommended that the Southwest urban renewal area overall could support, and would be improved by, some degree of intensification in land use.[42]

The owner of Capitol Park identified both problems, believing that the site should be retrofitted for greater building performance and redeveloped to accommodate new housing units. The attempt to address both of these things through a major program of renewal led directly to the conflict that developed between the property owner and preservationists. In the 1970s, the Capitol Park complex was divided into five sections. The section developed first, and that garnered most of the attention and plaudits when it opened, was renamed Potomac Place. In 2001 Monument Realty acquired Potomac Place. Their intention was to rehabilitate Chloethiel Smith's original slab apartment building, construct two new apartment buildings in the space between the main block and the town houses, and then sell the apartments as condominiums. The upgrade of the old building would involve significant investment in new building systems (especially heating, venting, and air-conditioning) and the replacement of all doors and windows. The overall thrust of the regeneration proposal for Capitol Park was consistent with current ideas about the desirability of improving the environmental and economic sustainability of such developments. Historic preservation as such, however, especially of landscape elements in the development, was simply not part of the plan.[43]

LANDSCAPE PRESERVATION VERSUS
ARCHITECTURAL INTENSIFICATION: A RACE

In December 2002 and January 2003 Monument successfully applied for site clearance and building permits. Less than two weeks later the DC

Preservation League (DCPL) submitted an application to the Historic Preservation Office to have the Potomac Place Apartments, including its associated open space, designated as a historic landmark. It included and highlighted the work of Dan Kiley, including the pavilion structure and the in situ artwork that it housed, a significant polychrome glass mosaic mural of a tree by the artist Leo Leonni. The original National Register of Historic Places nomination form, prepared by local Advisory Neighborhood Commissioner (ANC 2D) Richard B. Westbrook, was in fact dated December 9, 2002, which was prior to the date on which Monument lodged their permit applications. The property owner and preservation forces were evidently in a race at the end of 2002.[44]

While Monument won the race, in that they were awarded their permits, it would nevertheless prove to be a costly contest. After the historic landmark application was lodged, the Department of Consumer and Regulatory Affairs (DCRA) issued a stop work order. At this point DCRA also informed Monument that their permits did not include raze permits for the pavilion structure on the site (Map 13). In April 2003 the HPRB endorsed the historic landmark nomination. The approved nomination specified the park (site), pavilion (structure), and reflecting pool (object) as contributing historical resources.[45]

At the end of April 2003, the regeneration of the property arrived at an impasse. The site had a landmark listing that covered the best-known aspects of the Capitol Park development including the original apartment building by Smith and the defining elements of Kiley's landscape design— pavilion, patio, reflecting pool. On the other side of the ledger, the property owner possessed development permits that would allow them to proceed with work on the site, including on much of the area covered by Kiley's landscape design between the main apartment building and the town houses. The owners could not, however, raze the pavilion as they did not possess appropriate permits in relation to that structure. The implication of all this was that the developers could proceed with their project. But because the landmark registration included the pavilion, they would have to retain it and redesign their development to work around it. This denied them space for their project and, therefore, affected its feasibility as a whole. At the same time the pavilion and the landscape setting would basically be rendered worthless by the proposed development. The Mayor's Agent for historic preservation highlighted this contradiction in his deliberations on the matter.[46]

At this juncture the economic objectives of the proposal were compromised by the landmark listing, and the preservation objectives of the listing were undermined by a perfectly legal set of demolition and development permits. The situation seemed to be headed toward an unsatisfying compromise and a poor outcome for everyone involved.

The landmark listing and the impasse it caused did not divert Monument Realty. They remained committed to their original redevelopment

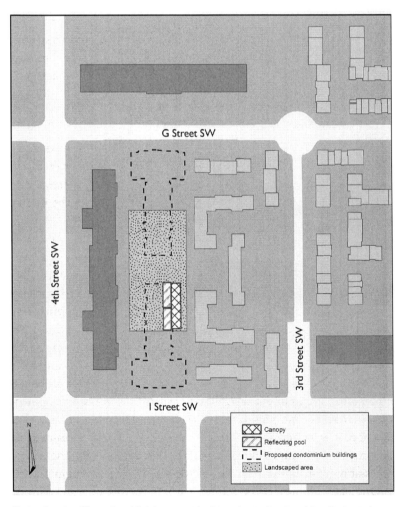

Map 13. Site plan of former Capitol Park Apartments, Southwest, showing locations of the reflecting pool, canopy, and new development proposed in 2002. Created by and copyright Matthew B. Gilmore.

proposal, and in May they applied for a raze permit for the pavilion so they could proceed as originally planned. The DCPL and Committee of 100 on the Federal City, however, opposed the application. Various legal maneuverings ensued related to both substantial and procedural issues. At this point the DC Historic Preservation Office intervened, initiating negotiations among the parties to try to find a more satisfactory resolution to the issue. On October 10, all parties arrived at a negotiated agreement that would permit Monument to demolish the pavilion as long as they agreed to move the glass mosaic mural that sat within the pavilion. Importantly they were also required to put $500,000 in escrow to support historic preservation in Washington, D.C., of which a certain amount was to be used to interpret Capitol Park and to promote the understanding of modernism in Washington.[47]

PRESERVING MODERNISM

Given that Capitol Park was a development that sought to usher in an urban future that did not come to pass, or did so in a very limited way, how should we understand its legacy? What has been protected? And what did the dispute and subsequent settlement mean for the intown environment and the identity of the city?

Capitol Park was undoubtedly an influential model within the overall pattern of Southwest urban renewal, but the Southwest renewal pattern was rejected as inappropriate everywhere else in the city. It was hailed in the architecture and planning literature but reviled by most neighborhood groups in Washington and subsequently abandoned as an approach by governments. It created strong communities, as promised, among the mostly prosperous group who moved there but depended upon the disruption and dispersal of the incumbent community of African Americans of modest means. It was identified as a key exemplar of successful modernist urban redevelopment but was subject to further redevelopment before it could be meaningfully protected. Its legacy, as one historian has described it, is "mixed," to say the least. But, as the HPRB's decision to list the property as a landmark suggests, its equivocal reputation should not necessarily exclude it from consideration as a historically significant place.[48]

Originally the idea of preserving parts of Southwest emerged just as many other preservation campaigns in Washington had. Residents, wary of unwanted change, looked to preservation as the best means for preventing it. Already in the mid-1990s some residents in the Southwest urban renewal area had entertained the idea of pursuing a historic district designation for their area. One architectural historian at the time argued that, on the face of it, those residents had a very good case. Southwest was innovative at a metropolitan level, highly regarded professionally, and relatively successful compared to other projects of its type nationally. But in the 1990s, considering the historical value of such places was uncommon. In 1991 the city's preservation office undertook a historic resources survey of the area that did not consider the urban renewal development, and only looked at the very small number of places in the area that had survived from before 1950.[49]

The modernist conception of the new Southwest at all levels almost automatically disqualified it from sympathetic appraisal and preservation consideration in the 1990s. One of the reasons Southwest is described as modernist is its formal innovation at the level of spatial organization—the disposition of dwellings, open space, and streets. Yet, as architectural historian Richard Longstreth observed in the 1990s, people were generally unable to perceive this new underlying environmental order because there is no obvious vantage point from which to perceive it. The sense of spatial enclosure that defined the nineteenth-century streetscape was completely absent. As a consequence, people—especially nonresidents—just could not "see" the spatial logic of Southwest and, therefore, did not value it. Planners, critics, and neighborhood preservationists continued to dismiss the Southwest approach to the city as wrongheaded just as they had in the 1970s and 1980s.[50]

The wheel has now turned. Far from preventing Capitol Park's recognition, modernist credentials are now considered an asset by many preservation specialists. This shift in perspective registered at several levels in recent years and infused local perception and evaluations of Southwest. Driven by new advocacy groups and organizations such as Docomomo (*Documentation and Conservation of the Modern Movement*) and the Twentieth Century Society, the recognition and preservation of modernist architecture quickly gathered strength in the final years of the twentieth century and has become a marked focus of recent preservation activity and scholarly output around the world.[51]

However, the status of designed landscapes that were often integral to the original conception of places such as Southwest have often not fared as well as the buildings to which they relate. While vital to the overall de-sign, the more ephemeral quality of landscape design has made mean-ingful preservation difficult to achieve. Yet if buildings are protected and the accompanying landscape destroyed or radically transformed, not only is the wider cultural significance of the whole place undermined, the building itself is often devalued as valuable aspects and prospects are lost as a consequence. While scholars and practitioners already recognized this danger by the turn of the century, asset owners have not been as sympathetic. The lower name recognition for key landscape architects such as Dan Kiley, in comparison with leading twentieth-century archi-tects, has also meant that wider public support has been more difficult to build for designed landscapes.[52]

While work by famous modernist architects has not always been easy to preserve, name recognition has driven a number of successful cases and high-profile campaigns. In Detroit, Mies van der Rohe's Lafayette Park, an urban renewal, private housing project developed according to similar community-design principles as Capitol Park, has been listed and entered on the National Register of Historic Places. Underlining the focus on architectural pedigree, the Lafayette Park housing is the centerpiece of a wider historic district called the Mies van der Rohe Residential Dis-trict. In the UK, threats to the Robin Hood Gardens housing estate by the celebrated late modern architects Alison and Peter Smithson mobilized a chorus of support from some of the best-known architects globally. In this case, however, the estate's reputation as a social and environmen-tal failure trumped architectural pedigree.[53] English Heritage chair Sandy Bruce-Lockhart told journalists in the wake of the controversy that Robin Hood Gardens "fails as a place for humans to live."[54]

Neither Chloethiel Woodard Smith nor Dan Kiley enjoy a reputation comparable to that of Mies van der Rohe or, for that matter, the Smith-sons. Nevertheless, the Capitol Park landmark nomination placed great emphasis on the reputation of the Capitol Park design and its designers. Prizes and public recognition were documented, sympathetic sobriquets from media coverage compiled and quoted, and the influence and associ-ations with the gods and heroes of twentieth-century architecture included to add weight to the nomination: Frank Lloyd Wright, Le Corbusier, Louis Kahn, and Walter Gropius all receive at least one mention in the nomination.[55]

As important as that design pedigree is, nobody who reflects seriously on the period can avoid the question of Southwest's social legacy. For some the urban renewal project was an assault on the city, and in particular on a poor but functioning black community, and that's what it will always be remembered as. That Southwest could be a politically potent symbol of universal, progressive urban redevelopment and then became shorthand for unjust and heavy-handed urban policy in the space of just a few years is something of an irony. It is a story that is nevertheless familiar in the history of modernism. Ambivalence is part of the heritage of modernist urbanism, which makes questions about what to keep and why especially fraught.

But the compromised preservation effort at Capitol Park is not only another case of the ambivalence generated by modernism. The agreement arrived at between the DCPL and the owners of Potomac Place became a catalyst for reimagining the scope of what the past looks like in Washington and, potentially at least, for rethinking the identity of the city. The funds that Monument Realty had to put in escrow to meet the terms of the settlement with DCPL as compensation for the destruction of the pavilion structure at Capitol Park funded a study of Washington modernism by the preservation consultants Robinson & Associates Inc. The study then informed a two-day symposium in January 2006, "DC Modern," organized by the DCPL and also funded by the Potomac Place settlement. The Robinson & Associates study was also the basis of a brochure highlighting modernist architecture and landscape design in D.C. (Figure 28). This and the symposium were both intended to raise the profile of modernism and to alert the development industry to the presence and significance of such work in Washington.

CONCLUSION

The means employed to renew central area real estate, improve housing, and drive urban investment in Washington, D.C., in the period 1965–2000 were based very firmly in the existing physical order of the city. For most of the city, instead of slum clearance there was stricter code enforcement. Instead of a focus on state intervention in the urban real estate market to stimulate construction of new dwellings, there was private market-led restoration. Instead of comprehensive, strategic planning and renewal there was statutory controls and uneven urban redevelopment.

Figure 28. Cover of the *Modernism in Washington* brochure, 2009. Produced by District of Columbia Office of Planning, based on a study by Robertson & Associates.

And instead of highway building for an auto-oriented future there was the Metro to underpin pedestrian viability. In other words, the three key projects of urban renewal—housing, roads, and slum demolition—were all stunted and much less implemented than advocates anticipated at midcentury. Citizen activism became as influential to the process, if not more so, than expert opinion. Private capital and small-scale investment was as significant as government and big developers (though obviously not for the development of the Metro). Importantly for this study, historic area preservation would be a more important shaper of urban form than large-scale clearance.

The preservation listing of Capitol Park, while compromised by the untimely landmark application and the resolution that followed, was in fact an assertion that the city should embrace certain forms and architectural gestures that cannot be assimilated to the "identifying legibility of Washington's inner town-house neighborhoods."[56] That is, the landmarking of parts of the renewal area proclaims that other visions and versions of what the city could be, visions such as that realized at Capitol Park, do in fact have a future. It suggests that the valorized nineteenth-century cityscape—valorized in terms of capital accumulation and in terms of cultural evaluation—should not be naturalized as the city's past, reified as its true identity, and promoted as the inevitable pattern for the future. The landmarking effort suggests, quite simply, that Washingtonians should not be satisfied to destroy the urban renewal landscape, despite its obvious defects and difficult history.

Preservation, Profits, and Loss

Washington, D.C., today is a city that in many ways was created by its historic preservation movement. The scope of the preservation process relative to the magnitude of the city was unparalleled elsewhere in North America. From the 1920s onward, Washington, D.C.'s neighborhood preservation groups set about renewing and preserving a cityscape that had just begun to mellow into its maturity. Successive waves of technological, social, and economic change initiated significant shifts in property value and local amenity across the period covered by this book. The preservation movement responded to those shifts very effectively. Beginning in Georgetown in the 1920s and 1930s its influence spread out across the terrain of the central city in the 1960s, 1970s, and 1980s, gradually influencing decision making across much of the central city. The intowners who engaged in the preservation effort reevaluated and repaired old row houses in aging neighborhoods with mixed reputations and interesting histories. They created organizations dedicated to their project, invested financial and personal resources, and vigorously promoted its cultural value. In doing so, by the year 2000, they had preserved a great swathe of the cityscape that most expert observers in 1950 regarded as obsolete and in need of complete reformation at the levels of housing, transport, and open space. By variously deflecting and resisting dilapidation and devaluation and by rejecting large-scale modernization, urban intensification, commercialization, and monumentalization, they remade their city and created what I have called historic capital.

Historic capital is an identifiable place, created during a clearly defined period. But more importantly it is a resource produced by the reevaluation, physical restoration, and preservation of the city's neighborhoods. This book is an attempt to understand and explain the making of historic capital in both senses. This matters because it tells us a lot about why the District of Columbia is what it is today: beautiful, well planned, convivial, architecturally conservative, as well as increasingly inaccessible to many of the people, especially African Americans and their families, who made it their home during the twentieth century. This inaccessibility or unaffordability is important because at the heart of the preservation story in Washington was the aspiration to protect and promote the idea that one could be at home there, build connections, and experience a sense of continuity. Preservation was not just about saving nice old houses. It was an expression of one's citizenship and connection to the particularity of place. But that sense of civic engagement and that preference were also deeply embedded in private property. The efficacy of housing restoration and historic preservation over the longer term depended in many ways on its success as a mechanism for regenerating the value of privately owned, central-area real estate. That success in turn circumscribed the social aspirations of the movement—continuity, social diversity, and strong civic connections. Over time making and maintaining a home in the central city became more difficult for those who did not own real estate or could not afford to improve the property they did own. While there were unquestionably mechanisms to join the preservation effort and express one's place-based citizenship without owning property, property ownership was very much the premise for the neighborhood preservation and restoration movement in Washington.

The preservationist emphasis on the value of privacy, the familial, and private property was a reaction against both state-sponsored urban transformation and commercial exploitation of urban space by private capital. To protect and promote historic capital, in other words, involved a clear rejection of bulldozer-driven urban renewal and of the federal predilection for architecture and urban design in the grand manner. The battle between residents of the Capitol Hill area and Congress over the proper scope of the federal imprint in the area was the most explicit example of this. The Capitol Hill Restoration Society (CHRS) expended considerable energy protecting local heritage and urban character against the expansion of the congressional footprint and with it Washington's monumental core. Historic capital was also a mode of creating or capturing value that rejected the creative destruction of large-scale private capital. Dupont Circle neighborhood activists quite deliberately resisted the steady northwesterly march of the city's downtown office district in the 1950s and 1960s. The preservation movement in Washington thus asserted the homeliness and intimacy of the intown areas in contrast to what they described as establishment monumentality and commercial banality.

Preservationists justified their endeavors, of course, not only by reference to the bad architecture they could stop or the good buildings they could keep. The remaking of the city using restoration and neighborhood preservation was a social process as much as a physical one. It was about the people and communities who valued those places and involved the creation of new organizations, such as the neighborhood-based restoration societies, and very self-conscious attempts to knit together new political coalitions in the city.

But like all urban transformation projects, there is a story of loss embedded within this account of preservation success and community formation. Historic capital is a kind of wealth produced by identifying and remaking historic places. But just as some of Washington's inhabitants accumulated historic capital, and sometimes even transformed it into financial capital, others were deprived or went without. The proponents of preserving Washington's intown neighborhoods rarely referred to those losses. To be sure, lost buildings and streetscapes were tabulated and documented. They were then frequently evoked to give energy to the preservation movement. The old Southwest, the houses and blocks near the U.S. Capitol, gracious clubs, commercial buildings, grand houses, and, disputed though it was, Rhodes Tavern, all became part of the archive of lost places that justified ongoing, preservationist vigilance.[1]

But the embedded story of human loss in *Historic Capital* is one that is much harder to uncover than the loss of buildings. Its traces are there, in expressions of resistance to the preservation project. But even those barely evoke the affective dimensions of living in the city. With bulldozer renewal there was explicit loss—of home, of neighborhood, and of community. But likewise, in the story of preservation, there is loss, even where buildings and neighborhoods were "saved." The social composition of many of Washington's neighborhoods changed as a result of, or in concert with, efforts to protect them as historic places. As they did people felt a sense of loss and perhaps even felt lost in a neighborhood and a city that had previously been deeply familiar.

In his collection of short stories, *Lost in the City*, Edward P. Jones evokes a city of shared places, familiar objects, and evanescent moods set in the same decades covered by *Historic Capital*. Washington's buildings and streets are not Jones's subject, but they animate and haunt the lives of his characters. Many of those characters possess little or no agency in the formal city-making or city-preserving process and experience their changing environment as a force of nature. Persistent rumors of property acquisition, demolition, and redevelopment in the late 1950s and early 1960s lend a precariousness to the events and lives that are depicted in the first story in the collection, "The Girl Who Raised Pigeons." Referring to the areas near the Jesuit high school, Gonzaga College, on North Capitol Street, Jones writes: "When the colored people and their homes were gone the wall and the tracks remained, and so did the high school, with the same boys being taught by the same priests."[2] The privilege of continuity and its institutions (presumptively white) is thus starkly contrasted with the imposed transience and loss experienced by African Americans. The experience of this contrasting prospect marks the book's characters and gives the city a powerful and quixotic presence in their lives.

A city is almost without exception a powerful presence in the life of its inhabitants. But the capacity to do and say something about it as a citizen or a property owner was an unevenly distributed resource across the period covered in *Historic Capital*. The privilege to say which parts of the city are historically significant and, therefore, worthy of protection and preservation is all the more important for not being the substance of one's basic material well-being. What do we keep? How do we look after places? And how do we explain the meaning and legacy of the places we keep? These were the things that were at stake for people in Washington's intown neighborhoods across the decades examined in this book. This became most explicit in the battle over historic district expansions in the inner Northwest in the late 1970s and early 1980s. These were not just discussions about which building or street was most intact. These were tussles over which social groups in the city could say what was important about the city's past and therefore how it should be in the future.

Scholars, journalists, and activists have explained such social conflict in recent decades by reference to the idea of gentrification. It has become a central explanatory concept employed to interpret class restructuring and the physical changes that have accompanied it. Today in Washington, where many formerly modest and affordable neighborhoods have seen housing costs grow exponentially since about 2000, concerns about gentrification are central to debates about the trajectory of the city. The rapid social change in places such as Shaw, Columbia Heights, and the environs of H Street Northeast have generated lively debate and a sustained critique of the city and its housing system.[3]

The idea of gentrification, however, is deeply contested. Quantitative social scientists have been more skeptical of its impact than journalists or researchers who focus on place perception. Those who see gentrification in terms of capital flows necessarily view the picture differently from those who focus on cultural tastes and the affective bonds of community. Others have pointed to the fuzziness and lack of analytical rigor associated with the concept. One of the more recent and more telling challenges to the standard story of gentrification has pointed out that gentrification affects small areas relative to the overall size and range of American urban environments. They also note that journalists, academics, and other urban elites tend to be front-row spectators or participants in the gentrification process in places where it has had a demonstrable and measurable impact, places such as Boston, New York, San Francisco, and Washington, D.C. Consequently, they have tended to give it undue emphasis, whereas crime, property devaluation, and employment opportunities are of greater interest to disadvantaged and working-class urbanites more widely. This is an important point, and it is true that for all the intown D.C. neighborhoods that have experienced rapid gentrification there are many others in the wider Washington metro area that have experienced persistent disadvantage or relative stability.[4]

What *Historic Capital* highlights, however, is that Washington's older intown neighborhoods did and do enjoy a special place in the life of the city. They are more representative than other areas and so have a greater capacity to stand in for the city as a whole. This is not simply the myopia of journalists and activists who are habitués of the inner city. It is the consequence of a long process of preserving and interpreting such places as representative. So when such places become unaffordable not only to current or former inhabitants, but to large segments of the metropolitan population, it is keenly felt. That representative place becomes distant and excludes the activities and people that once inhabited it with ease.

Of course as many urban pioneers and preservationists have noted over the years, their intention was never to boom the real estate of an area or displace the existing residents. Where it occurred it was mostly unexpected, at least in its scope and dimensions. The effects of their presence, in other words, were distinct from their intent. As one historian of gentrification in New York has noted, the larger changes to the environment and the associated rises in housing costs are, at least in part, "unintended consequences."[5] This is especially true when we are talking about the 1960s and 1970s, as most actors could not or would not have predicted the pattern of upscaling that followed. But follow it did. Indeed, my own evaluation of the preservation story in Washington is not so much that the neighborhood preservationists gentrified the city as such, but they made a city that was ripe for the kind of accelerated appreciation of real estate value that has become so pronounced in recent years.

The connections that exist between historic preservation and gentrification are ultimately to be found in the process of environmental and neighborhood improvement and locational advantage. Areas with distinctive architectural and environmental qualities that are also close to reliable centers of employment are undersupplied in U.S. cities. In a housing system dominated by private property ownership and competitive private financing, the presence of such qualities will almost always guarantee rising housing costs and a filtering up of properties into the hands of those with higher incomes or more wealth at their disposal. But this will happen whether or not those qualities are connected with historically significant places or are derived from other sources of housing amenity or environmental distinctiveness.

The correspondence between desirable locations and the preservation movement is, of course, far from coincidental. Likewise, the cultural taste for historic buildings is unquestionably bound up with class. But as we have seen in this study, shifts in taste and affection for this or that aspect of the past change over time, just as patterns of transportation, work, and consumption change. It is already very evident that the preservation project focused on Washington's intown residential districts and their nineteenth-century row-house fabric has basically expired.

It is too soon to say how the expiration of the restoration trend, as described in *Historic Capital*, is affecting Washington in the present. Certainly in the age of social media, propositions about community have changed. The social aspirations of the urban pioneers and other restorationists of the 1970s in particular now belong distinctly to an earlier period. The fate of historic capital in both senses is, therefore, unclear. Historic capital as a form of wealth may wither under new regimes of cultural evaluation. Likewise, historic capital as a distinct terrain within D.C., valued and understood as the locus for municipal identity and nonfederal urban character, may also slowly dissolve. New social configurations and patterns of development will certainly challenge its distinctiveness. But the historic districts that are perhaps the most powerful legacy of the preservation project in Washington from the 1920s until the present will, at the very least, be a source of ongoing legibility for that terrain.

The real question is how the shifting sense of what is valuable about the past might also reframe questions about what is right for the city's future. Planning and preservation in Washington were dramatically realigned by the ambitious government-led effort to regenerate the value of land via destructive urban renewal in Southwest. At present such bold, if flawed, thinking seems very remote. City leaders are largely content with market-driven, privately controlled modes of urban development. The terrain of *Historic Capital* has made that process seem very straightforward with the amenity afforded by the historic districts inviting ever new waves of real estate and commercial investment back to the center of the city. But it is possible for leaders to treat the current crisis—gentrification—with the same sense of urgency that extensive property devaluation inspired in the postwar decades. In a time of constrained budgets and constrained political autonomy in the District of Columbia, expansive state intervention is highly unlikely. But in 1957, when the urban renewal map was drawn up, the landscapes of dozens of historic districts containing tens of thousands of properties would have been unthinkable.

The way Washingtonians assessed the value and prospects of the intown environment changed very powerfully in the years immediately after that map was drawn. By 1960 hundreds were attending house and garden tours organized by the CHRS, and there was an expanding constituency of housing remodelers and preservation advocates. The rapid shift in thinking about how to regenerate the value of intown areas in the early 1960s was the premise for a fundamental recharting of policy and real estate dynamics in the subsequent decades. In other words, it is possible such a reevaluation could happen again. At present the terrain of gentrified row housing, the borders of intown, continue to expand in the city's Southeast and Northeast quadrants. But as the final chapter of this book demonstrated, other models and ideas of how people can live in the city and other visions of what is valuable about the past are now more salient than ever. Southwest no longer suggests exile from Washington's intown areas, and feature writers and bloggers find it sympathetic in ways that the previous generation did not. Could a reevaluated Southwest be the catalyst for a wider reconsideration of housing dynamics and urban life in Washington? It is possible. But it will be meaningless if this process of reevaluation goes no deeper than shifting what's hot in real estate. The measure of whether the legacy of the urban renewal period has become truly salient in the present will be its capacity to help inhabitants reimagine their conception of home and community and decision makers reorient urban and housing policy in Washington.

Acknowledgments

Much of the research that underpins this book was undertaken as part of a doctoral project in American studies at George Washington University. I should acknowledge in particular Richard Longstreth, Suleiman Osman, Chad Heap, and Chris Klemek for their advice during my time there. Fellow students at GWU, especially Kyle Riismandel, Jeremy Hill, and Sandra Heard, also provided a lively context for discussing ideas about American cities.

I developed parts of the manuscript while working at the University of Melbourne. Many thanks to colleagues in the Faculty of Architecture, Building, and Planning, especially David Nichols, Kim Torney, and Marianna Ristic, who read and commented on sections of the work. I am also grateful to Hannah Lewi, Julie Willis, and Philip Goad for their generous support and encouragement during my time at the University of Melbourne.

My current colleagues at the University of Sydney have likewise provided a stimulating intellectual environment. I am grateful to members of the museums and heritage research group, Steven Brown, Avril Alba, Helena Roberston, Jennifer Barrett, Julia Horne, Vicki Liebowitz, and Sandra Lösckhe. They offered an engaging setting to consider wider ideas about the social meaning of collections and preservation, and I am indebted to them for their very useful feedback on the book's introduction. When I first arrived at the University of Sydney in 2014 I had time to work on the book thanks to light teaching responsibilities, and for this I am grateful to John Redmond and the late Trevor Howells.

I have been assisted by numerous archivists and librarians over many years. I am especially grateful to Laura Berry at the Historical Society of Washington, D.C.'s Kiplinger Research Library and Jennifer King in the Special Collections Research Center at the Estelle and Melvin Gelman Library at George Washington University. I received great assistance and uncovered useful materials at the District of Columbia Preservation League and Special Collections at the University of Maryland library, and I am indebted to the staff in the Washingtoniana section of the Martin Luther King Jr. Memorial Library and the Prints and Photographs Collection of the Library of Congress. Perhaps the most significant archive utilized in this book, the Jessie Stearns Buscher collection, was held privately, and I am extremely grateful to Nancy Metzger for alerting me to this material and to both Nancy and her husband, Norman, for their hospitality and generosity in allowing me to use the materials in their home and borrow items from that collection when needed.

In the course of my research, I spoke in person or on the telephone to many active participants in the affairs of the city. I did not conduct formal interviews or rely on oral sources for the book, but the recollections and advice of this group about research materials and points of possible interest were invaluable. In addition to Nancy Metzger, I am grateful to Dick Wolfe, Charles Roberston, Richard Striner, Tersh Boasberg, and Dorn McGrath.

Matthew Gilmore made thirteen original maps for the book, each of them requiring several iterations. They are not only integral to the story but also provide a vital sense of spatial orientation within that story. Thank you, Matthew.

In addition to the libraries and archives already mentioned, I received assistance from many individuals and organizations with illustrations and permissions. They include Evan Harrington, Abigail Wiebenson, Sam Smith, Don Hawkins, the American Heritage Center at the University of Wyoming, and the National Society of the Colonial Dames of America. I received generous financial support from the Humanities Council of Washington, D.C., for pictures research and from the Society of Architectural Historians to support the making of maps and procurement of images and publication rights.

Pieter Martin at the University of Minnesota Press has been a champion of this project and a patient guide in realizing the finished product.

I am grateful to Anne Carter and Caitlin Newman at the Press for their timely assistance. In the final stages of manuscript preparation Chelsea Barnett provided invaluable research and editorial assistance here in Sydney. Chelsea, I hope I can return the favor when your manuscript is complete. Thank you.

Finally and most important, thanks to my friends and family, especially Honora, Terry, and Clare. Clare, you are my best reader, my favorite historian, and the center of our household.

Notes

INTRODUCTION

1. Sam Smith, *Captive Capital: Colonial Life in Modern Washington* (Bloomington: Indiana University Press, 1974), 3–36.

2. Charles Dickens, *American Notes* (1842; London: Collins Clear Type Press, 1920).

3. Douglas Haskell, "Saying Nothing, Going Nowhere," *Architectural Forum* III, no. 2 (August 1959): 135.

4. Paul Rudolph, "A View of Washington as a Capital—Or What Is Civic Design?," *Architectural Forum* 118, no. 1 (January 1963): 67.

5. Ada Louise Huxtable, "Architecture: The House that HUD Built," *New York Times*, September 22, 1968, 129.

6. Alistair Cooke, "Washington, DC," September 9, 1949, in *Letter from America: 1946–2004* (London: Penguin, 2004), 28.

7. Smith, *Captive Capital*, 3.

8. M. Christine Boyer, *The City of Collective Memory: Its Historical Imagery and Architectural Entertainments* (Cambridge, MA: MIT Press, 1994), 368–72.

9. Smith, *Captive Capital*, 4.

10. Ibid., 8.

11. Constance McLaughlin Green, *The Secret City: A History of Race Relations in the Nation's Capital* (Princeton, NJ: Princeton University Press, 1967).

12. Howard Gillette Jr., *Between Justice and Beauty: Race, Planning and the Failure of Urban Policy in Washington, D.C.* (Philadelphia: University of Pennsylvania Press, 2006).

13. Fredric M. Miller and Howard Gillette Jr., *Washington Seen: A Photographic History, 1875–1965* (Baltimore: Johns Hopkins University Press, 1995), 51–75.

14. Smith, *Captive Capital*, 37.

15. There are two books that have done this before. But both deal with the late nineteenth and early twentieth centuries before the preservation movement

matured into a major force in its own right. See Michael Holleran, *Boston's "Changeful Times": Origins of Preservation and Planning in America* (Baltimore: Johns Hopkins University Press, 1998); and Randall Mason, *The Once and Future New York: Historic Preservation and the Modern City* (Minneapolis: University of Minnesota Press, 2009).

16. Gillette, *Between Justice and Beauty*; Kate Masur, *An Example for All the Land: Emancipation and the Struggle over Equality in Washington, D.C.* (Chapel Hill: University of North Carolina Press, 2010).

17. Elaine Harwood and Alan Powers, eds., *The Heroic Period of Conservation*, Twentieth Century Architecture 7 (London: Twentieth Century Society, 2004).

18. William Holford, "In Search of a New Monumentality: A Symposium by Gregor Paulson, Henry-Russell Hitchcock, William Holford, Sigfried Giedion, Walter Gropius, Lucio Costa and Alfred Roth," *Architectural Review*, September 1948, 125.

19. John Brinckerhoff Jackson, *The Necessity for Ruins and Other Topics* (Amherst: University of Massachusetts Press, 1980), 89.

20. John Ruskin, *The Seven Lamps of Architecture* (1849; London: Century Books, 1988), 179.

21. Peter Blake, "Washington, D.C.," *Architecture Forum* 118, no. 1 (January 1963).

22. Lauren Berlant, *The Queen of America Goes to Washington City: Essays on Sex and Citizenship* (Durham, NC: Duke University Press, 1997), 29.

23. As quoted in Frederick Gutheim and Antoinette J. Lee, *Worthy of the Nation: Washington, DC, from L'Enfant to the National Capital Planning Commission*, 2nd ed. (Baltimore: Johns Hopkins University Press, 2006), 6.

24. Blake, "Washington, D.C.," 36.

25. Sarah Luria, *Capital Speculations: Writing and Building Washington, D.C.* (Lebanon, NH: University Press of New England, 2006).

26. On the theme of reflexive citizen opposition to modern architecture, see Bernard Huet, "L'architecture contre la ville," *AMC* 14 (1986): 10–13.

27. On the impact of Jim Crow on African American property, see N. D. B. Connolly, *A World More Concrete: Real Estate and the Remaking of Jim Crow South Florida* (Chicago: University of Chicago Press, 2014); Robert O. Self, *American Babylon: Race, Power and the Struggle for the Postwar City in California* (Princeton, NJ: Princeton University Press, 2003); and Beryl Satter, *Family Properties: Race, Real Estate, and the Exploitation of Black Urban America* (New York: Metropolitan Books, 2009); on Douglass and property, see Luria, *Capital Speculations*, 71–98.

28. Sharon Zukin, *Loft Living: Culture and Capital in Urban Change* (New Brunswick, NJ: Rutgers University Press, 1982); Neil Smith and Peter Williams, eds., *Gentrification of the City* (Boston: Allen & Unwin, 1986).

29. George Derek Musgrove, "History in a Time of Gentrification," *Journal of Urban History* 40, no. 6 (2014): 1155–60.

30. Sharon Zukin, "Why Neo-Cons Loved Communitarian Urbanist Jane Jacobs," *Architectural Review*, October 26, 2011, http://www.architectural-review.com/view/reviews/reputations/-jane-jacobs-1916–2006/8621634.article.

1. VALUE

1. See, for example, Jon A. Peterson, *The Birth of City Planning in the United States, 1840–1917* (Baltimore: Johns Hopkins University Press, 2003), 6; William H. Wilson, *The City Beautiful Movement* (Baltimore: Johns Hopkins University Press, 1989), 68–69; and Mark Gelernter, *A History of American Architecture: Buildings in Their Cultural and Technological Context* (Hanover, NH: University Press of New England, 1999), 204.

2. Mike Wallace, *Mickey Mouse History and Other Essays on American Memory* (Philadelphia: Temple University Press, 1996), 177–246.

3. John Reps, *Monumental Washington: The Planning and Development of the Capitol Center* (Princeton, NJ: Princeton University Press, 1967), 9–10, 26–27; also see Sarah Luria, *Capital Speculations: Writing and Building Washington, D.C.* (Lebanon, NH: University Press of New England, 2006), 3–5.

4. Alan Lessoff, *The Nation and Its City: Politics, "Corruption," and Progress in Washington, D.C., 1861–1902* (Baltimore: Johns Hopkins University Press, 1994), 72–101; William M. Maury, *Alexander "Boss" Shepherd and the Board of Public Works*, GW Washington Studies 3 (Washington DC: George Washington University, 1975); Sarah Pressey Noreen, *Public Street Illumination in Washington, D.C.: An Illustrated History*, GW Washington Studies 2 (Washington, D.C.: George Washington University, 1975).

5. Howard Gillette Jr., *Between Justice and Beauty: Race, Planning, and the Failure of Urban Policy in Washington, D.C.* (Philadelphia: University of Pennsylvania Press, 2006), 138–60; Richard Longstreth, "Brave New World: Southwest Washington and the Promise of Urban Renewal," in *Housing Washington: Two Centuries of Residential Development and Planning in the National Capital Area*, ed. Richard Longstreth (Chicago: Center for American Places, 2010), 255–80.

6. The literature dedicated to these cities is vast. But among the best for understanding the relationship between property and the physical forms and processes alluded to here are the following: Roy Rosenzweig and Elizabeth Blackmar, *The Park and the People: A History of Central Park* (Ithaca, NY: Cornell University Press, 1992); David M. Scobey, *Empire City: The Making and Meaning of the New York City Landscape* (Philadelphia: Temple University Press, 2002); Robert M. Fogelson, *Downtown: Its Rise and Fall, 1880–1950* (New Haven: Yale University Press, 2001); Reyner Banham, *Los Angeles: The Architecture of Four Ecologies* (London: Allen Lane, 1971); Robert O. Self, *American Babylon: Race, Power, and the Struggle for the Postwar City in California* (Princeton, NJ: Princeton University Press, 2003); Antero Pietila, *Not in My Neighborhood: How Bigotry Shaped a Great American City* (Chicago: Ivan R. Dee, 2010).

7. Gillette, *Between Justice and Beauty*, ix–xii.

8. Barclay G. Jones, "Preservation Economics and the District of Columbia: Controlling the Economic Effects of the Various Powers of Government on Preservation Efforts," in *The Washington Preservation Conference Proceedings* (Washington, D.C.: National Trust for Historic Preservation, 1972), 123–36.

9. National Capital Planning Commission (NCPC) and Frederic Gutheim, *Worthy of the Nation: The History of Planning for the National Capital* (Washington, D.C.: Smithsonian Institution Press, 1977), 287–343.

10. Norman Tyler, Ted J. Ligibel, and Ilene R. Tyler, *Historic Preservation: An Introduction to Its History, Principles, and Practice* (New York: W. W. Norton, 2000), 121–26.

11. Graeme Davison and Chris McConville, *A Heritage Handbook* (North Sydney: Allen & Unwin, 1991).

12. Patrick Wright, "Trafficking in History," in *Representing the Nation: A Reader*, ed. David Boswell and Jessica Evans (New York: Routledge, 1999), 125.

13. Mike Wallace, "Preservation Revisited," in *Mickey Mouse History and Other Essays*, 223–46.

14. Vince Michael, "Preserving the Future: Historic Districts in New York and Chicago in the late 20th Century" (PhD diss., University of Illinois, 2007).

15. Max Page and Randall Mason, "Introduction: Rethinking the Roots of the Historic Preservation Movement," in *Giving Preservation a History: Histories of Historic Preservation in the United States*, ed. Max Page and Randall Mason (New York: Routledge, 2004), 3.

16. Charles B. Hosmer's research is contained in two histories of the movement: *Presence of the Past: A History of the Preservation Movement in the United States before Williamsburg* (New York: Putnam, 1965), and *Preservation Comes of Age: From Williamsburg to the National Trust, 1926–1949* (Charlottesville: University Press of Virginia, 1981).

17. Kathryn Schneider Smith, "Georgetown: Washington's Oldest Neighborhood," in *Washington at Home: An Illustrated History of Neighborhoods in the Nation's Capital*, ed. Kathryn Schneider Smith, 2nd ed. (Baltimore: Johns Hopkins University Press, 2010), 27–28.

18. Kathryn Schneider Smith, *Port Town to Urban Neighborhood: The Georgetown Waterfront of Washington, D.C., 1880–1920* (Washington, D.C.: Center for Washington Area Studies of the George Washington University, 1989); Dennis E. Gale, "Restoration in Georgetown, Washington, D.C., 1915–1965" (PhD diss., George Washington University, 1982).

19. Elizabeth Kohl Draper, "Progress Report on the Restoration of Capitol Hill Southeast," *Records of the Columbia Historical Society, Washington, D.C.* 51/52 (1951–52): 134.

20. Donald Canty, "How Washington Is Run: An Ungovernment without Top or Bottom," *Architectural Forum* 118, no. 1 (January 1963): 53.

21. "Capitol Hill Has Its Own Brand of Gentility," *Washington Daily News*, January 5, 1970.

22. "Logan Circle: The Next Georgetown?," *Washington Post*, May 21, 1973.

23. "Real Estate 'Shell Game': Prices of Gutted D.C. Houses Rise Rapidly," *Washington Post*, October 29, 1979.

24. William A. Gordon, "Old Homes on Georgetown Heights," *Records of the Columbia Historical Society, Washington, D.C.* 18 (1915); Gordon, "Recollections of a Boyhood in Georgetown," *Records of the Columbia Historical Society, Washington, D.C.* 20 (1917): 121–40; NCPC and Gutheim, *Worthy of the Nation*, 191–92.

25. Gale, "Restoration in Georgetown," 72.

26. "We Present John Ihlder," National Association of Housing and Redevelopment Officials, Washington, D.C., (1945), 1, quoted in Barbara Gale Howick Fant, "Slum Reclamation and Housing Reform in the Nation's Capital, 1890–1940" (PhD diss., George Washington University, 1982), 148.

27. Fant, "Slum Reclamation and Housing Reform," 147–50; Gale, "Restoration in Georgetown," 71–73.

28. Georgetown Homeowners' Committee, *The Future of Georgetown* (1924), 7, Neighborhood Resources (Georgetown), Kiplinger Research Library, Historical Society of Washington, D.C.; "Right to Regulate Types of Buildings Urged by Sherrill," *Washington Post*, March 21, 1924.

29. Georgetown Homeowners' Committee, *The Future of Georgetown*, 3.

30. On the social and economic motivations of zoning, see Peter Hall, *Cities of Tomorrow: An Intellectual History of Urban Planning and Design since 1880* (Oxford: Blackwell, 1988); Sam Bass Warner Jr., *The Urban Wilderness: A History of the American City* (New York: Harper & Row, 1972), 28; and Michael, "Preserving the Future," 25–29.

31. Georgetown Homeowners' Committee, *The Future of Georgetown*, 4.

32. Ibid., 5 (emphasis added).

33. Michael, "Preserving the Future," 34. Daniel Bluestone has likewise emphasized the concurrent development and overlapping concerns expressed by planning and preservation controls. See Daniel Bluestone, *Buildings, Landscapes, and Memory: Case Studies in Historic Preservation* (New York: W. W. Norton, 2011), 110–13.

34. Mike Wallace, "Preserving the Past: A History of Historic Preservation in the United States," in *Mickey Mouse History and Other Essays*, 181–85.

35. On Ihlder as progressive and city-planning advocate, see Fant, "Slum Reclamation and Housing Reform," 145–78; Jane Jacobs, *The Death and Life of Great American Cities* (New York: Random House, 1961).

36. Gale, "Restoration in Georgetown," 75–76.

37. Fant, "Slum Reclamation and Housing Reform," 153; Gale, "Restoration in Georgetown," 72–78; "'B' Restricted Area Urged for Georgetown," *Washington Post*, April 22, 1924. Ihlder was conscious of parallel efforts in New York and Boston. On the activities of the Fifth Avenue Association, see Max Page, *The Creative Destruction of Manhattan, 1900–1940* (Chicago: University of Chicago Press, 1999). On early zoning efforts in Beacon Hill, see Michael Holleran, *Boston's "Changeful*

Times": Origins of Preservation and Planning in America (Baltimore: Johns Hopkins University Press, 1998), 262–65.

38. Georgetown Homeowners' Committee, *The Future of Georgetown*, 7; Gale, "Restoration in Georgetown," 72.

39. This appears somewhat at odds with the image of Ihlder as a reformer and "houser" who rejected the prevailing economic logic of the private construction industry. However, as Fant notes, this commitment was also mixed with a strong regard for the principles of comprehensive city planning. Fant, "Slum Reclamation and Housing Reform," 148–52; Gale, "Restoration in Georgetown," 77–78; Dupont Circle Citizens' Association, *Dupont Circle 1972* (Washington: Casillas Press, 1972), 12–13. On the "downzoning" of Cleveland Park, see "North Cleveland Park Citizens Have a Secret for Success," *Washington Post*, November 8, 1940.

40. Smith, "Georgetown," 28–30.

41. Louis Justement, *New Cities for Old: City Building in Terms of Space, Time and Money* (New York: McGraw Hill, 1946), 79.

42. For a detailed discussion of CIAM ideas and conferences from the 1920s onwards, see Eric Mumford, *The CIAM Discourse on Urbanism, 1928–1960* (Cambridge, MA: MIT Press, 2000), especially 59–117 regarding the functional city. TEAM X would challenge CIAM orthodoxies in the 1950s, and strict functionalism at the level of the city would gradually fall out of favor. But during and immediately after World War II, the idea of the superblock and the four functions were still a central reform platform advocated by most modernists.

43. Justement, *New Cities for Old*, 148.

44. Daniel Rodgers discusses the great expansion of municipal ownership and management of key urban assets and infrastructure in the period between the 1890s and the 1930s in a range of cities in Great Britain, Germany, and the United States in *Atlantic Crossings: Social Politics in a Progressive Age* (Cambridge, MA: Belknap Press, 1998), 112–208.

45. Justement, *New Cities for Old*, 34.

46. G. E. Kidder Smith, *Sweden Builds* (New York: Albert Bonniers, 1950), 22.

47. Justement does not draw the analogy himself, but the idea of rethinking construction and housing to closely reflect that of automobile manufacturing and consumption was widely discussed at the time. See, for example, Clarence Perry, *Housing for the Machine Age* (New York: Russell Sage Foundation, 1939), 25–40; and Herbert Matter, Charles Eames, and R. Buckminster Fuller, "Prefabricated Housing," *Arts and Architecture*, July 1944, 32–47.

48. Justement, *New Cities for Old*, 80.

49. Ibid., 98.

50. Ibid., 16; Fogelson, *Downtown*, 348.

51. Richard Longstreth, "The Difficult Legacy of Urban Renewal," *CRM: The Journal of Heritage Stewardship* 3, no. 1 (2006), 6–23; Longstreth, "Brave New World", 255; Francesca Rusello Ammon, "Commemoration amid Criticism: The

Mixed Legacy of Urban Renewal in Southwest Washington, D.C.," *Journal of Planning History* 8, no. 3 (2009): 175–220. For a discussion of the contrasting sense of abjection and order in Washington's landscape, see Margaret E. Farrar, "Making the City Beautiful: Aesthetic Reform and the (Dis)placement of Bodies," in *Embodied Utopias: Gender, Social Change, and the Modern Metropolis*, ed. Amy Bingaman, Lise Sanders, and Rebecca Zorach (London: Routledge, 2002), 37–54. On Washington's role as a national showcase, see Howard Gillette Jr., "A National Workshop for Urban Policy: The Metropolitanization of Washington, 1946–1968," *Public Historian* 7, no. 1 (1985): 7–27.

52. The key maps in this group were as follows: U.S. FHA, "District of Columbia, Median Age of Structures by Blocks" (1934), "District of Columbia, Average Rental for Occupied Dwelling by Blocks" (1937), "District of Columbia, Percent of Structures Needing Major Repairs or Unfit for Use" (1934), "Percent of Dwelling Units Occupied by Persons Other than White" (1934), and "District of Columbia, Spread of Colored Population" (1930), all held by Library of Congress, Geography and Map Reading Room. See also Ammon, "Commemoration amid Criticism," 179–81.

53. Longstreth, "Brave New World," 258–61; Ammon, "Commemoration amid Criticism."

54. Peterson, *Birth of City Planning in the United States*, 127–28.

55. Justement, *New Cities for Old*, 152.

56. Chalmers M. Roberts, "Builders Hit NCPC Plan to Redevelop SW. District," *Washington Post*, September 9, 1952, 1–2.

57. NCPC and Gutheim, *Worthy of the Nation*, 314–15.

58. "NCPC Acts to Advance Plan for Southwest," *Washington Post*, October 25, 1952; Jean M. White, "Past Won't Die in 1962 Renewal," *Washington Post*, February 1, 1962; Gutheim and Lee, *Worthy of the Nation*, 315–17.

59. Longstreth, "Brave New World"; Ammon, "Commemoration amid Criticism."

60. Baldwin used the term in a legendary television interview with Dr. Kenneth Clark on Boston Public Television, WGBH, in the summer of 1963. "Conversation with James Baldwin, A; James Baldwin Interview," June 24, 1963, WGBH Media Library & Archives, http://openvault.wgbh.org/catalog/V_C03ED1927DCF46B5A8C82275DF4239F9S. But versions of it were around at least as early as 1960. See, for example, Walter Fauntroy's reference to "urban removal—the removal of Negroes" in a newspaper interview in 1960. "Racial Effect of Renewal under Study," *Evening Star*, September 27, 1960.

61. James Q. Wilson, ed., *Urban Renewal: The Record and the Controversy* (Cambridge, MA: MIT Press, 1966), xiii. On the intellectual shifts that saw urban renewal policies come under attack, see Christopher Klemek, *The Transatlantic Collapse of Urban Renewal: Postwar Urbanism from New York to Berlin* (Chicago: University of Chicago Press, 2011), 79–127.

62. "Ministers Plan Attack on Southwest Renewal," *Washington Daily News*, November 2, 1960.

63. Paul S. Green and Shirley L. Green, "Old Southwest Remembered: The Photographs of Joseph Owen Curtis," *Washington History* 1, no. 2 (1989): 42–57.

64. Fredrick Gutheim, "The Growth of Historic Towns" (keynote address to the Annapolis Roundtable, St. John's College, Annapolis, MD), May 4, 1962, folder 116, container 3, Dupont Circle Citizen's Association Records, 1925–2000, Kiplinger Library, HSW.

65. Margaret Carroll, *Historic Preservation through Urban Renewal: How Urban Renewal Works, Two Areas of Emphasis, Broad Requirements, Preservation and Renewal in Action* (Washington, D.C.: Urban Renewal Administration, 1963), 27.

66. "Preservation and Renewal to Be Topics," *Washington Post*, September 7, 1963, F17.

67. Carroll, *Historic Preservation through Urban Renewal*, 27.

68. William W. Nash, *Residential Rehabilitation: Private Profits and Public Purposes* (New York: McGraw Hill, 1959); Providence City Plan Commission in Cooperation with the PPS and the Department of Housing and Urban Development, *College Hill: A Demonstration Study of Historic Area Renewal*, 2nd ed. (Providence: Charles G. Gowan Publishers for the Providence City Plan Commission, 1967), 7; Briann Greenfield, "Marketing the Past: Historic Preservation in Providence, Rhode Island," in Page and Mason, *Giving Preservation a History*, 163–84; Richard Longstreth, "Antoinette Forrester Downing, 14 July 1904–9 May 2001," *Journal of the Society of Architectural Historians* 61, no. 2 (2002): 260–62.

69. Providence City Plan Commission, *College Hill*, 225.

70. Greenfield, "Marketing the Past," 163–84; Longstreth, "Antoinette Forrester Downing," 260–62.

71. Longstreth, "Antoinette Forrester Downing," 261. This shift in the acknowledged agenda of historic preservation was first articulated in Wallace, "Preserving the Past." Vince Michael's doctoral research challenged the specific timeline set out by Wallace but confirmed the general trajectory outlined there.

72. See Isaac Burley and others, "Dollars and Sense: Preservation Economics," *Historic Preservation* 23, no. 2 (1971): 15–33; Jean M. White, "Washington's Past Is Still Present—But for How Long?" *Washington Post*, October 8, 1961, E3; Jean M. White, "Preserving a City by Renewal Is Theme of Parley," *Washington Post*, May 5, 1962, E1.

73. D. K. Patton, "New York City," *Historic Preservation* 21, no. 4 (1969): 15.

74. Leopold Adler, "Historic Savannah," *Historic Preservation* 21, no. 1 (1969): 17.

2. TASTE

1. Elisabeth Cheely, "Hill House Tour Has Party Air; Members and Residents Join 700," *Roll Call*, May 18, 1960, 8.

2. National Capital Planning Commission with Frederick Gutheim, *Worthy of the Nation: The History of Planning for the National Capital* (Washington, D.C.:

Smithsonian Institution Press, 1977), 271–79; Zachary M. Schrag, *The Great Society Subway: A History of the Washington Metro* (Baltimore: Johns Hopkins University Press, 2006), 35–43.

3. Cheely, "Hill House Tour Has Party Air"; CHRS, Home and Garden Tour Publicity Committee "Agenda," April 15, 1960, Jessie Stearns Buscher Papers (private collection, hereafter JSB Papers). Several pieces dedicated to house and garden tours in Dupont Circle and Logan Circle appeared annually in *The Intowner* throughout the 1970s and 1980s.

4. CHRS, *Capitol Hill Vigilantes,* folder 13, box 30, Capitol Hill Restoration Society Records (CHRS Papers), Special Collections Research Center, Estelle and Melvin Gelman Library, George Washington University.

5. Brownstone Revival Committee, "Back to the City: A Guide to Urban Preservation," in *Proceedings of the Back to the City Conference,* New York, September 13–16, 1974, folder 9, box 2, Frederic W. Gutheim Papers, Special Collections, Gelman Library, GWU; Neil Smith and Peter Williams, eds., *Gentrification of the City* (Boston: Allen & Unwin, 1986). On black pioneers, see Thomas Sugrue, *The Origins of the Urban Crisis: Race and Inequality in Postwar Detroit* (Princeton, NJ: Princeton University Press, 1996). Suleiman Osman has discussed the more complicated meaning of pioneer in the context of Brooklyn's gentrification from the late 1950s onward. See Suleiman Osman, *The Invention of Brownstone Brooklyn: Gentrification and the Search for Authenticity in Postwar New York* (Oxford: Oxford University Press, 2011), 192–96. In the 1980s prominent critics of gentrification such as Neil Smith made much of the use of the term "urban pioneering," arguing that it relies on a problematic, imaginary projection and reinscription of the idea of the white, civilizing pioneer heroically taming an uncivilized wilderness. But the idea of pioneering has been used in myriad urban situations—including as a description of the entry of blacks into formerly all-white neighborhoods.

6. CHRS, *Capitol Hill Vigilantes.*

7. "New Rat Control Program to Begin," *Capitol Hill News,* January 1968. In 1961 the "Cities Without Slums" campaign produced a "Clean-up, fix-up, paint-up" promotion that a number of central city neighborhood organizations in Washington adopted, including Mt. Pleasant Civic Association. See Mt. Pleasant Civic Association and Historic Mt. Pleasant Records, Washingtonian Archives, Martin Luther King Jr. Memorial Library, Washington, D.C. For background on the "No Slums in 10 Years" campaign, see Nicholas Bloom, *Merchant of Illusion: James Rouse, American Salesman of the Businessman's Utopia* (Columbus: Ohio State University Press, 2004), 78–81. On the widening restoration trend in the early 1960s, see "Restoration—A Chain Reaction," *Sunday Star,* September 17, 1961.

8. Charles Robertson on behalf of DCCA to National Capital Planning Commission, November 1980, folder 10, container 2, Dupont Circle Conservancy Records, Kiplinger Research Library, Historical Society of Washington, D.C.; DCCA and Dupont Circle Conservancy to Washington, D.C., Zoning Commission, July 1984, folder 14, container 2, Dupont Circle Conservancy Records, Kiplinger Library, HSW.

9. Neil Smith, *The New Urban Frontier: Gentrification and the Revanchist City* (London: Routledge, 1996), 57.

10. Joy Wheeler Dow, *American Renaissance: A Review of Domestic Architecture* (New York: W. T. Comstock, 1904), 161.

11. Richard Irvin Brumbaugh, "The American House in the Victorian Period," *Journal of the American Society of Architectural Historians* 2, no. 1 (1942): 27–30.

12. Robert J. Lewis, "The Neat and Orderly Colonial Facade," *Evening Star*, April 23, 1960, D1. On the colonial revival, see David Gebhard, "The American Colonial Revival in the 1930s," *Winterthur Portfolio* 22, nos. 2/3 (1987): 109–48; Bridget A. May, "Progressivism and the Colonial Revival: The Modern Colonial House, 1900–1920," *Winterthur Portfolio* 26, nos. 2/3 (1991): 107–22.

13. Deering Davis, Stephen P. Dorsey, and Ralph Cole Hall, *Georgetown Houses of the Federal Period: Washington, D.C., 1780–1830* (New York: Architectural Book Publishing, 1944), 18.

14. Ibid., 19.

15. William A. Gordon, "Recollections of a Boyhood in Georgetown," *Records of the Columbia Historical Society, Washington, D.C.* 20 (1917): 122.

16. William A. Gordon, "Old Homes on Georgetown Heights," *Records of the Columbia Historical Society, Washington, D.C.* 18 (1915): 91.

17. Davis, Dorsey, and Hall, *Georgetown Houses of the Federal Period*, 18.

18. Mary H. Northend, *Colonial Homes and Their Furnishings* (Boston: Little Brown, 1912), 236–37.

19. May, "Progressivism and the Colonial Revival," 109–10.

20. On the connection between the colonial revival and nationalism, also see Richard Guy Wilson, "Architecture and the Reinterpretation of the Past in the American Renaissance," *Winterthur Portfolio* 18, no. 1 (1983): 69–87.

21. Barbara Kirshenblatt-Gimblett, *Destination Culture: Tourism, Museums, and Heritage* (Berkeley: University of California Press, 1998), 259.

22. Henry H. Glassie, "Victorian Homes in Washington," *Records of the Columbia Historical Society, Washington, D.C.* 63/65 (1963–65): 348.

23. John Maass, *The Gingerbread Age: A View of Victorian America* (New York: Rinehart, 1957).

24. Lewis Mumford, *Sticks and Stones: A Study of American Architecture and Civilization* (New York: Dover, 1955), 46.

25. Morrison quoted in Glassie, "Victorian Homes in Washington," 363.

26. James Marston Fitch, *American Building: The Forces that Shape It* (Cambridge, MA: Riverside Press, 1948), 101.

27. Alan Gowans, *Images of American Living: Four Centuries of Architecture and Furniture as Cultural Expression* (Philadelphia: J. B. Lippincott, 1964), 337.

28. On the legacy of Victorian architecture and its preservation in the UK, see Nikolaus Boulting, "The Law's Delays: Conservationist Legislation in the British Isles," 26–27, and John Betjeman, "A Preservationist's Progress," 60–63, both in *The Future of the Past: Attitudes to Conservation, 1174–1974*, ed. Jane Fawcett

(New York: Watson-Guptill Publications, 1976); Wayne Andrews, *Architecture, Ambition and Americans: A Social History of American Architecture* (New York: Harper, 1955).

29. Glassie, "Victorian Homes in Washington," 320–65.

30. Louis Justement, *New Cities for Old: City Building in Terms of Space, Time and Money* (New York: McGraw Hill, 1946), 40.

31. Glassie, "Victorian Homes in Washington," 336–42.

32. Ibid., 320–65; "A Worthy City," *Washington Star*, September 17, 1961.

33. Wolf von Eckardt, "The Fabulous Facades of Logan Circle," *Washington Post*, April 29, 1972.

34. Elizabeth Kohl Draper, "Progress Report on the Restoration of Capitol Hill Southeast," *Records of the Columbia Historical Society, Washington, D.C.* 51/52 (1951–52): 134; Robert J. Lewis, "Restoration Areas: A Series," *Evening Star*, 1960; the four areas included in his series were Kalorama Triangle (August 27), Foggy Bottom (October 22), Capitol Hill (November 19), and Georgetown (December 31).

35. Richard Ernie Reed, *Return to the City: How to Restore Old Buildings and Ourselves in America's Historic Urban Neighborhoods* (Garden City, NY: Doubleday, 1979), xii.

36. Dennis E. Gale, "Restoration in Georgetown, Washington, D.C., 1915–1965" (PhD diss., George Washington University, 1982), 260–62.

37. Muriel Bowen, "Potomac Planning First Garden Tour," *Washington Post*, April 22, 1956, F16; "Alexandria to Showcase Nine Recent Restorations," *Sunday Star*, April 30, 1961, H8; "Featured on Tour in McLean," *Sunday Star*, April 30, 1961, G4; "Tour House," *Evening Star*, April 28, 1961; "Potomac Houses to Be Opened," *Evening Star*, April 23, 1961.

38. Mathilde D. Williams, *Georgetown 1621–1951: A Brief Outline of Its History* (Washington, D.C.: Peabody Library Association, 1951). On the links between modern heritage and patrimonial sentiment, see David Lowenthal, *The Heritage Crusade and the Spoils of History* (Cambridge: Cambridge University Press, 1998), 58. On the contrast drawn between the urban preservationist and the suburbanite, see Reed, *Return to the City*, 103–6.

39. Cheely, "Hill House Tour Has Party Air"; CHRS, "Agenda," April 15, 1960. Several pieces dedicated to house and garden tours in Dupont Circle and Logan Circle appeared annually in *The Intowner* throughout the 1970s and 1980s.

40. "Large Turnout Expected for Dupont Circle Tour," *The Intowner* 82 (July 1, 1973).

41. CHRS, "Annual Tour of Homes and Gardens," May 15, 1960, JSB Papers; CHRS, "Capitol Hill House and Garden Tour," May 6, 1962, JSB Papers; CHRS, "House and Garden Tour of Capitol Hill," May 3, 1964, JSB Papers; CHRS, "Capitol Hill House and Garden Tour," May 12, 1968, JSB Papers; CHRS, "19th Annual House and Garden Tour," May 9, 1976, Neighborhood Resources (Capitol Hill), Kiplinger Library, HSW. Barbara Held Inc. Real Estate was intimately involved

with the promotion of the tours and a major sponsor of the restoration movement on Capitol Hill. Their monthly newsletters through the late 1960s provide
a very clear picture of their collaboration with the CHRS, JSB Papers. Jesse
Stearns Buscher letter to Robert J. Lewis, real estate editor for the *Evening Star*,
JSB Papers, also makes clear the connections between real estate promotion,
media publicity, and restoration.

42. C. Dudley Brown, interview by Megan Rosenfeld, April 30, 2002, *Ruth
Anne Overbeck Capitol Hill History Project*, http://www.capitolhillhistory.org/
interviews/2002/brown_dudley.html.

43. CHRS, "House and Garden Tour of Capitol Hill," 1964.

44. Ibid.

45. Walter Benjamin, "Paris: Capital of the Nineteenth Century," in *Reflections: Essays, Aphorisms, Autobiographical Writings*, trans. Edmund Jephcott (New
York: Harcourt Brace Jovanovich, 1978), 154.

46. David K. Johnson, "Homosexual Citizens: Washington's Gay Community
Confronts the Civil Service," *Washington History* 6, no. 2 (1994–95): 51.

47. *Capitol Hill Spectator*, June 10, 1966, 5.

48. Gale, "Restoration in Georgetown," 251–59.

49. CHRS, House and Garden Tour house descriptions, 1960–64. See especially descriptions of individual properties in the booklet distributed to participants on the 1960 tour, JSB Papers.

50. "Col. Burns Unusual Antiques," *Sunday Star*, February, 21, 1960.

51. Ruth Anne Overbeck, "Capitol Hill: The Capitol Is Just Up the Street," in
Washington at Home: An Illustrated History of Neighborhoods in the Nation's Capital,
ed. Kathryn Schneider Smith, 2nd ed. (Baltimore: Johns Hopkins University
Press, 2011), 40; Marie McNair, "The Treat Was on the House," *Washington Post*,
February 13, 1960; "Restoration—A Chain Reaction."

52. CHRS, *Capitol Hill Vigilantes*.

53. Capitol Hill Southeast Citizens' Association, *Places and Persons on Capitol
Hill: Stories and Pictures of a Neighborhood* (Washington, D.C.: Capitol Hill Southeast Citizens' Association, 1960), 71–72.

54. Ibid., 72.

55. "Testimony of Thomas B. Simmons, AIA, AIP, President of the Capitol
Hill Restoration Society, INC., before the Joint Committee on Landmarks of the
National Capital," December 9, 1975, folder 16, box 1, Capitol Hill Restoration
Society Records (CHRS Papers), Special Collections, Gelman Library, GWU.

56. CHRS, "Capitol Hill House and Garden Tour" (1968–76), Neighborhood
Resources (Capitol Hill), Kiplinger Library, HSW; "Large Turnout Expected for
Dupont Circle Tour"; Brown, interview by Rosenfeld; Logan Circle Community
Association, "A Victorian Christmas: Logan Circle House Tour," December 10,
1978, Neighborhood Resources (Logan Circle), Kiplinger Library, HSW.

57. Jonathan Raban, *Soft City* (London: Hamilton, 1974).

58. CHRS, "Capitol Hill House and Garden Tour," 1968.

59. Barbara Held Inc., *Hill Happenings* (Washington, D.C., Barbara Held Real Estate newsletter), November 1970, JSB Papers.

60. Constance McLauglin Green, *Capitol Hill: A Heritage to Preserve* (House and Garden Tour brochure), May 3, 1964, JSB Papers.

61. William H. Whyte, *The Organization Man* (Garden City, NY: Doubleday, 1957); Jane Jacobs, *The Death and Life of Great American Cities* (New York: Random House, 1961); Betty Friedan, *The Feminine Mystique* (New York: W. W. Norton, 1963). For a more balanced historical perspective on suburbia, see Rosalyn Baxandall and Elizabeth Ewen, *Picture Windows: How the Suburbs Happened* (New York: Basic Books, 2000). Suleiman Osman has recently described the evolution of the idea of "historic diversity" in New York City in the twentieth century and its strong connection with ideas of authenticity. See *Invention of Brownstone Brooklyn*, 5–6.

62. "Hill House Tour Has Party Air"; Robert Hughes, "Ruth Ann Overbeck: Hill Historian and So Much More," *Hill Rag*, October 2001; Sam Smith, "Cauldron and Community: Joining the Hill in the 1960s" (lecture, November 12, 2002), *Ruth Ann Overbeck Capitol Hill History Project*, http://www.capitolhillhistory .org/lectures/sam_smith/index.html.

3. THE WHITE HOUSE AND ITS NEIGHBORHOOD

1. Frederic W. Gutheim, "The Growth of Historic Towns" (keynote address to the Annapolis Roundtable, St. John's College, Annapolis, MD), May 4, 1962, folder 116, container 3, Dupont Circle Citizen's Association Records, 1925–2000, Kiplinger Research Library, Historical Society of Washington, D.C.

2. Giedion first raised the issue in a 1946 lecture for the Royal Institute of British Architects, and the 1948 symposium discussed below was convened to solicit a wider range of views. J. M. Richards and others, "In Search of a New Monumentality," *Architectural Review*, September 1948, 117–27. Also see Lewis Mumford, "Monumentalism, Symbolism and Style," *Architectural Review*, April 1949, 173–80.

3. Henry-Russell Hitchcock in Richards and others, "In Search of a New Monumentality," 124.

4. J. M. Richards in Richards and others, "In Search of a New Monumentality," 117–22.

5. Gregor Paulsson in Richards and others, "In Search of a New Monumentality," 123.

6. Matthew Aitchison, "The Boyd Ultimatum," *AA Files*, no. 66 (2013): 59–67.

7. Jane Jacobs (with Carl Feiss and Frederick Gutheim), "Washington," *Architectural Forum* 102, no. 1 (January 1955): 92–112. A decade later John Reps certainly assumed that Washington's civic presence and meaning required ongoing development in a monumental manner. See John Reps, *Monumental Washington: The Planning and Development of the Capital Center* (Princeton, NJ: Princeton University Press, 1967).

8. Richard Guy Wilson, "High Noon on the Mall: Modernism versus Traditionalism, 1910–1970," in *The Mall in Washington, 1791–1991*, ed. Richard Longstreth (Washington, D.C.: National Gallery of Art, 1991), 163.

9. Kurt Helfrich, "Modernism for Washington? The Kennedys and the Redesign of Lafayette Square," *Washington History* 8, no. 1 (1996): 17.

10. Columbia Broadcasting System (CBS), *A Tour of the White House*, directed by Franklin J. Shaffner, aired February 14, 1962.

11. Quoted in Reps, *Monumental Washington*, 132.

12. Helfrich, "Modernism for Washington?," 16–37; Charles H. Atherton, "An Insider's Reflections on the Development of Washington, 1960–2004," *Washington History* 18, nos. 1/2 (2006): 48–60; Frederick Gutheim and Antoinette J. Lee, *Worthy of the Nation: Washington, DC, from L'Enfant to the National Capital Planning Commission*, 2nd ed. (Baltimore: Johns Hopkins University Press, 2006), 303–5.

13. Quoted in Helfrich, "Modernism for Washington?," 36.

14. Ibid., 21.

15. Hugh Sidey, "The First Lady Brings History and Beauty to the White House," *Life*, September 1, 1961, 62.

16. James A. Abbott and Elaine M. Rice, *Designing Camelot: The Kennedy White House Restoration* (New York: Van Nostrand Reinhold, 1998), 17–27.

17. Helfrich, "Modernism for Washington?," 29–30.

18. Ibid., 27–31; Atherton, "An Insider's Reflections on the Development of Washington," 48–60.

19. Helfrich, "Modernism for Washington?," 33.

20. "The Square Is Spared," *Washington Post*, October 1, 1962.

21. John F. Kennedy to Bernard L. Boutin, GSA, October 15, 1962, in Boutin, "Lafayette Square—The Final Word," in *Washington in Transition*, ed. Paul Thiry, special issue, *AIA Journal* 39, no. 1 (1963): 56.

22. Boutin, "Lafayette Square," 55–56; Allen Freeman, "'Fine Tuning' a Landmark of Adaptive Use: Ghirardelli Square Gets a Respectful Renovation," *AIA Journal* 75, no. 11 (1986): 66–71; Nan Ellin, *Postmodern Urbanism* (Cambridge, MA: Blackwell, 1996), 66.

23. Zachary M. Schrag, *The Great Society Subway: A History of the Washington Metro* (Baltimore: Johns Hopkins University Press, 2006), 44.

24. Gutheim and Lee, *Worthy of the Nation*, 296.

25. Ibid., 296–97; Schrag, *Great Society Subway*, 45.

26. Carl Feiss, "A Program for Landmarks Conservation in the District of Columbia: Recommendations to the National Capital Planning Commission on the Preservation of Historic Landmarks, Buildings, Monuments, Places and Districts of Historic, Architectural and Landscape Merit in Washington, DC," Washington, D.C., 1963, Special Collections Research Center, Estelle and Melvin Gelman Library, George Washington University.

27. Francis D. Lethbridge, "Goals of the Landmarks Committee," *Records of the Columbia Historical Society, Washington, D.C. 63/65* (1963–65): 448–51; William

Bushong, Judith Helm Robinson, and Julie Mueller, *A Centennial History of the Washington Chapter, the American Institute of Architects, 1887–1987* (Washington, D.C.: Washington Architectural Foundation Press, 1988), 87–90.

28. Francis D. Lethbridge, "Seeing the City in Time," *AIA Journal* 42, no. 2 (1964): 75.

29. Ibid., 72–73.

30. Ibid., 74.

31. Ibid., 73.

32. John Macarthur, "Townscape, Anti-scrape and Surrealism: Paul Nash and John Piper in *The Architectural Review*," *Journal of Architecture* 14, no. 3 (2009): 387–406. On the issue of fragmentation and authenticity, see Kurt W. Forster, "Monument/Memory and the Mortality of Architecture," *Oppositions* 25 (1982): 2–19.

33. Lethbridge, "Seeing the City in Time," 75.

34. JCL, "Landmarks of the National Capital, Preliminary List: Report to the National Capital Planning Commission and the Commission of Fine Arts by the Joint Committee on Landmarks," November 8, 1964, Commission of Fine Arts, Records and Research.

35. Lethbridge, "Goals of the Landmarks Committee," 450.

36. JCL, "Landmarks of the National Capital"; Lethbridge, "Goals of the Landmarks Committee," 449; Albert Rains and Laurance G. Henderson for the United States Conference of Mayors, *With Heritage So Rich* (New York: Random House, 1966).

37. JCL, "Landmarks of the National Capital," map insert; Julian Morrison, "Tour of Valued Landmark: Logan Has Come Full Circle," *Washington Daily News*, November 13, 1964.

38. Morrison, "Tour of Valued Landmark."

39. Howland quoted in "Logan Circle Seen New High-Rise Area," *Washington Post*, April 3, 1964; Morrison, "Tour of Valued Landmark."

40. Frederick Gutheim, "City and Capital—The Nature of the City of Washington," in Thiry, *Washington in Transition*, 87.

41. Robert J. Kerr III, "Historic Preservation in the Federal City," in Thiry, *Washington in Transition*, 105, and Gutheim, "City and Capital." Peter Larkham has noted that the idea of "sense of place" and genius loci exerted substantial influence on architectural and planning discourse during the 1960s in both England and the United States. See Peter J. Larkham, *Conservation and the City* (London: Routledge, 1996). The idea also receives extensive treatment in Dolores Hayden, *The Power of Place: Urban Landscapes as Public History* (Cambridge, MA: MIT Press, 1995).

42. Kerr, "Historic Preservation in the Federal City," 105; Gutheim, "City and Capital," 87.

43. Wolf von Eckardt, "2 Awards for House Design Won by Young Washington Architect," *Washington Post*, November 10, 1964; Hugh Newell Jacobsen, ed.,

A Guide to the Architecture of Washington, D.C. (Washington, D.C.: F. A. Praeger, 1965).

44. John F. Kennedy, "A Message from the President," to the membership of the American Institute of Architects (January 1963), in Thiry, *Washington in Transition*, 25.

45. Wolf von Eckardt, "All Elderly Stuff Fine Except Old Buildings," *Washington Post*, October 20, 1963, G8.

46. Sue Kohler, *The Commission of Fine Arts: A Brief History, 1910–1995* (Washington, D.C.: Commission of Fine Arts, 1996), 97–104.

47. Sinclair Lewis, preface to *Main Street* (New York: Harcourt, Brace and World, 1948).

48. Douglas Haskell, "Washington, D.C.," *Architecture Forum* 118, no. 1 (January 1963).

49. Carol Highsmith and Ted Landphair, *Pennsylvania Avenue: America's Main Street* (Washington, D.C.: American Institute of Architects Press, 1988), 14.

50. Ibid.

51. Ibid.; David Hathaway and Stephanie Ho, "Small but Resilient: Washington's Chinatown over the Years," *Washington History* 15, no. 1 (2003): 42–61; Helfrich, "Modernism for Washington?," 36.

52. Richard Longstreth, "The Neighborhood Shopping Center in Washington, D.C., 1930–1941," *Journal of the Society of Architectural Historians* 51, no. 1 (1992): 5–34.

53. Highsmith and Landphair, *Pennsylvania Avenue*, 121.

54. Ibid.

55. President's Council on Pennsylvania Avenue, *Pennsylvania Avenue: Report of the President's Council on Pennsylvania Avenue* (Washington, D.C.: US Government Printing Office, 1964), 18–19.

56. Quoted in Pennsylvania Avenue Development Corporation, "The Pennsylvania Avenue Plan, 1974," 7, https://www.nps.gov/nationalmallplan/Documents/Penn/PADC_PennAvePlan1974.pdf.

57. Gutheim and Lee, *Worthy of the Nation*, 323.

58. Wolf von Eckardt, "Why Can't We Keep the Old Post Office and Enjoy It?," *Washington Post*, March 8, 1970, F1.

59. Wolf von Eckardt, "Don't Tear It Down," *Washington Post*, November 30, 1974, C1.

60. Claudia Levy, "Rally Seeks to Save Old D.C. Landmark," *Washington Post*, April 19, 1971.

61. Von Eckardt, "Don't Tear It Down."

62. Carol F. Bickley, letter to the editor, *Washington Post*, November 27, 1974.

63. "Washington's Willard," *New York Times*, December 30, 1974.

64. *The Washington Preservation Conference Proceedings* (Washington, D.C.: National Trust for Historic Preservation and Latrobe Chapter of the Society for Architectural Historians, 1972).

65. In *The Washington Preservation Conference Proceedings*, see especially Antoinette Downing, "The Role of Public Agencies in Preservation in the District of Columbia," 111–18; James Marston Fitch, "Environmental Aspects of the Preservation of Historic Urban Centers," 143–61; Barclay G. Jones, "Preservation Economics and the District of Columbia: Controlling the Economic Effects of the Various Powers of Government on Preservation Efforts," 123–35; the papers contributed to the section called "Dialogue on a Major Preservation Issue: Capitol Hill," 31–42; Terry B. Moreton, "The People Speak," 57–60; and Richard B. Westbrook, "The National Capital Planning Commission's Historic Preservation Programs," 17–18. See also Russell V. Keune, "An Interview with Terry B. Moreton," *CRM: The Journal of Heritage Stewardship* 7, no. 2 (2010): 60–75.

66. Kirk Scharfenberg, "Council Studying Preservation Law," *Washington Post*, April 30, 1973, C1; Kirk Scharfenberg, "Council Moves to Save Key Buildings," *Washington Post*, September 14, 1973, C2.

67. "Home Fires Burn for Home Rule," *Washington Post*, June 4, 1973; Howard Gillette Jr., "Protest and Power in Washington, D.C.: The Troubled Legacy of Marion Barry," in *African-American Mayors: Race, Politics and the American City*, ed. David R. Colburn and Jeffrey S. Adler (Urbana: University of Illinois Press, 2001); Harry S. Jaffe and Tom Sherwood, *Dream City: Race, Power, and the Decline of Washington, D.C.* (New York: Simon & Schuster, 1994), 94–104.

68. Scharfenberg, "Council Moves to Save Key Buildings"; von Eckardt, "Don't Tear It Down."

4. RACE AND RESISTANCE

1. Briann Greenfield, "Marketing the Past: Historic Preservation in Providence, Rhode Island," in *Giving Preservation a History: Histories of Historic Preservation in the United States*, ed. Max Page and Randall Mason (New York: Routledge, 2004), 170.

2. Suleiman Osman, *The Invention of Brownstone Brooklyn: Gentrification and the Search for Authenticity in Postwar New York* (Oxford: Oxford University Press, 2011), 8; Frank H. Wilson, "Gentrification in Central Area Neighborhoods: Population and Housing Change in Washington, D.C., 1970–1980" (PhD diss., University of Michigan, 1985).

3. Sam Smith, *Captive Capital: Colonial Life in Modern Washington* (Bloomington: Indiana University Press, 1974), 85.

4. "White Octopus," *Capitol Hill News*, January 1968.

5. National Capital Planning Commission with Frederick Gutheim, *Worthy of the Nation: The History of Planning for the National Capital* (Washington, D.C.: Smithsonian Institution Press, 1977), 292; Sam Smith, "Cauldron and Community: Joining the Hill in the 1960s" (lecture, November 12, 2002), *Ruth Ann Overbeck History Project*, http://www.capitolhillhistory.org/lectures/sam_smith/index.html; Howard Gillette Jr., *Between Justice and Beauty: Race, Planning, and the Failure of Urban Policy in Washington, D.C.* (Philadelphia: University of Pennsylvania

Press, 2006), 174; Harry S. Jaffe and Tom Sherwood, *Dream City: Race, Power, and the Decline of Washington, D.C.* (New York: Simon & Schuster, 1994), 132.

6. "City Acts on SE Protest: Stops House, On Inspections," *Capitol East Gazette*, December 1967. For earlier recognition of the code enforcement problem, see "Urban Relocation," letter to the editor, *Washington Post*, December 20, 1955.

7. Peter Thomas Rohrbach, "Poignant Dilemma of Spontaneous Restoration," *City*, August–September 1970, 65–67.

8. Ibid., 65.

9. Capitol Hill Joint Committee, "Capitol Hill Prospectus," 17, folder 4, box 1, Capitol Hill Restoration Society Records (CHRS Papers), Special Collections Research Center, Estelle and Melvin Gelman Library, George Washington University.

10. "White Octopus," 7.

11. Philip A. Ridgely, letter to the editor, *City*, August–September 1970, republished in *Historic Preservation* 22, no. 4 (1970): 10.

12. The most oft-cited text is Paul Davidoff, "Advocacy and Pluralism in Planning," *Journal of the American Institute of Planners* 31, no. 4 (1965): 331–38. In Washington the best-known effort to implement such ideas was MICCO, which is discussed below.

13. The District of Columbia Redevelopment Land Agency, "Community Service and Family Relocation," 1966, Neighborhood Resources (Southwest), Kiplinger Research Library, Historical Society of Washington, D.C.

14. Mary A. Morton (words and music), "MICCO Theme Song," folder 2, box 26, Walter E. Fauntroy Papers, Special Collections, Gelman Library, GWU; "What Kind of Neighborhood Do You Want? The Choices for Shaw Residents in Urban Renewal," July 1968, folder 2, box 26, Fauntroy Papers, Special Collections, Gelman Library, GWU; Gillette, *Between Justice and Beauty*, 173–74.

15. Quoted in Gillette, *Between Justice and Beauty*, 175.

16. Frank B. Gilbert, "Real Estate Values," *Historic Preservation* 23, no. 2 (1971): 23.

17. Issac Burley and others, "Dollars and Sense: Preservation Economics," in special issue, *Historic Preservation* 23, no. 2 (1971): 15–33.

18. Noel Kane, "The Preservation of Population Diversity on Capitol Hill," in *The Washington Preservation Conference Proceedings* (Washington, D.C.: National Trust for Historic Preservation and Latrobe Chapter of the Society for Architectural Historians, 1972), 37.

19. Quoted in Mara Charkasky, "On the Formation of the Dupont Circle Historic District," 1984, 19, Neighborhood Resources (Dupont Circle), Kiplinger Library, HSW.

20. Wilson, "Gentrification in Central Area Neighborhoods," 183–84.

21. Kane, "The Preservation of Population Diversity on Capitol Hill," 38.

22. For in-depth social research on Washington's inner city in the 1970s, see Dennis E. Gale, *The Back-to-the-City Movement Revisited: A Survey of Recent Home-buyers in the Capitol Hill Neighborhood of Washington, D.C.* (Washington, D.C.: Department of Urban and Regional Planning, George Washington University, 1977); Dennis E. Gale, *Washington, D.C.: Inner-City Revitalization and Minority Sub-urbanization* (Philadelphia: Temple University Press, 1987), 10–27; Wilson, "Gen-trification in Central Area Neighborhoods," 112–43.

23. "AMO Officers Charged by Frain with Racist Line," *The Intowner* 94 (April 1974).

24. Capitol Hill Joint Committee, "Capitol Hill Prospectus," 17.

25. Rohrbach, "Poignant Dilemma of Spontaneous Restoration," 65; "City Acts on SE Protest."

26. "Renaissance on Capitol Hill," *Christian Science Monitor*, August 25, 1967; Carol Pogash, *Urban Death or Resurrection*, Annual Report (Washington, D.C.: American Institute of Planners, 1970), excerpted from a speech given to the League of California Cities, folder 9, box 2, Frederic W. Gutheim Papers, Special Collections, Gelman Library, GWU; "Back to the City: A Guide to Urban Pres-ervation," in *Proceedings of the Back to the City Conference*, New York, September 13–16, 1974, folder 9, box 2, Gutheim Papers, Special Collections, Gelman Library, GWU; "Why More and More People are Coming Back to Cities," *U.S. News and World Report*, August 9, 1977, 69; Neal R. Pierce, "Nation's Cities Poised for Stun-ning Comeback," *Nation's Cities*, March 1979; Shirley Bradway Laska and Daphne Spain, *Back to the City: Issues in Neighborhood Renovation* (New York: Pergamon Press, 1980). Neighborhood newspapers covered the involvement of real estate interests extensively, but metropolitan dailies also featured real estate agents in articles about the restoration trend. For example, "Capitol Hill Couple Love Older Houses," *Washington Post*, November 23, 1968.

27. Kathleen Menzie Lesko, Valerie Babb, and Carroll R. Gibbs, *Black George-town Remembered: A History of Its Black Community from the Founding of "The Town of George" in 1751 to the Present Day* (Washington, D.C.: Georgetown University Press, 1991).

28. Sabiyha Prince, *African Americans and Gentrification in Washington, D.C.: Race, Class and Social Justice in the Nation's Capital* (Farnham: Ashgate, 2014); Wil-liam Raspberry, "Slumdwellers and the Middle-Class Crunch," *Washington Post*, November 10, 1975, A27; Linda Wheeler, "Dupont Circle: Losing the Artist's Touch," *Washington Post*, March 22, 1980, B1; Wolf von Eckardt, "Logan Circle: Test Case for American Cities," *Washington Post*, December 29, 1973; Michael Tomlan, *Historic Preservation: Caring for our Expanding Legacy* (Cham: Springer, 2015), 72–75.

29. Arthur P. Ziegler Jr., *Historic Preservation in Inner City Areas: A Manual of Practice* (Pittsburgh: Alleghany Press, 1971), 66.

30. On advocacy planning, see Christopher Klemek, *The Transatlantic Collapse of Urban Renewal: Postwar Urbanism from New York to Berlin* (Chicago: University

of Chicago Press, 2011), 187–201. For antiblockbusting tactics, see Rosalyn Baxandall and Elizabeth Ewen, *Picture Windows: How the Suburbs Happened* (New York: Basic Books, 2000); and Thomas Sugrue, *The Origins of the Urban Crisis: Race and Inequality in Postwar Detroit* (Princeton, NJ: Princeton University Press, 1996), 190–97.

31. Lee Adler and Emma Adler, *Savannah Renaissance* (Charleston, SC: Wyrick, 2003), 66–74.

32. "Historic District: Anacostia's Uniontown Isn't Georgetown but Its Charm Will Now Be Preserved," *Washington Star*, November 29, 1973; Fredric Miller and Howard Gillette Jr., *Washington Seen: A Photographic History, 1875–1965* (Baltimore: Johns Hopkins University Press, 1995), 214–15; Howard Gillette Jr., "Old Anacostia: Washington's First Suburb," in *Washington at Home: An Illustrated History of Neighborhoods in the Nation's Capital*, ed. Kathryn Schneider Smith (Northbridge, CA: Windsor Publications, 1988), 97–105; Ronald M. Johnson, "LeDroit Park: Premier Black Community," in Smith, *Washington at Home*, 138–47.

33. "LeDroit Park Residents Resent Notoriety from 'Ramblers' Gang," *Washington Star*, January 26, 1961.

34. Woody West and Earl Byrd, "Place of Dreams and Nightmares," *Washington Star*, February 28, 1974.

35. Robin Elisabeth Datel, "Preservation and a Sense of Orientation for American Cities," *Geographical Review* 75, no. 2 (1985): 130.

36. Quarles quoted in "Why Black History?" *Washington Afro-American*, February 17, 1973.

37. Ron Powell and William D. Cunningham, *Black Guide to Washington* (Washington, D.C.: Washingtonian Books, 1975), 2.

38. "Zeta Phi Beta Sorority Incorporated Is Committed to Black History," *Washington Afro-American*, February 17, 1973; "Sightseers View Black Historical Sites," *Washington Afro-American*, October 5, 1974.

39. West and Byrd, "Place of Dreams and Nightmares"; Carr, Lynch & Associates, "A Program of Neighborhood Conservation for the Anacostia and LeDroit Park Historic Districts," submitted to D.C. Department of Housing and Community Development, November 15, 1978, 61, Neighborhood Resources (Anacostia), Kiplinger Library, HSW.

40. Penn Central Transportation Co. v. New York City, 438 U.S. 104 (1978).

41. Jeremy W. Dutra, "You Can't Tear It Down: The Origins of the D.C. Historic Preservation Act," *Georgetown Law Historic Preservation Papers Series*, 2002, http://scholarship.law.georgetown.edu/hpps_papers/1.

42. Jaffe and Sherwood, *Dream City*, 79; Gillette, *Between Justice and Beauty*, 192.

43. Gillette, *Between Justice and Beauty*, 192.

44. Anne Oman, "New Law Protects District Landmarks," *Washington Post*, March 8, 1979, D1.

45. Peter Pearl, "District Officials Oppose Expanding Historic Area," *Washington Post*, May 18, 1983, C1.

46. Charles Robertson to Edna Frazier-Cromwell, January 18, 1983, folder 41, container 2, Dupont Circle Conservancy Records, Kiplinger Library, HSW.

47. John B. Ritch III to Ernest Harper, March 1983, folder 41, container 2, Dupont Circle Conservancy Records, Kiplinger Library, HSW; Dupont Circle Conservancy to Carol Schifrin, March 1983, folder 41, container 2, Dupont Circle Conservancy Records, Kiplinger Library, HSW.

48. Dennis E. Gale, *The Impact of Historic District Designation in Washington, D.C.*, Occasional Paper 6 (Washington, D.C.: Center for Washington Area Studies, George Washington University, 1989), 24.

49. Eric W. Allison, "Gentrification and Historic Districts: Public Policy Consideration in the Designation of Historic Districts in New York City" (PhD diss., Columbia University, 2005).

50. Akram M. Ijla, "The Impact of Local History Designation on Residential Property Values: An Analysis of Three Slow-Growth and Three Fast-Growth Central Cities in the United States" (PhD diss., Cleveland State University, 2008).

51. Donovan D. Rypkema, "The (Economic) Value of National Register Listing," *CRM* 25, no. 1 (2002): 6–7.

52. Edna Frazier-Cromwell (on behalf of 14th and U Street Coalition Inc.) to Charles Robertson, November 18, 1982, folder 42, container 2, Dupont Circle Conservancy Records, Kiplinger Library, HSW.

53. Anne Chase, "Shaw Leaders Oppose Plans for Historic District," *Washington Post*, April 27, 1983, DC1.

54. Anne H. Oman, "Residents Support Legislation to Protect Landmark Buildings," *Washington Post*, August 3, 1978, DC5.

55. Whayne Quin to Joint Committee on Landmarks, May 1983, folder 54, container 2, Dupont Circle Conservancy Records, Kiplinger Library, HSW. Also see Whayne Quin, "Historic Preservation: The Need for Reform," *Realtor*, November 1981.

56. Counsel for Antonelli to Joint Committee on Landmarks, November 17, 1979, folder 57, container 2, Dupont Circle Conservancy Records, Kiplinger Library, HSW.

57. A & G Limited Partnership, Petitioner, v. Joint Committee on Landmarks of the National Capital, Respondent, 449 A.2d 291, no. 80-1 (D.C. Ct. App. 1981), *DigitalGeorgetown*, http://hdl.handle.net/10822/761666; Dutra, "You Can't Tear It Down."

58. Quin, "Historic Preservation."

59. Whayne Quin to Joint Committee on Landmarks, June 10, 1982, folder 54, container 2, Dupont Circle Conservancy Records, Kiplinger Library, HSW.

60. Washington Board of Realtors, "A Comprehensive Preservation Plan for Washington," folder 12, container 1, Dupont Circle Conservancy Records, Kiplinger Library, HSW.

5. WHOSE NEIGHBORHOOD? WHOSE HISTORY?

1. John J. Schulter, "Second Time Around May Be Better for All," *The Intowner* 123 (December 1976).

2. Pessimism and alarm about the state of the city after the 1968 riots was not confined to the mainstream, white press but also characterized the *Washington Afro-American* coverage of the events. See for example Mary E. Stratford, "District Rioting Unleashed Ugly Emotions," April 9, 1968, and "Stores Looted, Rocks Thrown at D.C. Police," April 9, 1968.

3. Schulter, "Second Time Around May Be Better for All."

4. Ibid.

5. Neil R. Pierce, "Nation's Cities Poised for Stunning Comeback," *The Intowner* 134 (March 1978).

6. William Raspberry, "Slumdwellers and the Middle-Class Crunch," *Washington Post*, November 10 1975, A27; Linda Wheeler, "Dupont Circle: Losing the Artist's Touch," *Washington Post*, March 22 1980, B1.

7. Dennis E. Gale has argued that preservation interests came to occupy the position previously claimed by social justice arguments in key decisions about urban policy. While I don't think this political explanation fully accounts for changes affecting the city in this period, I agree with the basic trajectory he outlines. Dennis E. Gale, *Washington, D.C.: Inner-City Revitalization and Minority Suburbanization* (Philadelphia: Temple University Press, 1987), 43.

8. National Trust for Historic Preservation in the United States, *America's Forgotten Architecture* (Washington, D.C.: The National Trust, 1976), 42.

9. Ibid.

10. This concern with the totality of the urban environment appeared in the architecture discourse via Ian Nairn, "Outrage," *Architectural Review*, June 1955; and Peter Blake, *God's Own Junkyard: The Planned Deterioration of America's Landscape* (New York: Holt, Rinehart and Winston, 1964). Rachel Carson's *Silent Spring* also appeared in the early 1960s and popularized the idea of an interconnected and fragile ecology to a much wider public. See Rachel Carson, *Silent Spring* (New York: Houghton Mifflin, 1962).

11. William Murtagh, "Aesthetic and Social Dimensions of Historic Districts," in *Historic Districts: Identification, Social Aspects and Preservation* (Washington, D.C.: National Trust for Historic Preservation, 1975).

12. Herbert Gans, "Preserving Everyone's Noo Yawk," *New York Times*, January 28, 1975; Ada Louise Huxtable, "Preserving Noo Yawk Landmarks," *New York Times*, February 4, 1975.

13. For a full discussion of the exchange between Huxtable and Gans, see Dolores Hayden, *The Power of Place: Urban Landscapes as Public History* (Cambridge, MA: MIT Press, 1995); Herbert J. Gans, *The Urban Villagers: Group and Class in the Life of Italian-Americans* (New York: Free Press, 1962).

14. Suleiman Osman, "The Decade of the Neighborhood," in *Rightward Bound: Making America Conservative in the 1970s*, ed. Bruce Schulman and Julian E.

Zelizer (Cambridge, MA: Harvard University Press, 2008), 106–27; U.S. Department of the Interior, "National Register of Historic Places—Nomination Form—LeDroit Park Historic District," 1973, Neighborhood Resources (Anacostia), Kiplinger Research Library, Historical Society of Washington, D.C.; U.S. Department of the Interior, "National Register of Historic Places—Nomination Form—The Anacostia Historic District," March 1978, Neighborhood Resources (Anacostia), Kiplinger Library, HSW; Carr, Lynch & Associates, "A Program of Neighborhood Conservation for the Anacostia and LeDroit Park Historic Districts," submitted to D.C. Department of Housing and Community Development, November 15, 1978, Neighborhood Resources (Anacostia), Kiplinger Library, HSW.

15. National Trust for Historic Preservation in the United States, *A Guide to Delineating Edges of Historic Districts* (Washington, D.C.: Preservation Press, 1976); Miles Glendinning, *The Conservation Movement: A History of Architectural Preservation, Antiquity to Modernity* (New York: Routledge, 2013), 259–358.

16. National Trust for Historic Preservation, *A Guide to Delineating Edges of Historic Districts*; Paul Sprague and Linda Legner, eds., *Historic Districts Conference: Unity Temple, Oak Park, Illinois* (Oak Park, IL: Oak Park Landmarks Commission and the National Trust for Historic Preservation, 1974); Anne Derry and others, *Guidelines for Local Surveys: A Basis for Preservation Planning* (Washington, D.C.: U.S. Department of the Interior, 1977).

17. "Senate Office to Replace This Slum," *Washington Post*, July 27, 1948; "Washington Eyes Space for New Senate Building," *Christian Science Monitor*, August 9, 1948; "E. Capitol Mall Plan Dropped; N.Y. Ave. Federal Site Urged," *Evening Star*, July 1, 1961; "Congress Grand Plan for New Capitol Hill", *U.S. News & World Report*, April 16, 1962, 74–77; "Rising Living Standards for Congressmen, Too," *U.S. News & World Report*, January 25, 1965, 44–48; "Capitol Hill: It Keeps on Spreading," *U.S. News & World Report*, October 2, 1972, 58. For critical accounts of the failure to connect monumental and everyday on Capitol Hill and the Mall, see Donald Canty, "How Washington Is Run: An Ungovernment without Top or Bottom," *Architectural Forum* 118, no. 1 (January 1963): 49–56; and Norma Evenson, "Monumental Spaces," in *The Mall in Washington, 1791–1991*, ed. Richard Longstreth (Washington, D.C.: National Gallery of Art, 1991), 19–36.

18. William McGaffin, "Burgeoning Offices Laid to Committees," *Washington Post*, October 19, 1958, A14.

19. Willard Clopton, "Capitol Hill Homeowners Revolt," *Washington Post*, January 4, 1961, B1; CHRS, "Resolution passed by the CHRS, January 9, 1961," Jessie Stearns Buscher Papers; "Capitol Hill Homeowners Protest Appraisals," *Roll Call*, January 11, 1961; "Hill Society Hits Bargain Hunt on Land," *Washington Post*, January 10, 1961, B2.

20. "The Emperor of Capitol Hill," *Architectural Forum* 129, no. 2 (1968): 80–85; Richard L. Lyons, "The Congressional Sweat Set Opens Fancy New Rayburn Gymnasium: It Even Includes a Pool," *Washington Post*, March 12, 1965, A1; George Lardner Jr., "Capitol Architect Shrugs off Jibes," *Washington Times*, June 9, 1965, A27.

21. "Masters without a Masterplan," *Washington Post*, June 3, 1971, A18.

22. Thomas B. Simmons, "Thoughts for Congress Before It Rapes the Hill," *Washington Star*, March 13, 1977, F1.

23. William Worthy, *The Rape of Our Neighborhoods: And How Communities Are Resisting Take-Overs by Colleges, Hospitals, Churches, Businesses and Public Agencies* (New York: William Morrow, 1976).

24. Simmons, "Thoughts for Congress Before It Rapes the Hill," F1.

25. S. Oliver Goodman, "300 Trade Groups Headquartered Here," *Washington Post*, October 3, 1956, 64.

26. "Builders to Dedicate Headquarters," *Washington Post*, April 13, 1957, D1; Wolf von Eckardt, "A Home for Housing," *Washington Post*, February 2, 1974, B1. On Brookings, see correspondence between the Dupont Circle Conservancy's Charles Robertson and Brookings, folders 46–49, container 2, Dupont Circle Conservancy Records, Kiplinger Library, HSW.

27. William H. Jones, "First Building Set to Open in Big Downtown Complex," *Washington Post*, May 6, 1977, E1; John B. Willman, "DC Office Space Market Sizzling," *Washington Post*, April 18, 1979, D8.

28. Joseph R. Passonneau, *Washington through Two Centuries: A History in Maps and Images* (New York: Monacelli Press, 2004).

29. DCCA, Annual Report of the Secretary, June 1, 1973 – June 1, 1974, folder 116, container 3, Dupont Circle Citizens' Association Records, Kiplinger Library, HSW; Dupont Circle Citizens' Association, *The Reporter* 35, no. 2 (1974): 2.

30. For a historical perspective on the riots, see Howard Gillette Jr., *Between Justice and Beauty: Race, Planning, and the Failure of Urban Policy in Washington, D.C.* (Philadelphia: University of Pennsylvania Press, 2006), 179–83; a more journalistic account from the time is Ben W. Gilbert, *Ten Blocks from the White House: An Anatomy of the Washington Riots of 1968* (New York: F. A. Praeger, 1968).

31. Francis D. Lethbridge, "Goals of the Landmarks Committee," *Records of the Columbia Historical Society, Washington, D.C.* 63/65 (1963–65): 448–51; Carl Feiss, "A Program for Landmarks Conservation in the District of Columbia: Recommendations to the National Capital Planning Commission on the Preservation of Historic Landmarks, Buildings, Monuments, Places and Districts of Historic, Architectural and Landscape Merit in Washington, DC," Washington, D.C., 1963, Special Collections Research Center, Estelle and Melvin Gelman Library, George Washington University.

32. "Capitol Hill Historic District nomination form," July 1976, Neighborhood Resources (Capitol Hill), Kiplinger Library, HSW. The source for the quote was Letitia W. Brown, "Residence Patterns of Negroes in the District of Columbia, 1800–1860," *Records of the Columbia Historical Society, Washington, D.C.* 69/70 (1969–70): 66–79.

33. "Capitol Hill Historic District nomination form," July 1976.

34. Peter Thomas Rohrbach, "Poignant Dilemma of Spontaneous Restoration," *City*, August–September 1970, 65–67.

35. "Capitol Hill Historic District nomination form," July 1976. James Borchert's research, conducted at roughly the same time as the historic district research, makes clear that the Capitol Hill neighborhoods were characterized by a clear pattern of dwelling based on race in the late nineteenth century, with African Americans inhabiting interior blocks and alleyways and whites the main streets. See Borchert, "Alley Landscapes in Washington," in *Common Places: Readings in American Vernacular Architecture*, ed. Dell Upton and John Michael Vlach (Athens: University of Georgia Press, 1986), 281–91. For an example of how black history was given a place within the pageant of the American past in Washington during the lead up to bicentennial, see Ron Powell and William D. Cunningham, *Black Guide to Washington* (Washington, D.C.: Washingtonian Books, 1975), produced with assistance from the Afro-American Bicentennial Corporation. For a historical analysis of the production of historical meaning through the bicentennial celebrations, see John Bodnar, *Remaking America: Public Memory, Commemoration, and Patriotism in the Twentieth Century* (Princeton, NJ: Princeton University Press, 1992), 226–44.

36. "Dupont Circle Historic District Nomination Form," January 1976, Neighborhood Resources (Dupont Circle), Kiplinger Library, HSW. On Alvarez, see DCCA, Annual Report of the Secretary, June 1, 1973 – June 1, 1974; Mara Cherkasky, "For Sale to Colored: Racial Change on S Street, NW," *Washington History* 8, no. 2 (1996–97): 40–57.

37. HPO Staff Report, Dupont Circle Historic District, March 1977, Neighborhood Resources (Dupont Circle), Kiplinger Library, HSW.

38. Lee Daub and others to Henry Brylawski, Chairman of Joint Committee on Landmarks, June 30, 1977, folder 38, container 2, Dupont Circle Conservancy Records, Kiplinger Library, HSW.

39. Charles Robertson to Chairman of Joint Committee on Landmarks, ca. March 12, 1978, folder 38, container 2, Dupont Circle Conservancy Records, Kiplinger Library, HSW.

40. On the formation of the Dupont Circle Conservancy, see Articles of Incorporation, folder 12, container 1, Dupont Circle Conservancy Records, Kiplinger Library, HSW; and Correspondence between Charles Robertson and Dennis Brown, folder 12, container 1, Dupont Circle Conservancy Records, Kiplinger Library, HSW. On the reaction of large-scale real estate interests, see Washington Board of Realtors, "Proposal: A Reasonable Approach to the Effects of Historic Preservation," March 1982, folder 12, container 2, Dupont Circle Conservancy Records, Kiplinger Library, HSW. The most vociferous opponent of historic districts in the real estate business at the time was lawyer Whayne Quin. For his view on the situation, see his "Historic Preservation: The Need for Reform," *Realtor*, November 1981.

41. Edna Frazier-Cromwell to Dupont Circle Conservancy, October 1982, folder 40, container 2, Dupont Circle Conservancy Records, Kiplinger Library, HSW.

42. Charles Robertson to Edna Frazier-Cromwell, January 18, 1983, folder 41, container 2, Dupont Circle Conservancy Records, Kiplinger Library, HSW.

43. Richard Friedman to Carole Schifrin, ca. February 1982, folder 42, container 2, Dupont Circle Conservancy Records, Kiplinger Library, HSW.

44. Anne Chase, "Shaw Leaders Oppose Plans for Historic District," *Washington Post*, April 27, 1983, DC1–DC4.

45. Ibid., DC1. ShawPAC, which joined the 14th and U Street Coalition in this battle, replaced the Model Inner City Community Organization (MICCO) as the official advocate for Shaw residents in the urban redevelopment process. See "ShawPac Is Formed," *Washington Afro-American*, August 10, 1974.

46. Chase, "Shaw Leaders Oppose Plans for Historic District," DC1.

47. On the "black aristocracy," see Michael Andrew Fitzpatrick, "'A Great Agitation for Business': Black Economic Development in Shaw," *Washington History* 2, no. 2 (1990–91): 48–73, and Morris MacGregor, *The Emergence of a Black Catholic Community: St. Augustine's in Washington* (Washington, D.C.: Catholic University of America Press, 1999), 360–63. A WTOP Editorial, "Black Power," broadcast on August 22, 1968, spelled out the stakes of what black power might mean for urban redevelopment. See Transcript of "Black Power," 1968, folder 12, box 26, Walter E. Fauntroy Papers, Special Collections, Gelman Library, GWU. For a broader overview of black power in local political discourse, see "Black Power and the Struggle for Home Rule, 1970–2000," in *The Black Washingtonians: The Anacostia Museum Illustrated Chronology*, Smithsonian Anacostia Museum and Center for African American History and Culture (Hoboken: J. Wiley, 2005), 295–300.

48. 14th and U Street Coalition flyer, 1982, folder 42, container 2, Dupont Circle Conservancy Records, Kiplinger Library, HSW.

49. Katherine Eccles to Charles Robertson, December 7, 1982, folder 40, container 2, Dupont Circle Conservancy Records, Kiplinger Library, HSW.

50. Among the documents they collected were a newspaper article—"Illegal Election-Moves Charged," *Washington Times*, February 23, 1983—and a letter: Mrs. William Johnston to Edna Frazier-Cromwell, folder 42, container 2, Dupont Circle Conservancy Records, Kiplinger Library, HSW. The events were also covered in the black press, but no wrongdoing was reported. See "School Board Fills Vacancy: Frazier-Cromwell Picked," *Washington Afro-American*, June 4, 1983.

51. Richard Friedman to Dupont Circle Conservancy, April 19, 1983, folder 42, container 2, Dupont Circle Conservancy Records, Kiplinger Library, HSW.

52. HPO, "DC Inventory of Historic Sites," https://planning.dc.gov/page/dc-inventory-historic-sites.

53. Blair A. Ruble, *Washington's U Street: A Biography* (Washington, D.C.: Woodrow Wilson Center Press; Baltimore: Johns Hopkins University Press, 2010).

54. Pat Press, "New People for Old Houses?," *Washington Post*, November 27, 1983, B8.

55. See correspondence regarding the historic district bid as well as nomination forms and other documents related to hearings, folders 96–104, container 3,

Historic Mt. Pleasant Inc. Records, MS 547, Kiplinger Library, HSW; Randy Mintz, "Mount Pleasant Divided on Historic District Designation," *Washington Post*, September 13, 1984, DC6; Courtland Milloy, "Pleasant, but Not Historic," *Washington Post*, June 19, 1986, DC1; Valca Valentine, "New Historic Status Comes to Mount Pleasant," *Washington Post*, October 25, 1986, E1.

6. RHODES TAVERN AND THE PROBLEM WITH PRESERVATION IN THE 1980S

1. Citizens' Committee to Save Historic Rhodes Tavern, "A Heritage Destroyed: 185 Years of D.C., U.S. History End with Rhodes Razing," *Rhodes Record* 1, no. 1 (September 10, 1985): 1.

2. Ibid.

3. Citizens' Committee to Save Historic Rhodes Tavern, "How Rhodes Got Razed and How Home Rule Got Bruised in the Process," *Rhodes Record* 1, no. 1 (September 10, 1985): 3.

4. Phil McCombs and Anne H. Oman, "$40 Million Mall Is Planned," *Washington Post*, November 12, 1977, A1; Neil Harris, *Capital Culture: J. Carter Brown, the National Gallery of Art, and the Reinvention of the Museum Experience* (Chicago: University of Chicago Press, 2013), 337–43; National Register of Historic Places, Inventory Nomination Form, "National Metropolitan Bank Building," September 13, 1978, National Park Service, http://npgallery.nps.gov/pdfhost/docs/NRHP/Text/78003059.pdf; National Register of Historic Places, Inventory Nomination Form, "Chase's Theater and Riggs Building," September 17, 1978, *Historic Washington*, http://www.historicwashington.org/docs/Historic%20Landmark%20Application/Chase's%20Theater%20and%20Riggs%20Building.pdf.

5. National Register of Historic Places, Inventory Nomination Form, "National Metropolitan Bank Building," 1978, and National Register of Historic Places, Inventory Nomination Form, "Chase's Theater and Riggs Building," 1978.

6. D.C. Regulation 73-25: "Before the Director may issue a permit to demolish or alter the exterior of . . . a building or structure listed on the city's inventory of historic sites . . . the Director shall submit the application for a permit to the Commissioner of the District of Columbia and shall place notice of the application for a permit in the District of Columbia Register. The Commissioner, or his designated agent, acting with the advice of the District of Columbia Professional Review Committee for nominations to the National Register of Historic Places . . . shall within sixty (60) days determine whether the alteration or demolition of the building, structure or place is contrary to the public interest and should be delayed for a designated period of up to 180 days following such determination to permit the District of Columbia's State Historic Preservation Officer and the Professional Review Committee to negotiate with the owner or owners of the building, structure or place and civic groups, public agencies, and interested citizens to find a means of preserving the building, structure or place. Before issuing any order delaying such demolition or alteration, the Commissioner or his designated agent shall afford the applicant and any interested

parties an opportunity to offer any evidence they may desire to present concerning the proposed order." Title 5A-1, § 109.10, D.C. Building Code.

7. Zachary M. Schrag, *The Great Society Subway: A History of the Washington Metro* (Baltimore: Johns Hopkins University Press, 2006), 204–6.

8. McCombs and Oman, "$40 Million Mall Is Planned," A1. Jerry Knight also gave extensive coverage to Carr and the downtown real estate revival in the period. See, for example, Jerry Knight, "Carr Hails a Renaissance in DC," *Washington Post*, December 21, 1978, F1.

9. Oliver T. Carr Jr., "Save Metropolitan Square," *Washington Post*, October 9, 1983, C8.

10. Dana Hedgpeth, "Carr Empire's Changing Skyline," *Washington Post*, November 20, 2006, http://www.washingtonpost.com/wp-dyn/content/article/2006/11/19/AR2006111900752.html; Wolf von Eckardt, "Big Stakes in a New City Game," *Washington Post*, March 4, 1978, B1; Schrag, *Great Society Subway*, 204.

11. Anne H. Oman, "Building Preservation Sought in Commercial Complex Project," *Washington Post*, February 23, 1978, DC4.

12. Von Eckardt, "Big Stakes in a New City Game," B1. On the delay in demolition regulation, D.C. Regulation 73-25, see Jeremy W. Dutra, "You Can't Tear It Down: The Origins of the D.C. Historic Preservation Act," *Georgetown Law Historic Preservation Papers Series*, 2002, http://scholarship.law.georgetown.edu/hpps_papers/1. On Betts Abel, see von Eckardt, "Big Stakes in a New City Game," B1.

13. The decision in Citizens Committee to Save Historic Rhodes Tavern, Petitioner, v. District of Columbia Department of Housing and Community Development, Respondent, 432 A.2d 710, no. 80-179 (D.C. Ct. App. 1981) contains an excellent summary of the facts in the dispute up until October of 1980; available from Leagle, http://www.leagle.com/decision/19811142432A2d710_11137.

14. Anne H. Oman, "Arts Commission Won't Oppose Demolition of the Rhodes Tavern," *Washington Post*, March 9, 1978, DC4; von Eckardt, "Big Stakes in a New City Game," B1.

15. Paul Hodge, "10 DC Landmarks Listed as Historic Sites," *Washington Post*, March 25, 1969, C4; Dutra, "You Can't Tear It Down"; von Eckardt, "Big Stakes in a New City Game," B1.

16. Dutra, "You Can't Tear It Down," 29.

17. D.C. Code Ann. § 6-1102(11).

18. Citizens Committee to Save Historic Rhodes Tavern v. District of Columbia Department of Housing and Community Development, 432 A.2d 710, no. 80-179 (DC Ct. App. 1981), cert. denied, 454 US 1054 (1981).

19. Anne Oman, "History of Tavern the Focus of Move to Save it," *Washington Post*, May 18, 1978, DC2; "Historic Tavern Once Housed Congressmen," *Roll Call*, September 24, 1981.

20. National Capital Planning Commission and District of Columbia Redevelopment Land Agency, *Downtown Urban Renewal Area: Landmarks* (Washington, D.C.: Government Printing Office, 1970), 57–59; Richard Squires, "Rhodes Tavern

and the History of Washington, D.C.," and Nelson Rimensnyder, "Rhodes Tavern and the History of the Planning Development and Institutions of the Nation's Capital, 1799–1981" (conference papers, Washington, D.C.), February 13, 1982, folder 10, box 2, Citizens Committee to Save Historic Rhodes Tavern, Special Collections Research Center, Estelle and Melvin Gelman Library, George Washington University.

21. National Capital Planning Commission, *Downtown Urban Renewal Area*, 57.

22. Rimensnyder, "Rhodes Tavern and the History of the Planning, Development and Institutions of the Nation's Capital," 863–82.

23. National Capital Planning Commission, *Downtown Urban Renewal Area*, 57–58.

24. Squires, "Rhodes Tavern and the History of Washington, D.C."; Citizens' Committee to Save Historic Rhodes Tavern, "A Heritage Destroyed."

25. Joseph P. Mastrangelo, "Parading About the Rhodes," *Washington Post*, August 25, 1978, C5.

26. Linda Wheeler, "Maverick Fights to Save an Old but Ugly Tavern," *Washington Post*, July 7, 1981, B1.

27. On history painting, nationalism, and historical meaning, see Mark Salber Phillips, *On Historical Distance* (New Haven: Yale University Press, 2013), and Bain Attwood, *Possession: Batman's Treaty and the Matter of History* (Carlton: Miegunyah Press, 2009).

28. Randall Mason, *The Once and Future New York: Historic Preservation and the Modern City* (Minneapolis: University of Minnesota Press, 2009), 4.

29. The quote was used as an epigraph by Nelson Rimensnyder in his "Rhodes Tavern Initiative 11: A History" (Washington, D.C., 1984), Pamphlet Collection, Kiplinger Research Library, Historical Society of Washington, D.C.

30. Robert B. Gair, letter to the editor, *Washington Post*, August 17, 1978.

31. Citizens' Committee to Save Historic Rhodes Tavern, "How Rhodes Got Razed," 3.

32. Wolf von Eckardt, "Conservation Quandry: Not Every Building Should be Saved," *Washington Post*, August 5, 1978, D1.

33. Shalom Baranes, letter to the editor, *Washington Post*, September 7, 1984.

34. Linda Wheeler, "To Tear Down or Not: Rhodes Tavern Tests New D.C. Law on Landmarks," *Washington Post*, December 16, 1979, D1.

35. Oman, "Arts Commission Won't Oppose Demolition of the Rhodes Tavern," DC4.

36. Joseph N. Grano Jr., "The Case for Saving Rhodes Tavern," *Washington Star*, March 22, 1980.

37. Ibid.

38. Citizens' Committee to Save Historic Rhodes Tavern, "How Rhodes Got Razed," 3.

39. Grano, "Case for Saving Rhodes Tavern."

40. Wheeler, "Maverick Fights to Save an Old but Ugly Tavern," B1.

41. "A resolution to preserve and restore the first Town Hall of the City of Washington, DC, the historic Rhodes Tavern," H. Res. 532, 97th Congress (1982).

42. "History Buffs Losing Bout to Save Washington Tavern," *Pittsburgh Press*, April 6, 1980; "Preserving D.C. Tavern: Historic Landmark or Missing Tooth: Debate Rages," *Boston Globe*, May 9, 1980.

43. "Rhodes Tavern Was D.C.'s Early City Hall and Site of Elections", *Washington Afro-American*, June 5, 1982.

44. Opening lines of text of "Initiative Measure No.11," By the People of the District of Columbia. Reprinted in Rimensnyder, "Rhodes Tavern Initiative 11."

45. Charles Robertson to Joseph Grano, September 23, 1982, folder 12, container 2, Dupont Circle Conservancy Records, Kiplinger Library, HSW.

46. Leila J. Smith, "A Preservation Action Group for All Washington," in *The Washington Preservation Conference Proceedings* (Washington, D.C.: National Trust for Historic Preservation, 1972), 71. On DTID! campaigns to save the Franklin School and Willard Hotel, see Anne H. Oman, "Saving the Pieces of Urban History," *Washington Post*, December 1, 1977, DC1.

47. Fernando Barrueta, "Why Washington Is Moving East," *Design Action* 1, no. 1 (1982): 10. The Demonet Building, for example, was purchased by Japanese investors in 1986. Recent scholarly analysis of Japanese real estate investment in American cities in this period reveals that many firms paid inflated prices because of the relatively high costs of Japanese real estate. This had the effect of escalating the cost of land in downtown Washington and making capital readily available for private redevelopment of commercial real estate. See Roger Farrelly, "Organization, Motivations and Case Studies of Japanese Direct Investment in Real Estate, 1985–1994," Pacific Economic Paper, no. 282, Japan-Australia Research Centre, Australian National University.

48. "An All-Purpose Name," *Washington Post*, July 15, 1984, C2.

49. Roger Lewis, "Modifying Landmark Buildings Inevitably Involves Compromises," *Washington Post*, November 15, 1986, E18.

50. Anne Veigle, "Battle Lines Blur as Preservation Goes from Street to Boardroom," *Washington Times*, September 20, 1988.

51. Daniel Bluestone, *Buildings, Landscapes, and Memory: Case Studies in Historic Preservation* (New York: W. W. Norton, 2011), 104–31; Michael Holleran, *Boston's "Changeful Times": Origins of Preservation and Planning in America* (Baltimore: Johns Hopkins University Press, 1998); Mason, *Once and Future New York*.

52. James F. Clarity and Warren Weaver Jr., "What's in a Name?," *New York Times*, September 14 1984, A24.

53. Veigle, "Battle Lines Blur."

54. Ibid.; Richard Longstreth, "Capital Gains, Capital Challenges: Historic Preservation in Washington since 1979," foreword to James Goode, *Capital Losses: A Cultural History of Washington's Destroyed Buildings*, 2nd ed. (Washington, D.C.: Smithsonian Institution Press, 2003), xiii–xvi.

55. Richard Striner, "Historic Preservation and the Challenge of Ethical Coherence," in *Ethics in Preservation: Lectures Presented at the Annual Meeting of the National Council for Preservation Education,* Indianapolis, Indiana, October 23, 1993, http://www.preservenet.cornell.edu/edu/Ethics_pres.pdf, 5.

56. Richard Striner and Anna Carter to full membership of D.C. Alliance for Preservation, October 19, 1989, folder 154, container 4, Dupont Circle Conservancy Records, Kiplinger Library, HSW.

57. Striner, "Historic Preservation and the Challenge of Ethical Coherence," 5.

58. Edmund Burke, *Reflections on the Revolution in France, and on the Proceedings in Certain Societies in London Relative to that Event* (1790; Harmondsworth: Penguin, 1969), paragraph 165.

59. Charles Robertson to Richard Striner and Anna Carter, D.C. Alliance for Preservation, September 19, 1989, folder 168, container 4, Dupont Circle Conservancy Records, Kiplinger Library, HSW.

60. Charles Robertson, remarks at "The People Speak" session of the Second Washington Preservation Conference, folder 12, container 1, Dupont Circle Conservancy Records, Kiplinger Library, HSW.

61. Charles Robertson, draft rules of procedure for the JCL under DC Law 2-144, folder 12, and Dupont Circle Conservancy to DC Zoning Commission, December 1984, folder 14, series 2, Dupont Circle Conservancy Records, Kiplinger Library, HSW.

62. A conservancy funding application for a Grants-in-Aid program in 1984 contained a list of names and occupations of the conservancy's principal members. See folder 15, series 2, Dupont Circle Conservancy Records, Kiplinger Library, HSW. The idea of preservation as curation was not the conservancy's idea. It was championed by the best-known preservation educator and writer of the period, James Marston Fitch. See James Marston Fitch, *Historic Preservation: Curatorial Management of the Built World* (New York: McGraw-Hill, 1982).

63. Wheeler, "Maverick Fights to Save an Old but Ugly Tavern," B1.

64. Colin Rowe and Fred Koetter, *Collage City* (Cambridge, MA: MIT Press, 1978), 97.

65. On the impact of the Historic Preservation Tax Credit, see Mike Wallace, "Preserving the Past: A History of Historic Preservation in the United States," in *Mickey Mouse History and Other Essays on American Memory* (Philadelphia: Temple University Press, 1996), 201–03.

66. Caroline Constant, "Designing with History: Recent DC Architecture," *Design Action* 1, no. 1 (1982): 1–3. On the ubiquity of Shalom Baranes's work in Washington, see Benjamin Forgey, "The Architect Who's All Over the D.C. Map," *Washington Post,* August 18, 2002, G1.

7. MODERNIST URBANISM AS HISTORY

1. Mayor's Agent for the District of Columbia Historic Landmark and Historic District Protection Act, "Application of Potomac Place II LLC for the

Demolition of the Pool Canopy at 800 4th Street, Southwest," HPA No. 2003-004; 2003-008, *DigitalGeorgetown*, http://hdl.handle.net/10822/761611; Chloethiel Woodard Smith, "Cities in Search of Form," *AIA Journal* 35, no. 3 (1961): 74–79. Also see exhibition materials connected to Smith, *Two on Two at the Octagon: Design for the Urban Environment* (Washington DC: DC Preservation League Records, January 16–March 18, 1979).

2. On Interbau or the IBA, see Florian Urban, "Recovering Essence through Demolition: The 'Organic' City in Postwar West Berlin," *Journal of the Society of Architectural Historians* 63, no. 3 (2004): 354–69; Greg Castillo, "Making a Spectacle of Restraint: The Deutschland Pavilion at the 1958 Brussels Exposition," *Journal of Contemporary History* 47, no. 1 (2012): 97–119. On the pedigree of designers in the Southwest urban renewal project, see Keith Melder, "Southwest: Where History Stopped," in *Washington at Home: An Illustrated History of Neighborhoods in the Nation's Capital*, ed. Kathryn Schneider Smith, 2nd ed. (Baltimore: Johns Hopkins University Press, 2010), 101–3; Richard Longstreth, "Brave New World: Southwest Washington and the Promise of Urban Renewal," in *Housing Washington: Two Centuries of Residential Development and Planning in the National Capital Area*, ed. Richard Longstreth (Chicago: Center for American Places, 2010), 255–80.

3. The most comprehensive historical account of the "sick cities" idea and its implications for the architecture and planning discourse in the 1940s is in Andrew M. Shanken, *194X: Architecture, Planning, and Consumer Culture on the American Home Front* (Minneapolis: University of Minnesota Press, 2009). The "sick city" idea was specifically articulated in reference to Washington, D.C., by Louis Justement in *New Cities for Old: City Building in Terms of Space, Time and Money* (New York: McGraw Hill, 1946), 3–6. It was still current in the popular press in the 1960s when *Look* published a special issue on the subject. The issue also included a piece on Chloethiel Woodard Smith. See John Peter, "Our Sick Cities and How They Can be Cured," *Look*, September 21, 1965, 27–33, and "Leading Lady on Urban Renewal," *Look*, September 21, 1965, 75–79.

4. Sam Smith, *Captive Capital: Colonial Life in Modern Washington* (Bloomington: Indiana University Press, 1974), 216–18.

5. Dennis E. Gale, *Washington, D.C.: Inner-City Revitalization and Minority Suburbanization* (Philadelphia: Temple University Press, 1987), 58.

6. Alexander M. Padro, "Preserving Our More Recent Past," *Washington Post*, March 23, 2003, B8.

7. Justement, *New Cities for Old*, 98.

8. José Luis Sert, *Can Our Cities Survive? An ABC of Urban Problems, Their Analysis, Their Solutions* (Cambridge, MA: Harvard University Press, 1944); Henry S. Churchill, *The City Is the People* (New York: Harcourt Brace, 1945); Justement, *New Cities for Old*; Shanken, *194X*, 62–69; Christopher Klemek, *The Transatlantic Collapse of Urban Renewal: Postwar Urbanism from New York to Berlin* (Chicago: University of Chicago Press, 2011), 52–61.

9. Wolf von Eckardt, "New Southwest a Bundle of Boons," *Washington Post*, October 30, 1962.

10. John B. Willman, "New Apartments Add to Maturity of Southwest," *Washington Post*, February 4, 1961, B1–B2.

11. Robert J. Lewis, "Another New Best Address," *Washington Star*, January 7, 1961.

12. "Southwest Washington: Finest Urban Renewal Effort in the Country," *Architectural Forum* 118, no. 1 (January 1963): 85.

13. Ibid.

14. Justement, *New Cities for Old*, 3.

15. Shannon & Luchs Realtors "The Capitol Park Town Houses" (advertisement).

16. Ibid.

17. "Southwest Washington," 85; Carolyn Lewis, "It's Humphrey's Move this Time," *Washington Post*, October 22, 1966, C1.

18. National Capital Planning Commission with Frederick Gutheim, *Worthy of the Nation: The History of Planning for the National Capital* (Washington, D.C.: Smithsonian Institution Press, 1977), 199; Howard Gillette Jr., *Between Justice and Beauty: Race, Planning and the Failure of Urban Policy in Washington, D.C.* (Philadelphia: University of Pennsylvania Press, 2006), 142–43.

19. Francesca Rusello Ammon, "Commemoration amid Criticism: The Mixed Legacy of Urban Renewal in Southwest Washington, D.C.," *Journal of Planning History* 8, no. 3 (2009): 183–84; Longstreth, "Brave New World," 258–62; Gillette, *Between Justice and Beauty*, 161–62.

20. Berman v. Parker, 348 U.S. 26 (1954); Gillette, *Between Justice and Beauty*, 157; Carol M. Rose, "Preservation and Community: New Directions in the Law of Historic Preservation," *Stanford Law Review* 33, no. 3 (1981): 473–534.

21. Rose, "Preservation and Community," 486.

22. Longstreth, "Brave New World," 257.

23. Bernard J. Frieden, *The Future of Old Neighborhoods: Rebuilding for a Changing Population* (Cambridge, MA: Joint Centre for Urban Studies, MIT Press, 1964); Jane Jacobs, *The Death and Life of Great American Cities* (New York: Random House, 1961), 24.

24. Wolf von Eckardt, "A New View from the Capitol," *New Republic*, January 5, 1963, 21.

25. Jacobs, *The Death and Life of Great American Cities*; Herbert J. Gans, "The Failure of Urban Renewal," in *Urban Renewal: The Record and the Controversy*, ed. James Q. Wilson (Cambridge, MA: MIT Press, 1966), 537–57; Herbert J. Gans, *The Urban Villagers: Group and Class in the Life of Italian-Americans* (New York: Free Press, 1962). Paul S. Green and Shirley L. Green echo the observations of Jacobs and Gans in their account of the old Southwest: "Old Southwest Remembered: The Photographs of Joseph Owen Curtis," *Washington History* 1, no. 2 (1989): 42–57.

26. Martin Anderson, *The Federal Bulldozer: A Critical Analysis of Urban Renewal, 1949–1962* (Cambridge, MA: MIT Press, 1964); Klemek, *Transatlantic Collapse of Urban Renewal*, 179–81.

27. Gillette, *Between Justice and Beauty*, 163.

28. Ammon, "Commemoration amid Criticism," 199.

29. Gillette, *Between Justice and Beauty*, 171–73.

30. "Catholic Group Heads Attack on Southwest Renewal," *Washington Post*, February 13, 1961, B7.

31. Gillette, *Between Justice and Beauty*, 176; Frederick Gutheim and Antoinette J. Lee, *Worthy of the Nation: Washington, DC, from L'Enfant to the National Capital Planning Commission*, 2nd ed. (Baltimore: Johns Hopkins University Press, 2006), 312; Mary A. Morton (words and music), "MICCO Theme Song," folder 2, box 26, Walter E. Fauntroy Papers, Special Collections Research Center, Estelle and Melvin Gelman Library, George Washington University; WTOP Editorial, August 22 and 23, 1968, folder 12, box 26, Fauntroy Papers, Special Collections, Gelman Library, GWU; and "What Kind of Neighborhood Do You Want? The Choices for Shaw Residents in Urban Renewal," July 1968, folder 2, box 26, Fauntroy Papers, Special Collections, Gelman Library, GWU; Gillette, *Between Justice and Beauty*, 173–74.

32. Garnet W. Jex, *The Bulldozer and the Rose* (Washington, D.C., 1958), slides, Kiplinger Research Library, Historical Society of Washington, D.C. On similar kinds of representation of urban renewal areas, see Samuel Zipp, *Manhattan Projects: The Rise and Fall of Urban Renewal in Cold War New York* (New York: Oxford University Press, 2010), 84–88.

33. Duncan Spencer, "Two Waterfronts: Or Why Alexandria Is River's Fun Side," *Roll Call*, May 28, 1998.

34. Melder, "Southwest"; Longstreth, "Brave New World"; Ammon, "Commemoration amid Criticism."

35. Ammon, "Commemoration amid Criticism," 198.

36. ULI, *Southwest Washington, D.C.: A Strategy for Revitalizing Waterside Mall and the Waterfront* (Washington, D.C.: ULI, 1998), 33.

37. This was openly acknowledged by the city in a 2006 report. See Government of the District of Columbia, *Homes for an Inclusive City: A Comprehensive Housing Strategy for Washington, D.C.* (Washington, D.C.: Comprehensive Housing Strategy Taskforce, 2006), https://www.brookings.edu/wp-content/uploads/2016/06/housingstrategy_fullreport.pdf.

38. Melder, "Southwest"; ULI, *Southwest Washington*, 4.

39. ULI, *Southwest Washington*, 31–33.

40. Margaret Feldman to Tersh Boasberg, April 17, 2003, folder 12, container 2, Margaret Feldman Collection, MS 759, Kiplinger Library, HSW.

41. Jane Freundel Levey, *River Farms to Urban Towers: Southwest Heritage Trail* (Washington, D.C.: Cultural Tourism DC, 2004).

42. On the regeneration and preservation of modernist "tower in the park" development, see Michael McClelland, Graeme Stewart, and Asrai Ord, "Reassessing the Recent Past: Tower Neighborhood Renewal in Toronto," in *Special Issue on Modern Heritage*, ed. Thomas C. Jester and David N. Fixler, special issue, *APT Bulletin: The Journal of Preservation Technology* 42, no. 2/3 (2011): 9–14, and

Amanda Murphy, "Renewing Urban Renewal: A Case Study in Southwest D.C.," *Blueprints* 26, no. 1 (2007–8): 10–13.

43. Mayor's Agent for Historic Preservation, "Application of Potomac Place II LLC for the Demolition of the Pool Canopy."

44. Mayor's Agent for Historic Preservation, National Register of Historic Places, Registration Form, "Capitol Park," DC Preservation League Records.

45. Mayor's Agent for Historic Preservation, "Application of Potomac Place II LLC for the Demolition of the Pool Canopy."

46. Mayor's Agent for Historic Preservation, "Application of the Potomac Place Land LLC for the Demolition of the Pool Canopy—Applicants Proposed Findings of Fact, Conclusions of Law, and Decision and Order," June 27, 2003, DC Preservation League Records.

47. Mayor's Agent for Historic Preservation, "Application of Potomac Place Land II LLC for the Demolition of the Pool Canopy," "Decisions and Order." This last item includes the terms of the agreement made between the parties.

48. Ammon, "Commemoration amid Criticism," 175–220. Also see Richard Longstreth, "The Difficult Legacy of Urban Renewal," *CRM: The Journal of Heritage Stewardship* 3, no. 1 (2006): 6–23.

49. Richard Longstreth, "I Can't See It; I Don't Understand It; and It Doesn't Look Old to Me," *Historic Preservation Forum Journal* 10, no. 1 (1995): 6–15; Varna G. Boyd and Louana M. Lackey, "Archaeological and Architectural Evaluation and Recommendations," in *Archaeological Survey of the Southwest Quadrant of the District of Columbia, submitted to the District of Columbia Historic Preservation Division*, ed. Elizabeth A. Moore and Charles W. McNett (Washington, D.C.: District of Columbia Historic Preservation Office 1992).

50. Longstreth, "I Can't See It," 38.

51. Major surveys of the field include Theodore H. M. Prudon, *Preservation of Modern Architecture* (Hoboken, NJ: Wiley & Sons, 2008); Miles Glendinning, *The Conservation Movement: A History of Architectural Preservation, Antiquity to Modernity* (New York: Routledge, 2013); Allen Cunningham, ed., *Modern Movement Heritage* (London: E. & F. N. Spon, 1998); Dennis Sharp and Catherine Cooke, eds., *The Modern Movement in Architecture: Selections from the DOCOMOMO Registers* (Rotterdam: 010 Publishers, 2000). Several special issues of major journals in the field have also treated the preservation of modernism in some detail. See, for example, Hannah Lewi, ed., *Keeping the Past Public*, special issue, *Journal of Architecture* 15, no. 5 (2010); Thomas C. Jester and David N. Fixler, eds., *Special Issue on Modern Heritage*, special issue, *APT Bulletin: The Journal of Preservation Technology* 42, no. 2/3 (2011); International Committee for Documentation and Conservation of Buildings, Sites and Neighbourhoods of the Modern Movement, *Urbanism, Gardens & Landscape*, special issue, *DOCOMOMO Journal* 16 (1997).

52. Charles Birnbaum, ed., *Preserving Modern Landscape Architecture II: Making Postwar Landscapes Visible* (Washington, D.C.: Spacemaker Press, 2004).

53. National Register of Historic Places, Mies van der Rohe Residential District, Lafayette Park, Item No. 96000809, https://npgallery.nps.gov/NRHP/Asset

Detail/NRIS/96000809; Will Hurst, "Only Listing will Save Robin Hood Gardens," *Building Design*, February 21, 2008, http://www.bdonline.co.uk/only-listing-can-save-robin-hood-gardens/3106993.article; Steven Rose, "Don't Knock Brutalism," *The Guardian*, June 26, 2008, https://www.theguardian.com/artanddesign/artblog/2008/jun/26/dontknockbrutalism.

54. Will Hurst, "English Heritage Defends Its Failure to Back Robin Hood Gardens," *Building Design*, May 16, 2008, http://www.bdonline.co.uk/english-heritage-defends-its-failure-to-back-robin-hood-gardens/3113844.article.

55. National Register of Historic Places, Registration Form, "Capitol Park," DC Preservation League Records.

56. Gale, *Washington, D.C.*, 58.

CONCLUSION

1. James Goode, *Capital Losses: A Cultural History of Washington's Destroyed Buildings*, 2nd ed. (Washington, D.C.: Smithsonian Institution Press, 2003).

2. Edward P. Jones, "The Girl Who Raised Pigeons," in *Lost in the City: Stories* (New York: Harper Collins, 1993), 12.

3. Sabiyha Prince, *African Americans and Gentrification in Washington, D.C.: Race, Class and Social Justice in the Nation's Capital* (Farnham: Ashgate, 2014).

4. John Buntin, "The Myth of Gentrification: It's Extremely Rare and Not as Bad for the Poor as You Think," *Slate.com*, January 14, 2015, http://www.slate.com/articles/news_and_politics/politics/2015/01/the_gentrification_myth_it_s_rare_and_not_as_bad_for_the_poor_as_people.html; Richard Florida, "The Closest Look Yet at Gentrification and Displacement," *Citylab.com*, November 2, 2015, http://www.citylab.com/housing/2015/11/the-closest-look-yet-at-gentrification-and-displacement/413356/; Richard Florida, "The Complicated Link between Gentrification and Displacement," *Citylab.com*, September 8, 2015, http://www.citylab.com/housing/2015/09/the-complicated-link-between-gentrification-and-displacement/404161/; Emily Badger, "It's Time to Give up the Most Loaded Least Understood Word in Urban Policy: Gentrification," *Washington Post*, December 17, 2014, https://www.washingtonpost.com/news/wonk/wp/2014/12/17/its-time-to-give-up-the-emptiest-word-in-urban-policy-gentrification/; Chris Myers Asch and George Derek Musgrove, "Not Gone, Not Forgotten: Struggling over History in a Gentrifying D.C." *Washington Post*, October 19, 2012, https://www.washingtonpost.com/blogs/therootdc/post/not-gone-not-forgotten-struggling-over-history-in-a-gentrifying-dc/2012/10/18/09ad8c24-1941-11e2-b97b-3ae53cdeaf69_blog.html.

5. Suleiman Osman, *The Invention of Brownstone Brooklyn: Gentrification and the Search for Authenticity in Postwar New York* (Oxford: Oxford University Press, 2011), 16.

Index

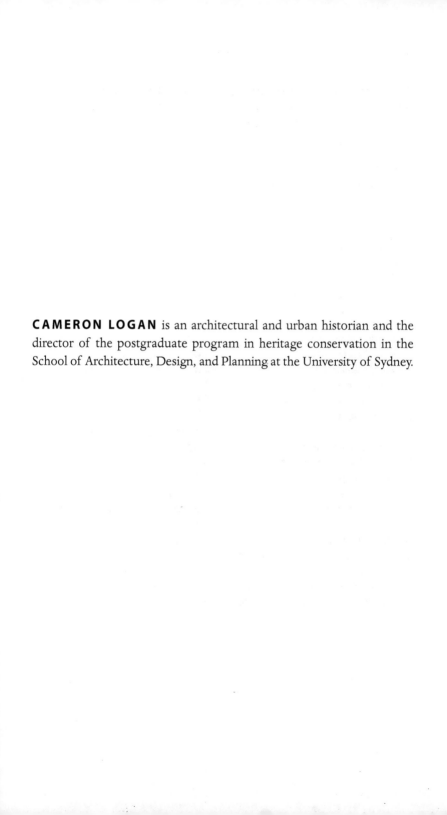

CAMERON LOGAN is an architectural and urban historian and the director of the postgraduate program in heritage conservation in the School of Architecture, Design, and Planning at the University of Sydney.

6/6/18